Calling WPC Crockford

Calling WPC Crockford:

THE STORY OF A 1950s POLICEWOMAN

Ruth D'Alessandro

WELBECK

Published by Welbeck
An imprint of Welbeck Non-Fiction Limited,
part of Welbeck Publishing Group.
Based in London and Sydney.

First published by Welbeck in 2022

A CIP catalogue record for this book is available from the British Library

ISBN
Paperback – 9781787399099
eBook – 9781787399655

Typeset by Roger Walker
Printed in Great Britain by CPI Books, Chatham, Kent

10 9 8 7 6 5 4 3 2 1

The Forest Stewardship Council® is an international
nongovernmental organisation that promotes environmentally
appropriate, socially beneficial, and economically viable management
of the world's forests. To learn more, visit www.fsc.org

www.welbeckpublishing.com

For my daughters Sophia and Eleanor:
This is what Grandma Gwen did as a WPC

Contents

Author's foreword

by Ruth D'Alessandro

When you grow up in a police family, as I did, you grow up with stories. The same stories are told over and over again: to you, to dinner guests, with police colleagues and when criticising television crime dramas. You never forget them, especially when told them as a child, as I was. They don't become embellished over time, because they don't need to be. They are strong enough in their own right.

My mother, Gwendoline Crockford, was a woman police constable in the Berkshire Constabulary in the early 1950s. In the mid-1950s, she was selected for detective training and served as the force's first woman detective until 1960 when she was then promoted, back into uniform, to woman police sergeant. She left the force in 1962 when she married my father, a police constable. Her public service spanned that fascinating, and often-overlooked period, of social history when Britain emerged from the darkness of wartime and post-war austerity into the light of a social revolution, with the newly formed NHS and the welfare state, up to the more permissive early years of the Swinging Sixties.

Mum's stories were funny, dramatic and often shocking. Whether retrieving a human skeleton from the woods, attending post-mortems, dealing with many neglected children, abandoned babies and abused women, going undercover to catch thieves, investigating burglaries or experiencing the manhunt for a serial child killer, they were always told calmly, kindly and with forensic detail.

I was always going to sit Mum down one day and write an end-to-end chronology of her time in the police. There would be plenty of time for that, I thought. Then cancer suddenly took her in 2004 at the age of 74 and all I was left with was memories and stories, some books and a small file of newspaper cuttings and photographs.

On International Women's Day in 2017, I posted a photograph of my mum on social media with the caption, "So on International Women's Day, here's a pioneer – the first-ever woman detective in the Berkshire Constabulary – and my mum. If only she was still around to write her memoir, 'Call the Sergeant'."

Friends commented, "Why don't *you* do it, then?"

How on earth was I going to do that? I spent a few weeks wallowing in sadness and regret that I hadn't truly appreciated what a remarkable woman Mum was, and that I hadn't documented her police career properly. But her story kept nagging at me, tugging at my elbow, a voice in my head saying, over and over, "Write it anyway."

I've heard it said that writers don't choose their story, the story chooses them, so I thought I'd give it a go, particularly as most 1950s police memoirs are by officers

2

in the Metropolitan Police; very few are about regional constabularies.

Some police archives are complete and well-preserved. Unfortunately, those of the Berkshire Constabulary – which was amalgamated with four other constabularies to become the Thames Valley Police in 1968 – are not. Amalgamations, refurbishments and even historic basement floods meant there was little relevant archive material available and some was inaccessible.

Undeterred, I headed for the British Library to access original local Berkshire newspapers of the time. I was astounded, and delighted, to find many of my mother's stories reported in black and white, sometimes with her namechecked, sometimes not, but pretty much just as she had told them.

I also researched and read voraciously anything about 1950s policing that I could find – out-of-print books, journals, academic papers and online forums– to build up as complete a picture of Berkshire policing at that time as I could. I appreciate that there may be details I have got wrong – the history of 1950s policewomen is patchy at best. From my research and conversations with Mum, procedures and inter-agency collaborations were much looser back then, with women police such a rarity that they really could carve out their own ways of doing things. This would be unthinkable nowadays.

While *Calling WPC Crockford* is painstakingly researched, and closely based on real events that my mother experienced in the 1950s, it is a work of storytelling. I have fictionalised a few characters, relationships and incidents, changed some names, locations and timescales to protect any relatives still connected with Wokingham. But much of what you will read is true and a reflection of a time long past. And if you think some of the stories are a little far-fetched, those are probably the true ones.

PART 1

CHAPTER 1

Why on earth did I choose to become a policewoman?

Mr Hitler, dominating my formative years, helped make my decision. I was 10 at the end of 1939 and 16 in 1945. The nightmare began on 3 September 1939, a Sunday that felt different, when I settled onto a bottom-numbing pew in All Saints Church with Mum, Dad, my younger sisters Barbara and Jean and older brother Ron.

People were less chatty and more serious than usual, brows furrowed. A polished wooden wireless balanced on the edge of the pulpit, the churchwarden tinkering with a dial. Waiting was unbearable; I felt sure we were starting late. I couldn't see a clock, had no watch and didn't feel I could ask Dad what the time was, so grim-faced was he.

The vicar climbed the steps into the pulpit. Neville Chamberlain, the British Prime Minister, would deliver an announcement, he said. He turned the volume dial.

"This is London. You will now hear a statement from the Prime Minister.

"I am speaking to you from the Cabinet Room at 10 Downing Street. This morning the British Ambassador in Berlin handed the German government a final note stating that unless we heard from them by 11 o'clock that they were prepared at once to withdraw their troops from Poland, a state of war would exist between us. I have to tell you now that no such undertaking has been received, and that consequently this country is at war with Germany..."

Gasps and sobs rose from the congregation. I felt my tummy turn over and my forehead prickle. Mum hurriedly brushed away a tear. Dad shook his head, whispering, "Not again, please God, not again," as Mr Chamberlain continued speaking, his voice cracking under the gravity of his words. The rest of the speech passed in a blur. Us children looked at each other, wide-eyed, wondering what to do. Our parents stood, ramrod-stiff and a foot apart, paralysed by their thoughts, as other families hugged and clung to each other.

To ram home the message and our new reality, air raid sirens began to wail outside as if we were about to be attacked from above, panicking the congregation and scattering us, albeit in an orderly fashion, out of church. I can remember little about where we went or what we did for the rest of that day, a traumatic memory that I blocked out. What I do remember was how confused and powerless I felt. Even at nine years old, I knew I never wanted to feel that powerless again.

Then, nothing happened. We had braced ourselves for all-out German attack, civil defence plans deployed and air raid precautions imposed, along with rationing and conscription. Everything seemed designed to make us uncomfortable and even the youngest of us felt a sense of anticlimax.

7

"This is more of a sitzkrieg than a Blitzkreig," said Dad.

My brother giggled. "It's the Bore War, isn't it?"

We put up with eight months of inertia until the following May, when Germany attacked western Europe and the war got going.

Of course, we kept calm and carried on like everyone else, enduring air raid sirens, the blackouts and rationing. Mum gave our meat, butter, egg and cheese rations to Dad as he had to go out to work and then do his bit in both the Home Guard and the Special Constabulary.[1] We constantly went to bed hungry. Mum occasionally brought home a slab of greasy-looking dark "beef" that she soaked in the sink overnight, steamed, soaked again, sliced and covered in Bisto. We could barely get our knives through it, and when we did start chewing, the tough flesh released a flavour like cod liver oil. Hungry as we were, we dreaded this for tea. I found out later it was whale meat.

Although we were spared London's Blitz, we still spent nights lying awake fearing the Luftwaffe would come and bomb nearby Woodley Aerodrome. Someone built an air raid shelter in the next street but we never went in it. Our parents thought it was safer for me and Barbara to sleep crammed into the cupboard under the stairs, saying the staircase would remain standing even if the house was bombed out. We lay on the hard floorboards

---

1 The Special Constabulary is a force of trained, part-time volunteer police officers. "Specials" come from all walks of civilian life.

with the spiders, cold and uncomfortable, listening for the low thrum of approaching enemy aircraft.

I thought we were going to be killed one night when a Luftwaffe pilot ditched his bombs over some local farmland – we heard the deafening whine and a series of thuds as the stick of bombs landed. Miraculously, nobody was killed and the army defused the single unexploded bomb that landed on the road. Rumour that the pilot had ditched his bombs out of fear and flown back to Germany scared gave us hope that the enemy may be fallible and we could beat him after all.

I was an inquisitive child (nosy, Mum would say), desperate to make sense of the war from fragments of news. My parents didn't buy a national newspaper. We were only allowed the wireless on when they said we could and visits to the cinema to see the Pathé newsreels were few and far between. In a way, this limited news media meant we experienced less "information overload" than nowadays, although reports we did read grew in our imaginations and haunted us for weeks.

One wartime report affected me deeply. On a sunny day in June 1942, I was standing, bored, in the bread queue by the newspaper stand, scanning the front pages for something to read. The German government had announced that it had wiped the Czechoslovak town of Lidice off the map to avenge the assassination of Nazi leader Reinhard Heydrich. All the men had been shot, the women sent to concentration camps and the children placed in "appropriate educational institutions" – whatever they were – before the town was levelled to the ground.

Lidice was a small town like Wokingham. The townsfolk there were probably just like the townsfolk here. I looked around. Mr Danvers, the jolly window cleaner, cycled past with his ladder on his shoulder – he would have been shot. Esme Cripps, just ahead of me in the queue with her freckled twin boys, would have been dragged away screaming from her children to her fate in Ravensbrück; her boys, separated and crying for their mother, taken somewhere unknown. The Victorian Gothic red brick town hall would have disappeared under the wheels of bulldozers. At that moment, I knew that a massacre like Lidice could happen here if Hitler invaded and it would be children just like me and my sisters and my friends who would suffer the most. I began to think, if we could win the war and survive, I'd like to be on the side of the mothers and children to stop anything like this happening again.

I left school at 14 for my first job as a girl Friday at a local sawmill, which wasn't as grim as it sounds. Good-natured Italian prisoners of war, captured in Libya and relieved to be out of the conflict, skipped between monstrous, spinning circular saws with blurred metal teeth, feeding in tree trunks with bare hands. I enjoyed my time there; not only did it give me office experience to get my next job, it taught me that people are surprising. The "enemies" in our midst were just like us, making the best of a situation, grateful to be safe until the war ended.

Going to university after the war never crossed my mind. Daughters of plumbers didn't do that. I was expected to get a job to supplement the family income, marry a nice young man with a trade and settle down to become a housewife and mother. But for some reason, the law attracted me and I wanted to work in the legal profession. My sawmill job had given me skills at filing, writing up invoices, answering the telephone and even some basic typing, although I merely pecked at the keys with two fingers. To get a respectable solicitor's office job, I needed to be able to type properly. I did a shorthand typing course at night school, learning to touch-type fast, and to convert dictation into scribbles that looked more like Arabic script than English. That Mum would no longer be able to read my diary was an unexpected advantage of mastering shorthand.

Soon I was offered a shorthand typist job at a solicitors' office in the town on 30 shillings a week. I'd hoped to be answering the telephone and filling in the solicitors' diaries, but I was placed in the small upstairs typing pool with three other girls, doing nothing but dictation and typing.

We chipped our manicured nails banging away on the sticky, clunky, 20-year-old Imperial typewriter keys. The senior partner refused to replace them with newer, Italian Olivetti models because he didn't want to put money in the pockets of "former enemies". For six long years, I filled hundreds of notebooks with scribbled solicitors' dictations and typed countless legal documents. I prided myself on my accuracy and rarely needed to correct my work, although the junior partner tended to have second thoughts just before signing a letter, which meant typing the whole thing up again.

I lived at home with Mum, Dad and my two sisters while I worked at the solicitors' office. Our brother was away on National Service so our youngest sister had his box room and I was happy to share with Barbara – in a bedroom this time, not in the understairs cupboard. We found the same things funny, an essential safety valve for coping throughout our parents' tense, humourless marriage.

As children, bodily functions had been taboo in our family: anyone who laughed at farts got a smack, which of course made them risky and even funnier. Barbara could keep a poker face, whereas I would dissolve into puce-faced, uncontrollable, punishable giggling. Some Sundays, Barbara and I had to play piano duets, sitting side by side, for dreary relatives. Barbara's favourite trick was to let off a silent fart that only I could smell, hoping I would crack and disgrace myself. Much as I cursed her devilment then, I learned emotional control in a risky situation – useful as a policewoman.

Mum charged Barbara and me half our weekly salaries in rent and we still had to hand over our ration coupons. Like during the war, our rations were saved up to give to Dad, even though Barbara and I were out working and getting hungry too. But we had our own money now and that meant fish and chips, which weren't rationed. Usually, we bought extra portions for the rest of the family from Somerscales fish bar, although some days when they had been particularly horrible, we'd sit on a park bench and scoff the lot ourselves, straight out of the newspaper, pickled eggs and all.

I don't know why I believed that working in a solicitors' office would lead to a glittering legal career. It was 1950, when the dawn of a hopeful new decade had come and gone, and we still felt hungry, threadbare, bombed out and exhausted. Where was the brave new world that we all dreamed about once the war was over? Here I was, six years after VE Day, still bashing out the same old letters and legal documents into the new decade. I kept counting my blessings that I was lucky to have a job, a roof over my head and nobody in my family killed, but I couldn't stop the nagging, guilty thoughts that I could be doing something *better*.

Sometimes the smallest changes in life can deliver the most significant consequences. One of the typing pool girls left to get married and I moved into her desk by the window. The solicitors' office faced the front entrance of the imposing Wokingham police station. I spent much of my day when I wasn't typing gazing out of the window at the daily rhythms of its comings and goings. I was captivated: through the doors went policemen marching in thieves and drunks, women occasionally crying, stray dogs dragged in on bits of string, members of the public with boxes and bundles – one man went in carrying a large snake at arm's length – and scruffy children running in and out laughing. At 2 p.m., a column of smart policemen would march out, dispersing to their respective beats, and it was easy to spot the detectives – they really did wear trilbies and belted mackintoshes, just like in the movies.

One officer particularly caught my eye – a woman police sergeant. Dad knew of her through his role as a Special – she was the only WPS in Berkshire, in charge of the woman police constables in several stations. I admired her poise and her smart, surprisingly modern-looking uniform. She looked professional, but feminine. I liked that look. She had an air of cool-headed capability and people appeared to treat her with respect, men raising their hats to her as they passed. I imagined that she could have been a nurse, a land girl or at least in the Women's Royal Voluntary Service during the war, doing her bit, getting stuck in. I wished I'd been a bit older to have had those opportunities, rather than spending the whole war feeling scared and out of control.

One afternoon, late, the junior partner changed his mind twice about an intricate conveyancing letter I had typed for him and shouted at me for being slow finishing it. I hated being shouted at and all those scared, out-of-control feelings came flooding back. I'd had enough of the junior partner and his petulant moods. I'd had enough of typing. I knew what I was going to do next: I was going to join the police.

CHAPTER 2

The skeleton in the coppice

October 1953

I was typing a pub brawl report in the front office when I heard the heavy door of the police station crash open. Children's voices.

"A skeleton! We found a skeleton!"

Looking up from my typewriter through the open door, I saw the "Ferals" – as we called the familiar, scruffy gang of mischievous local kids – rush into the lobby, tripping and shouting over each other. The eldest, John, sprouting the fluffy beginnings of a moustache, banged unnecessarily urgently on the bell. Three younger boys leapt onto the hard seats and jumped up and down.

Sergeant Lamb wasn't at the desk. When one of them pulled the public information poster about potato-destroying Colorado beetles off the noticeboard, I'd had enough. I took a final drag on my Kensitas cigarette, stubbed it out and went out front.

The only girl, small, blonde Dora, stood on tiptoes, scratching at her matted hair and trying to peer over the counter, while another pale, slim teenage boy with a frightened face tried to merge into the background.

"What on *earth* is going on here?" I demanded in my most authoritative voice.

The kids crowded round the desk, jostling each other, blurting out a few intelligible words:

"Missus Policeman Miss ... skeleton! ... found a skeleton ... in the woods ... looked as if it was gonna chase us ... scary teeth..."

"A skeleton? Really?" I asked. "What sort of skeleton is it this time?"

The volume of the children's chatter rose.

"Excuse me butting in, WPC Crockford, but not this skeleton lark again." Sergeant Lamb's best ex-Regimental Sergeant Major's voice boomed out over the cacophony of voices as he hurried out of the gents'. The chorus of chatter briefly halted. "If you're pulling my leg once more, you lot, your parents will be hearing from *me*!"

"No, no, really, you got to believe us this time, Mister Sergeant Sir," said Charlie, the flaxen-haired boy, bounding up to the desk, his blue eyes wide and pleading. He looked Sarge in the eye, then at me. Something about him felt sincere and our usual cynicism wavered.

"So," said Sarge, "where are we supposed to find this skeleton with scary teeth?"

"In High Copse woods! By them grain store things..." chattered the Ferals.

We managed to scribble down some directions. Sarge squinted at the local OS map pinned to the wall.

"That sounds like Fowler's land," he said. "It's private property and the gravel path's not a public thoroughfare."

"All right then," I said to the children. "If I go to the

woods to find this skeleton, who's going to come with me?"

There was silence, then, "No ... Not me ... not me ... I don't wanna ... Me neither ... I don't wanna to see the skeleton again..." chorused some of the children, shaking their heads. Others just looked frightened. They certainly didn't want to go anywhere near it again.

John looked at the wall clock. "We're late, let's scarper!" he ordered. And, as one, they tumbled out of the station as fast as they had arrived.

The lobby was now silent and empty. A chill gust of wind swirled some dry leaves in through the open door. All that remained of the Ferals' chaotic visit were muddy footprints and some scattered poster fragments.

Sarge tutted.

I went to the door and looked out. Rectory Road was quiet, no sign of them. Fast and lithe, they would be halfway to their homes or more mischief by now.

"Well, what do we make of that little episode, Sarge?" I asked. "Isn't this the third time in as many months the Ferals have been in with tales about finding a skeleton?"

"Hmm. They're probably still mucking about. It could be a deer or that Mrs Watkins's missing St Bernard. But something about that little blond lad's face makes me think there may be something more to it."

I also had a strange feeling about this latest skeleton report. We often had kids coming into the station saying they'd found bones or items of clothing, that their dad had given them a good hiding, or they'd found some dirty magazines in the bushes. Sergeant Lamb usually sent them away with a flea in their ear, but not before he had confiscated the magazines. This felt different.

"All right, could you cycle down there and go and have a look, WPC Crockford? But don't go on your own, those woods are damn sinister at the best of times. WPC Baxter's in the locker room – see if she'll come with you."

I saw Pattie's reflection in the locker room mirror before she noticed me. She was primping her eyebrows and pouting, checking her barely-there lipstick that she hoped Sergeant Robertshaw wouldn't notice. She turned sideways and tugged her tunic over her bust, huffing.

"You look great, Pats, honestly," I said, making her jump.

"Oh, hi, Gwen. Do you think so? I'm wearing a new uplift brassière but now my tunic buttons look even more like nippies."

She was right, and now she pointed them out, they were impossible to unsee. Whoever designed our uniform had based it on the men's tunic with the same round silver buttons on each breast pocket and little thought for the female form. If you were fairly flat-chested, like me, they didn't notice, but anyone bustier, like Pattie, appeared to have metal-tipped bosoms.

"Blokes keep gawping at my bust. I asked that lechy PC Higgs what he was staring at and he said he was just appreciating a fine pair of constabulary buttons. Can you believe it?"

I tutted. *Typical Higgs*.

"Anyway," I said, "I've got something to take your mind off him. We've had a report of a skeleton in some woods. Probably a missing dog remains, but Sarge thinks

18

it's worth us taking a look. Fancy a twilight jaunt to some spooky woods? I'd rather not go on my own."

"Fear not! WPC Patricia Baxter is here to protect you with her police-issue metal nipples!" She laughed, pushing her chest out. "Glad it's me and you investigating this skeleton, not Higgs."

"He'd probably 'accidentally' stick his hand on your knee instead of the gearstick, then make you wait in the car."

"He would. But then, *he'd* wait in the car and make *me* go into the woods."

The mid-afternoon October sun was sinking behind the treeline as Pattie and I arrived at High Copse Farm's twin grain silos. It was blowy, leaves coming off the trees with each gust. The autumn air carried a back-to-school smell: cool, damp and slightly mildewy, with a tinge of bonfire smoke. I shivered slightly in my thin tunic.

We set off down the short gravel path into the woods, sturdy shoes clumping just out of step.

"Looks like a track over there, Pattie, to our left."

We stopped by the double barbed wire fence. Clearly, something or someone had squeezed under the wire, flattening the ground elder. Slender as we were, after years of rationing, we couldn't fit under it and we had uniform dry cleaning to consider, too. The fence went on, unbroken, all around the wood. Climbing over it was the only option.

I went first, rolling the pleats of my voluminous uniform skirt up to mid-thigh to get my leg over the top. With what I felt was a gymnastic scissor action, I swung my other leg deftly over the barbs and stepped down into the leaves.

Pattie gathered and rolled her skirt right up over her stocking tops before she tackled the fence. As she swung her second leg over, she caught her thigh on the upper barbs, scratching herself deeply and ripping her stockings.

"Ow! Sodding hell! There goes my last pair of regulation stockings."

"Never mind your stockings, Pattie, you're bleeding all over the place – here, have my hanky."

Pattie stemmed the blood with my handkerchief, tucking it into her stocking as a makeshift bandage.

Skirts rolled back down, we stumbled off into the hazel coppice, crunching through leaves and twigs. The light was fading now, giving the woods a suffocating, misty, grey atmosphere. Sinister, just as Sarge had said. Blackbirds, settling down to roost for the night, chi-iked warnings and a hidden pheasant shrieked its strident call and whirred upwards, making us both jump.

We continued deeper into the wood. The air grew damper, more bosky, with a musty sweetish smell. I took out my torch. Pattie had forgotten hers.

"I'm not sure we're going to find anything now," I said. "It's too dark."

But Pattie was standing stock-still ahead of me, hand raised.

"Gwen . . . Gwen! Shine that torch over here." She beckoned to me.

I directed the beam across the woodland floor, towards the base of a beech tree. It lit up a tatty old boot thrown on the ground, then another close by. Some dark cotton material somehow connected the boots to a pile of leaves further up. As I gingerly shone the torchlight upwards, we both gasped and recoiled as it illuminated a slack-jawed skeletal human face, its sunken, dead eyeholes glaring, as if part of the tree trunk. Strands of dishevelled white hair sprouted from the desiccated skin remaining on the scalp, giving it the appearance of a nightmarish ceremonial shrunken head howling in horror at being discovered.

"That's not a sodding St Bernard!" blurted Pattie.

No, this skeleton was human, probably male judging by the boot size and remnants of a tweed jacket, and it was clear that it had been in the woods for a few months. It had been a perfect summer for decomposing and desiccating a body. Woodland creatures had nibbled at this unfortunate too – he was missing both hands and his arms looked as though something carnivorous had gnawed on the bones.

"What are we going to do with him, Gwen? He's been here for a while. Can't see the harm in leaving him for another night, can you?"

"We can't do anything with him until we get the police surgeon and a team down here. And now the Ferals have found him, don't you think they're going to tell all their pals, who'll want to come and have a good look too? Maybe poke him with sticks? He deserves a bit of dignity, not another night alone in the woods."

Thanks to Sergeant Lamb's hunch that this might be something, he had sent a team in a police van to High Copse Farm to meet us. Detective Inspector Larry

Dankworth arrived with other officers and a local GP, Dr Wickes, who doubled up as a police surgeon to certify unexpected deaths. Bennett, a clues officer, arrived on a bike with his equipment in a wooden box on the front.

One PC unfolded a stepladder from the van and set it up over the fence, making access to the woods easier. Bennett helped him unload several lamps to illuminate the scene. Hearing their voices, I waved my torch at them to signal our location.

At the scene, DI Dankworth said, "That'll be all, Crockford and Baxter, we'll take it from here. You can go back and wait by the van now."

"But excuse me, Inspector," I said, "we're probationer WPCs. We know all the theory about procedure when a body like this is discovered. It's essential we put it into practice."

"Procedure is, Crockford," said Dankworth, "Dr Wickes here certifies death. Dr Wickes – does this man look dead to you?"

"Well yes, I don't think he's going to be getting up any time soon . . ."

"And then with Bennett, the clues officer, we look around the scene for . . . clues. Looks like an old tramp's wandered off into the woods and died. Seen it before. I'd be surprised if it's anything more suspicious than that. We need officers at the entrance to the scene to keep the prying eyes of the public away, so off you go, ladies. We'll talk you through the rest of the procedure when we've finished."

We waited by the police van in the gloom, smoking Pattie's cigarettes, irritated and bored. Bennett's flashgun lit up the woods periodically as he took photographs. No members of the public with prying eyes turned up.

The team came out of the woods and started packing up their equipment.

Dankworth eventually spoke to us. "Pretty much as I thought. Looks like some old roadster has died in there. Possibly a suicide. We found an almost-empty bottle of whisky and an empty pill bottle next to him – writing on it is as near as dammit illegible. We've taken those for closer examination."

Dankworth headed for the farmhouse to make a telephone call. When he returned, his team was ready to go, engine running. Bennett had already cycled off.

As he got into the passenger seat of the police van, Dankworth turned to us: "You've asked me for dead body experience, so I'm letting you have it. The undertaker is coming to collect the body. If you could retrieve it from the woods and get it as far as the lane, they'll take it from there. I've left you a couple of lamps so you can see what you're doing. Cheers. Cheerio."

And the van went off.

"Well, that's typical," I said. "They do the interesting bit and we clear up."

Tired, and reluctant to deal with the skeleton again, we approached the woods. The stepladder had been packed up and taken away, leaving us on the wrong side of the fence again.

"I really don't believe this," complained Pattie. "Doesn't anyone have the slightest consideration for anyone else? We're going to have to get over that sodding thing again."

We felt like crying, but we took deep breaths.

"Let's get it over with." I brushed away a tear of mild hysteria. "Try not to lose any more blood – I've run out of hankies."

With a minimal amount of blood loss, we were back at the skeleton.

"And what the hell are we supposed to use to collect the body, Gwen?" asked Pattie, starting to look a little bit sick.

My own stomach turned over. "Dankworth and his merry band of clowns haven't left us anything, have they? We're going to have to carry this old boy out with our bare hands."

"I don't fancy giving him a piggyback," complained Pattie.

"He's not going to be heavy, that's for sure," I replied. "I think I saw a bit of corrugated iron on the ground further back. Let's see if we can find that."

We pulled a sheet of rusted corrugated iron out of the leaf litter. It was longer than we thought, but narrow, and would be a challenge keeping the body on it.

Laying the sheet down beside the skeleton, we tried to work out how best to lift him onto it, as he was sitting up at a 90-degree angle. However we laid him down, his bottom, head and feet would dangle over the sides. Remembering an encyclopaedia picture I'd seen of a Mexican Day of the Dead ceremonial cadaver, we could try carrying him aloft in a sitting position.

Pattie agreed and tugged at the skeleton's trouser legs while I pulled his shoulders away from the tree trunk.

Trying to ignore the exodus of scuttling beetles and larvae from under his tattered, mildewed shirt and the slugs in his nasal cavity, we shuffled the skeleton onto the corrugated iron sheet, where he sat bolt upright and open-jawed, like one of the undead dragged from the grave, aghast at this treatment.

I shone a lamp around to make sure we hadn't missed anything. We picked up the boots with his feet still inside, but by now not attached to his legs, what looked like an arm bone and a second empty Macallan whisky bottle that was wedged under the body.

"Blimey, that's an expensive Scotch, Gwen," said Pattie. "My posh uncle up West drinks that."

"Makes a change from meths. A tramp with a discerning palate."

Pattie sniffed. "Probably pinched it."

I took these artefacts of a life's final scene and placed them next to the cadaver. We balanced the lamps on the sheet, but they kept toppling over and were next to useless.

Just as we, his uniformed bearers, lifted him off the ground, there was a soft cracking pop and the skeleton's top half fell backwards onto the sheet. Foul-smelling liquid leaked out and pooled in the ruts of the corrugated iron.

"I think we broke him in half, Pattie." I giggled shakily, horrified.

"Ugh!" Pattie gagged at the stench.

"At least he's laying down properly now."

We set off back to the path, discovering that we had to keep the corrugated iron completely level to stop the rancid ooze running off the ends and onto our uniform and shoes. Amazing how the fear of being soaked in cadaver juices concentrated the mind. When we reached the barbed-wire fence, our feet were mercifully dry, unlike our skirts.

The next problem was getting the skeleton over that wretched fence. We balanced the corrugated sheet on top of the wire. As we leaned over to lower it, the barbs dug viciously into our upper arms and shins. We both shouted in pain. Pattie, by his legs, could hold it no longer and dropped her end, catapulting the skeleton's head through the air and onto the path. It rolled for a few yards before settling, facing upwards and silently scream-ing at the dark sky, in front of some hobnailed boots.

Farmer Fowler had walked down to see how we were getting on. Although used to farming's sights and smells, he stepped back in horror when he saw the skull, hand over his mouth. His sheepdog sniffed and snarled at the macabre object, unsure whether to treat it as a bone or a human, then cringed away from us two dishevelled, bleeding women tumbling over the barbed wire after the decapitated corpse.

Fowler stammered, "Well, that's never a bloody St Bernard, is it?"

Just then, a private ambulance arrived, moving slowly along the stony lane, its headlamps illuminating the bizarre scene. Two serious and efficient undertakers in dark suits with black ties stepped out, taking cursory glances at the crumpled headless corpse on one end of the corrugated iron and the detached skull. They unloaded a coffin shell and some polythene sheeting.

"We could have done with some of that earlier," I said.

"You mean you moved this body on that sheet?" asked the undertaker, catching his colleague's eye with a horrified stare.

"Er, yes, from the woods," responded Pattie. "Our colleagues drove off without leaving us anything to collect him with."

"We'll take over from you, ladies," said the undertaker. "I expect you've had enough of this gentleman now."

"Bet you're both looking forward to a long hot bath tonight," said the younger undertaker, grinning.

"And getting this uniform off," said Pattie, stretching, making the undertaker grin a little more at her constabulary buttons.

"But not the dry-cleaning bill." I sighed, looking at the streaks of unspeakable fluids on my skirt.

We watched the ambulance trundle away.

"Poor bloke," said Pattie. "No hands for fingerprints, no identification papers."

"Forensics might just about be able to detect a blood group from his teeth," I said. "After all this, I wonder if we'll ever find out who this old boy was and why he ended up dying out here all on his own."

CHAPTER 3

Joining and training

I applied to the Berkshire Constabulary at the County Police Headquarters in Reading and received an invitation to a selection board.

"Well done, my girl! Chip off the old block!" said Dad, pointing to his Specials uniform, about to go on duty. "The best of luck to you. A word of advice for when they ask you why you want to join the police force – don't say, 'because I want to help people.' They'll tell you to go off and be a nurse or a probation officer if that's your sole object. Your job is to know and uphold law and order, first and foremost. Don't forget that."

"I really don't know what's wrong with your solicitors' job, Gwen," said Mum. "You've been all right there for the last six years . . ."

"I might not even get selected, Mum, and if I don't, I'll stay at the solicitors'," I said.

But I couldn't bear the thought of that. I had to make this happen.

The County Police Headquarters in Reading were shabby and dated compared to Wokingham's handsome Edwardian police station, but the blue lamp outside and general bustle was the same. It had that distinctive police-station smell I would become so familiar with – a mix of boot polish, typewriter ribbon, sweat, tobacco smoke and disinfectant.

I followed a sergeant along a series of dingy corridors to an examination room set up with single desks like a classroom. Some men were already seated at their desks, exam papers face down. Nobody looked at anyone else. It was as if we'd turned the clock back 15 years and were nervous schoolchildren again.

All the desks filled up apart from one by the door. The examining sergeant looked at his watch.

"Well, you're all present and correct, bar one. You can turn your papers over and begin."

Just as I was getting stuck into the arithmetic section, I heard a distant trip-trapping of heels on parquet, getting faster as it approached, skidding just outside the door.

A puce-faced woman, strands of strawberry blonde hair escaping from a messy bun, wearing a fur-collared camel coat and carrying an oversized handbag burst in, full of apology. All eyes turned to her.

"I'm so sorry ... I missed the first bus ... then I couldn't find the station," she panted. "Ooh – have you started?"

The sergeant wordlessly indicated the empty desk.

The woman sat down, rustling as she tried unsuccessfully to make her coat stay on the back of the chair, and rummaging in her handbag for a pencil case. We turned back to focusing on our maths problems. There was a clunk and skittering sounds as the pencil case fell on the floor and its contents bounced everywhere.

With a sharp intake of breath, the examining sergeant marched to her desk and picked up her scattered stationery.

"I'm so sorry," whispered the woman. "I'm all fingers and thumbs this morning."

Arithmetic paper completed, we took an intelligence test and a dictation that sounded like some sort of court proceedings report. General knowledge was pretty straightforward: name members of the Cabinet, county towns in the south of England, countries in the British Empire. There were some questions on the Cold War, which we were living through; I wrote an essay about whether atomic bombs would ever be used in anger again, concluding that no nation would be so stupid as to drop another bomb first.

Following the exam was a selection board interview with some silver-bedecked, top brass and the chief constable, Commander Humphry Legge, an imposing, aristocratic man with a lazy, plummy accent and an iron handshake.

After small talk about Wokingham, voluntary work and my family, he asked, "Why do you want to join the police force?"

My mind raced. *Don't say you want to help people. Don't say you want to help people . . .*

"I want a job that is both demanding and rewarding, upholding law and order, helping the police to deliver exceptional service to the public, who have very high expectations of us," I said.

Thanks, Dad.

Commander Legge sat up, smiling, looking me in the eye.

And with that, he concluded the interview with another iron grip.

The day ended with a medical. I took a seat outside the examination room as instructed and I could hear loud, nervous giggles coming from inside. After a few minutes, the door opened and the strawberry blonde woman from the exam came out, thumb pressed over a plaster.

"They even want your blood, they do." She giggled, slightly breathless. "How did you get on? I think I messed up some of the questions. Hugh Gaitskell's the Home Secretary, isn't he?"

"I think it's James Chuter Ede," I said.

"Oh bugger, I got that wrong, then. Oh well . . ." she said.

I was about to chat when the doctor called me in for my medical. He took my blood pressure and a vial of blood out of my arm, then measured my height (bang on 5'4", the minimum for a WPC) and weight. When I came out, the woman had gone. I doubted I would see her again.

As I left for work a few weeks later, the postman called, "Letter for you, Miss Crockford."

He handed me a small brown envelope with BERKSHIRE CONSTABULARY on the front.

"Hope you've not been getting yourself into any pickles." He winked at me.

"Oh, I'm sure I shall be," I replied, tearing open the envelope.

Madam,
With reference to your application to join this Force, I
am directed by the Chief Constable to inform you that
you will be appointed as a Probationary Constable as
from 16 September, 1951. You should, therefore, report
at this office at 9.15 a.m on Monday, 17 September.

I was in! I'd passed selection. I was going to join the police force, assuming the senior partner would give me a good reference, that I was "honest, sober and respectable". The partners were huddled in a meeting when I arrived at work, so I took the opportunity to type out my resignation and acknowledge the superintendent's letter. I looked out of the window at the police officers going in and out of the station.

That was going to be me soon.

At 9.10 a.m. on Monday, 17 September, I walked through the doors of County Police Headquarters with my documents. A sergeant showed me into a reception room filled with a sea of grey demob suits. I seemed to be the only woman there. Some of the men turned to look at me. Some smiled pleasantly and nodded; others, stony-faced, looked me up and down and turned back to chat to their pals. I helped myself to a cup of coffee, but passed on the biscuits – I was too nervous to eat.

"Cooee!" I heard a woman's voice calling across the room and saw a waving hand. Heads turned. The strawberry blonde from selection was moving towards me through the grey throng with a rich tea clamped between her lips, juggling her handbag, cup and saucer. She took the biscuit out of her mouth and placed it on the slopped coffee in the saucer.

"Hello! Remember me? We were at selection together? I'm Patricia Baxter, but please call me Pattie. Nice to see you again!"

Patricia Baxter held out her hand with its beautifully French manicured nails. I shook it.

"Hello, Pattie. Yes, I do remember you." *How could I forget?* "I'm Gwen Crockford."

"Looks like I got away with Hugh Gaitskell, doesn't it?" she giggled.

And being 20 minutes late for the exam, I thought. But there was a kind of endearingly clumsy warmth about Pattie.

"Is it just us? The only two girlies? With all these boys?" Pattie glanced around, catching the eye of a Gary Cooperesque recruit, who winked back at her. She giggled again. "I think we're going to have some fun on this training course."

Fun was the last thing on my mind. I couldn't wait to get stuck into learning all about the law, courtroom process, policing the beat, taking statements and investigating burglaries and murders.

We went in groups into a panelled hall and were given a small Bible to hold in our right hands. In front of a magistrate, we chanted an oath off a card:

"... And that while I continue to hold the said office,

I will discharge the duties thereof to the best of my skill and knowledge faithfully, according to law, without fear, favour, affection, malice or ill will…"

We had our official photographs taken. Pattie couldn't resist putting her head on one side, pouting, and when the photos were developed, she looked like a Marilyn Monroe impersonator after a heavy night out. My effort to appear a steely, don't-mess-with-me officer of the law just gave me the resting bitch face of a female Stasi guard. People pointed and laughed at our photos on the station board for years.

The next day, we were on a train heading to Staffordshire to the police depot at Mill Meece, a converted WW2 Admiralty camp, for our 13-week training course. Like most ex-forces camps, it consisted of a series of single-storey prefabricated huts set around a large parade ground and playing fields.

A sergeant showed us to our quarters. I was expecting – and dreading – a long dormitory of iron beds, but each of us 18 women recruits had our own bright, single study bedroom with a washbasin and a window. Hot showers were available 24/7 in the shared bathrooms and I may as well have just stepped into The Savoy. I was so delighted with our accommodation. Pattie was right – this could be fun.

"Beds are a bit narrow, though, aren't they?" complained Pattie, popping her head round my door.

"We'll be so exhausted after a day of training we'll just fall dead asleep into them and won't even notice," I replied.

"Speak for yourself." She chuckled and disappeared next door to arrange her make-up.

The Mill Meece police course was more like army training than I expected. We had to be in full polished uniform for breakfast at eight, then on parade at 8.40 before inspection. We seemed to do an awful lot of military-style marching up and down, being shouted at by a drill sergeant. We felt ridiculous square-bashing in billowing skirts. Arms and legs floating out of time, we looked like a row of uniformed Sugar Plum Fairies prancing across the parade ground, compared to our male colleagues in trousers who mastered that clumpy, keeping-in-step thing immediately.

At nine, after the daily marching debacle, we began lectures: the intricacies of the licensing laws; road traffic regulations; the Children and Young Persons Act, which was to be my constant companion for the next decade; an eye-popping week about sex crimes and deviance; forensics; customs of the various law courts and how to prepare cases, and rural skills such as spotting animal diseases.

Our first, somewhat bizarre lecture, by a pompous little instructor from the Birmingham City force was all about "upholding the dignity of the service". Apparently, we should sleep with open windows, cultivate a BBC standard of speech and recognise that "punctuality is a must". I glared meaningfully at Pattie, who was examining her nails.

We backed up what we learned in lectures with after-dinner study, much of it learning definitions by rote. The 18 of us would sit along the corridor of our hut with our mighty reference tomes – *Moriarty's Police Law* and the even weightier *Stone's Justices' Manual* – testing each other on various offences and shouting back the definitions. Larceny was our particular bugbear – it covered more than 30 crimes, as disparate as cattle rustling, breaking into a place of worship, embezzling Post Office packages, demanding money with menaces and stealing ore from mines. We had to know all these off by heart and often just confused each other.

"Bloody hell, it's like your worst nightmare game of Cluedo," cried Pattie. "It was Professor Plum who killed the dog down the coal mine with a house-breaking implement after stealing a statue."

After lectures, we had practical sessions – first aid, jujitsu for self-defence (which sounds impressive, but really just taught us how to throw someone over our shoulder, or get an armlock on them), role-play arrests and mock courtroom cases. We were bussed off on a couple of day trips: one to sit through the proceedings of a magistrates' court, the other to visit a funeral director's morgue and see a dead body for ourselves.

Before we got to the morgue, we'd been reassured that we wouldn't be attending a post-mortem, or be shown someone who'd died in a horrific accident. But none of us felt like chatting as we stood in a semicircle around a mortuary table where a sheet-covered body lay. Pattie looked pale and shifted from foot to foot. Just to prolong our discomfort, the funeral director – clearly a man who had no ability to read a room – began his introduction with, "Well, of course it was back in 1194 that the office of coroner, originally 'coronator' or 'crowner', derived from the Latin word 'corona' was established . . ." and droned on for a good 10 minutes about the officialdom of death, oblivious to our anxious intakes of breath.

When he eventually removed the sheet, we exhaled collective relief at the sight of a tiny, elderly lady who just looked as if she was having a pleasant afternoon nap. No smell, no horror, perfectly peaceful. Somebody's mum, granny, sister, daughter. One of the girls teared up as the director covered the body with the sheet again. And then we all got back on the bus.

Little did we appreciate that many of the dead bodies we would encounter in our careers wouldn't be as intact or unviolated as this dear lady.

It wasn't entirely all work and no play at Mill Meece for 13 weeks, though. We could go into Stoke for the evening as long as we were back before lights out, or into Stafford on the weekend. Us girls were taken on a tour of the nearby Wedgwood china factory – we were in the heart of the Staffordshire "Potteries" after all. I bought my family's Christmas presents in the factory shop.

The highlight of the week was the Friday night dance in the assembly hut. Because new recruits arrived every week as the top group graduated, there were always new people to socialise with. As we went through our course, we grew in confidence to advise and reassure the raw recruits, some of whom – especially those destined for the colonial services – seemed far more worldly-wise than us. With more men than women at the dances, us girls barely sat out a single number, and could pick and choose the best-looking partners, or those least likely to bruise our toes.

Relationships inevitably formed. Several of the girls in our hut had surreptitious romances with the male recruits and I must admit my head was turned by Geoffrey, a lad from the Durham constabulary who I danced with regularly and partnered up with for whist drives. We'd read the same books, had the same interest in current events and came from the same type of repressive, religious, old-fashioned family that prevented us having anything more than a chaste kiss after my passing out parade. Probably just as well I didn't fall head-over-heels for Geoffrey as he was destined to set sail for a career in the Rhodesian police force immediately after training.

Pattie, on the other hand, had fallen hook, line and sinker for Jim, the Gary Cooperesque recruit who had winked at her on the first day in Reading. They would nip off to the local pub together and went dancing in Stoke one evening, missed the last bus and had to walk for three hours back to the depot. How they weren't spotted squeezing through the hedge at four in the morning said less about Pattie and Jim and more about Mill Meece's security.

One Thursday evening, almost midnight, I was struggling to memorise the details of the Town Police Clauses Act – things you can't do in the streets. Everyone else had gone to bed – I thought. I could hear muffled giggling coming from Pattie's room next door and a masculine low chuckling. Then a rhythmic squeaking sound like bedsprings started and more giggling. There was no way I could focus on learning the various forms of public nuisance with that going on. I lay on my bed with a pillow over my ears. After a while, it stopped and I started to doze off. Then, the clunking sound of Pattie's window opening jerked me awake once more and I opened my own window to see what was going on. There was Jim, hanging halfway out.

"What the . . ." I said as Pattie appeared, urgently shushing me.

"Hey! You there!" A distant shout from the drill sergeant, who must have been outside on night patrol duty. Jim dropped to the ground behind some low bushes and commando-crawled rapidly away into the darkness.

"You there! What's going on?" The drill sergeant marched up to Pattie's window.

"Did I see some personage exiting your room, miss?" He looked left and right, but Jim was well away now.

"Oh no, I think you must be mistaken, Sergeant," said Pattie, with her sweetest smile.

"Well, why is your window wide open in the middle of winter?"

"Sergeant, we were told in our first lecture that to uphold the dignity of the police service, we have to sleep with open windows. So that's what I'm doing. And Gwen here is opening hers before she goes to sleep, isn't that right, Gwen?"

I nodded dumbly, not wanting to dob Pattie in, but I cursed her as I nearly froze to death leaving my window open all that night.

Our time at Mill Meece was drawing to a close. We had been assessed throughout the 13 weeks and there were just some final written exams to pass before we qualified. On the day before we passed out, our overall results were posted:

WPC G.A. Crockford   84 per cent
WPC P.M. Baxter   51 per cent

"Ooh, by the skin of my teeth," said Pattie. "Well done you, though."

"You passed!" I said. "We really start learning to be policewomen now."

We marched up and down as badly as ever to a military band on our passing out parade before a farewell reception in the assembly hall. Some of the girls cried as they bade farewell to their beaus. Pattie and Jim disappeared into her room one last time and I kissed Geoffrey, wishing him a safe passage to Africa.

On the train back to Wokingham for Christmas, I couldn't believe 13 weeks had gone by so quickly and I'd learned so much. The real challenge would be putting it all into practice in real life situations.

CHAPTER 4

Nurse Suzette McDaniel

I'd looked forward to coming home for Christmas after Mill Meece. I felt I had learned so much, grown in confidence and found my independence. I'd loved having my own room, space to be me, hot showers on tap and the respect, camaraderie and support of the other recruits. I'd grown up.

Then I got back to Seaford Road. Back to the arguments, the tin bath, the snide comments, sharing a bedroom again and my younger sister "borrowing" what little make-up I had. Nothing had changed, but for me everything had changed.

Christmas dinner, after a couple of glasses of sherry, descended into old familiar rows about what some relative did, didn't do or said in 1938, with Dad getting so exasperated he slammed his spoon down in his pudding bowl so hard he spattered us all with custard.

"I'm going out. Get away from you lot," he shouted, picking up his hat and coat and flouncing out of the front door, tripping on the doormat.

"Yes, and don't bother coming back," yelled Mum.

I quietly went upstairs. After I'd sponged the custard off my cardigan, I opened my suitcase and took out my uniform and newly-issued warrant card to remind myself that I was an adult, with responsibilities.

My younger sister Jean appeared at the bedroom door. "I haven't seen you in your uniform. Would you put it on for me?"

I showed her how to tie the tie, fix the detachable collar with studs and fasten the epaulettes. I put my hat on at the correct angle. I hoped I looked feminine yet professional.

"You look like a real lady policeman, Sis," said Jean, beaming.

"She looks like a police *man* in that uniform." Mum's voice. She had crept upstairs behind Jean. "Good job you've got yourself a vocation to rely on. With your attitude and looks, no man will want to come anywhere near you." And she went into her bedroom to lie down, complaining of one of her "heads".

That evening I scoured the local newspaper's lodgings column. I would rather give rent money and my ration coupons to a stranger than my mother any longer. At least I'd get a room to myself, and a lot less drama.

I put down my suitcase outside an imposing mock-Tudor house in Murdoch Road and jangled the ship's bell. Mrs Cunningham, all floral in headscarf and housecoat, flung open the door and beckoned me in.

"Come in. Come in, dear. I've got your room all ready," she trilled.

I hesitated momentarily before crossing the threshold into a new house, a new job, a new life. I followed my new landlady up dark oak stairs to the first landing, where there were two closed doors and an open one into a light, airy room. A small desk stood by the window and a mighty mahogany wardrobe took up all of one wall. There was a single bed draped with a thick, gold, brocade eiderdown in the middle of the room and a beatific Jesus blessing a tree full of tropical birds beamed from a picture above the bedstead.

"Bathroom for your landing is to your left," said Mrs Cunningham. "You'll need to switch the immersion heater on an hour before you want a bath."

This was the height of modern sophistication. To be able to summon up hot water at the flick of a switch, after years of a kettle-filled tin bath in front of the fire at Seaford Road. I'd revelled in the hot showers at training school and now I could choose when I had a hot bath. Life was on the up.

"You'll have to agree with Suzette when you need to use the bathroom, what with her shifts and your shifts."

"Suzette?"

"Ah, yes, dear Suzette. She's in the room next to you, sharing the landing. A nurse at Wokingham Hospital. She comes and goes at funny times of the day and night."

Ah, I thought, *it'll be nice to share with another member of the emergency services*. Police, nurses and firemen have a kind of all-in-it-together camaraderie born out of dealing with both the worst and the best of what the job throws at them.

Mrs Cunningham dropped her voice to a conspiratorial whisper, "She's a *coloured* girl, you know."

I didn't really know what to say to that. I'd read in the newspapers that lots of West Indians had come over after the war to work, but I hadn't met any before.

"Well, I look forward to meeting her," I said.

"Get yourself unpacked. Supper's at seven. When you're ready, pop down and I'll show you where everything is."

"Thanks, Mrs Cunningham."

I closed my door as her floral form bustled off down the stairs and looked around my spartan new home. I unpacked my clothes into the wardrobe, hung my uniform on the back of the door, then sat on the edge of the bed, contemplating my new life. I'd loved training school – the book learning, the role plays, the interaction with the other recruits, Pattie's exploits, having a room to myself.

I couldn't wait to get started in the job, yet I had a sudden sinking feeling that I would forget it all in a real-life situation. Would I really cut it on the beat? I tried to recite those definitions of larceny to bolster my confidence and found to my dismay that I couldn't recall half of them. What if my first case was a theft? I looked at Beatific Jesus for some sort of sign that everything was going to be all right, but He just kept smiling at His birds.

A gentle knocking on the door brought me out of the rabbit hole of doubt I'd gone down. *It's probably Mrs Cunningham dropping some towels off*, I thought. I opened the door to a short, tubby woman with golden skin, freckles and a generous smile.

"Hello, I'm Suzette," she said. "You must be Gwen, my new landing mate? The policewoman?"

I could almost hear Mrs Cunningham's words to her, "She's a police *woman*, you know."

We shook hands. Her handshake was firm, warm and soft.

"How do you do, Suzette, it's lovely to meet you."

"Sorry, I was asleep when you arrived. I'm on nights now so I don't surface much before late afternoon. Just to ask you – I'm going to put the immersion on now for my bath, do you want one later? If so, I'll leave it on for you."

"That would be very kind, thank you."

"I'm in for supper tonight so we can have a proper chat then. My shift doesn't start until 10. I've never met a policewoman before – it must be such an interesting job." She smiled and went into the bathroom.

I felt a bit of impostor syndrome – I couldn't call myself a proper policewoman yet. But Suzette was sweet and welcoming. That would do for now.

The downstairs at Mrs Cunningham's lodging house looked as if it had been untouched since the Victorian era: all dark, heavy furniture, oriental rugs, button-back armchairs and lacy antimacassars. Some would call the style dated; I thought it was quite upmarket after Seaford Road's tatty, kicked-about-by-a-family-of-six furnishings.

"You'll take your meals in here," instructed Mrs Cunningham, indicating a long dining table flanked by carved oak sideboards. She launched into an overcomplicated explanation of how she would serve me and Suzette breakfasts and suppers to align with our shifts. I glazed over, but it seemed to involve keeping a plate of food warm for hours over a simmering saucepan of water with the lid on top.

45

Suzette and I settled opposite each other across the table at seven, in that awkward, best-behaviour politeness that comes from being in a different place with unfamiliar people. Supper was a greyish beef stew that seemed to be 80 per cent swede, with boiled potatoes and cabbage. With Mrs Cunningham hanging about behind the kitchen door, no doubt waiting to hear approving noises about her food, I surreptitiously pushed the chunks of swede about, trying to find some meat.

Suzette watched me, her eyes twinkling and a smile playing on her lips.

"You looking for the beef?" she whispered.

"I am." I blushed slightly, not wanting to appear rude or ungrateful.

"You're going to be looking for a long time." Suzette snorted into her glass of water and I started to laugh. She continued, "I've been looking since 1949," my shoulders started to shake, "and I still haven't found any."

That was it. I was in fits of silent laughter, my eyes filling with tears, not daring to breathe in case I snorted and hovering Mrs Cunningham heard. Suzette was silently laughing and pointing at my helplessness.

And that's how the ice broke on one of my longest and best friendships.

Over apple crumble that actually had apples in it, Suzette recounted how she had responded to the plea for Commonwealth medical professionals to staff the newly-formed NHS, left her family and sailed over from Barbados in 1949. After she'd told me about her hardworking mother, idle father and sisters she'd left back on their farm, coping with the economic downturn on the island wrought by the 1944 hurricane, her eyes glistened and she hesitated. She was clearly struggling to say something else, but I didn't want this warm, funny person who had done so much to welcome me to be upset. There would be plenty of time to share each other's burdens, trials and tribulations, so I swiftly changed the subject.

"You must have some incredible nursing stories to tell, though?"

Suzette's smile returned. "I'll need to get to know you better before I tell you some of the naughtier ones, Gwen. But today I had to say goodbye to one of my oldest and favourite patients."

"I'm sorry to hear that," I said. "It must be hard when a patient dies."

"Oh no, he didn't die. He was discharged home from hospital with his vile son-in-law. Probably a fate worse than death."

"I'm guessing there's a story here, Suzette?"

"Kind of. My patient was dear Mr Jenkins, an elderly gentleman, going senile, bless him. A veteran of the Sudan Campaign and a survivor of the Battle of Omdurman in 1898 – a true Victorian, I suppose. Sometimes he would be lucid, but occasionally he would regress into his younger days. His eyes would become wild and fearful and he'd clasp the sheets and quote Kipling poetry at me as I made his bed or settled him on a bedpan. Poor love. His body was in Wokingham Hospital, but his mind was back in the Sudan, reliving his skirmish with the Mahdi's army.

"One day Mr Jenkins's son-in-law, Basil Gill – some sort of local dignitary connected with the council – was visiting, just as he was coming out of one of his funny turns. I tucked him in and left them chatting. When he'd gone, Matron called me into her office.

"'Nurse McDaniel, I'm sorry to say I've had a complaint from Mr Gill.'

"'A complaint? What . . .'

"'He thinks his father-in-law would be more comfortable being looked after by an "English" nurse, as he thinks you give him flashbacks to his army days in Sudan and it's not good for his heart.'

"'Would Mr Jenkins feel more comfortable, or is it really Mr Gill who would feel more comfortable?' I asked. I think Matron got where I was coming from.

"'I know,' she said, sighing, 'but what can you do? Gill is quite high up in the council and corporations, and we don't want to rock the boat, so if you could just make yourself scarce from around Mr Jenkins during visiting hours, everybody's happy, then, aren't they?'

"So every visiting hours, I busied myself with other patients, and as soon as Gill had gone I went back to nursing his father-in-law. But you know what? When Mr Jenkins was discharged from hospital today, Gill was pushing him along in a wheelchair and I happened to be coming down the corridor towards them. Gill didn't know where to look, but Mr Jenkins had one of his moments of clarity. He made him stop the wheelchair, then he reached out his skinny arms to me for a hug – which I gave him, of course – and thanked me for looking after him. 'Basil,' he'd said, 'this is my nurse! The best nurse any man could have. She has been magnificent, and I shall miss her.'

"'I'll miss you too, Mr Jenkins,' I said, 'keep yourself well.'

"Gill's face! He couldn't have looked more embittered if he had been sucking on a lemon." Suzette laughed.

Despite her relentlessly cheery exterior, it was clear that Suzette didn't always have an easy time of things at work. But word of her kind, caring and cheerful personality got round and made everyone want a Barbadian nurse to look after them.

In fact, Suzette would become a Wokingham treasure, not only because she was one of the first West Indians to come and live in the town, but also because she radiated sunshine, even in a dismal British winter. By spending the war in Barbados, she hadn't been ground down by grey Britain's deprivation, doodlebugs and digging for victory. For me, she was a refreshing change from my other friends and family whose constant Blitz-spirit moaning – once useful for keeping going in the darkest hour – had continued into peacetime.

It was after nine o'clock. We could hear Mrs Cunningham clattering about putting the final bits of crockery back in the cupboards. Two hours had passed in a flash, chatting about our families and our work. I felt my anecdotes about the solicitors' office were so boring compared with Suzette's nursing ones. Surely police work would be eventful and I'd have some tales to tell?

Suzette jumped up from the table. "Lordy, is that the time? I need to get to the hospital. Well, that was fun chatting to you, we'll do it again soon!"

I would have cheerfully gone out of the door there and then with Suzette to get stuck into my first day, rather than spending this first night sick with apprehension. Despite the unfamiliar cracks, creaks and groans of the old house's nocturnal cooling, I managed to sleep, dreaming of a contented Mr Jenkins floating in the azure waters off a palm-fringed Barbados beach, with Suzette waving to him from the shore.

CHAPTER 5

On the job

It was 8.50 a.m., on 2 January 1952. I sheltered for a few minutes on the stone steps beneath Wokingham Police Station's magnificent Arts and Crafts pagoda entrance, drawing deeply on a cigarette to calm my first day jitters. I glanced up at my old solicitors' office window opposite. Someone – a new girl – was watching me over her typewriter. I wondered what she was thinking.

The less imposing public door to the station front desk was to the right of the pagoda, with its blue lamp above and COUNTY POLICE carved into its stone lintel. It was here I had to report. I approached the front desk. I couldn't see many officers, but I heard behind-the-scenes bustle.

"One of our shiny new recruits, miss?" asked the kindly desk sergeant, noticing my uniform under my scarf and unbuttoned big coat.

"Er, yes, it's my first day," I said. "Hello, I'm Gwen … I mean WPC Crockford."

"I'm Sergeant Alan Lamb. You're early. That's good. Punctuality is a must, you know. Sign into the duty book here, please. Then if you'd like to wait in that room, your training sergeant will be down to show you the ropes and introduce you to everyone."

51

I scribbled my name, then stood in what looked like a panelled interview room off the lobby and watched the clock hand jump to nine o'clock. I heard the station door open and some familiar hurrying feet clumping up to the desk.

"Another one of our shiny new recruits, miss?" I heard Sergeant Lamb say. "Well, aren't we the lucky ones today?"

"WPC Patricia Baxter reporting for duty, Sah!"

I didn't need to be in the lobby to know that Pattie had saluted Sergeant Lamb.

"I'm Sergeant Alan Lamb," I heard him say. "You're on time by the skin of your teeth, Constable. Punctuality is a must."

It was good to see Pattie again. We hugged each other. Mill Meece had been a blast, made all the more entertaining by her presence. Lord knows what she would be like to work with.

A tall, barrel-chested policeman with thick, dark hair, a broad smile and an extensive row of medal ribbons above his breast pocket entered the room. Goodness, was he imposing. Even Pattie was silent.

"I'm Sergeant Hartwell, and with WPS Robertshaw, who'll be along later, I'll be your training sergeant for your two probationary years. We'll be supervising and assessing you, and with luck, graft and you passing your three exams, we'll turn you into two fully-fledged police officers."

Bob, as we could call him, took us round the busy, labyrinthine police station complex. The magistrates' court and probation office took up half of the building and the station itself was arranged over three floors with a sweeping flight of stone stairs in the middle.

I initially lost count of the number of offices and back rooms: the front office, charge office, separate women's office, CID, switchboard, interview rooms, offices for the station clerk, superintendent and inspector (who lived in a police house on the complex), attic storeroom, cell block, canteen and kitchen. Outside, maintenance garages lined the station yard for the array of vehicles: Black Maria police vans, small patrol cars and a fast pursuit car. A row of kennels housed some stray dogs.

We met so many people that morning that even I had trouble remembering who was who. Some characters stood out right from the start: PC Henry Falconer was a leaner, more serious version of Bob Hartwell, with Brylcreemed hair and a downturned mouth that made him seem permanently unhappy.

"Ex-servicemen, those two," Sergeant Lamb told me. "Bob and Henry's intake after the war are the finest recruits our constabulary has ever had."

Henry's medal ribbons were as impressive as Bob's. Clearly, the two men were fit, capable officers who had come through the war and they commanded respect. The same couldn't be said for PC Higgs. A thin, pale youngster with freckles, frizzy hair and a silly grin, he spent too much time looking me and Pattie up and down. We didn't fancy being left alone in a room with him.

We looked through glass doors into the CID offices. A blond, rangy detective inspector was pointing at some mug shots and enlarged fingerprints pinned to a cork board, gesticulating to another detective.

"I won't interrupt DI Dankworth in full flow," said Bob. "You'll get to meet him properly when you do your two weeks' CID placements. Or if he needs you before that."

We had to stand to attention when Superintendent Barker came out of his office. A lugubrious, moon-faced man with dark circles under his eyes, he mumbled a welcome to his two new WPCs before trotting down the stairs. Pattie and I looked at each other.

"So now you've met the super," Bob lowered his voice, "or, as we call him, The EF."

"The EF?" asked Pattie.

"It's short for Eternal Flame," said Bob.

We were still puzzled.

"Because he never goes out."

The time came to meet WPS Robertshaw. Bob took us to the women's office, where she awaited us. A statuesque woman with strong features, steely blue eyes and military poise, she was as commanding in person as she was when I had watched her from my window. Professional yet feminine. Her handshake was stronger than Commander Legge's.

"How do you do? Welcome to Wokingham. Sorry I couldn't be here first thing. I was settling a new WPC in at Crowthorne. I'm now responsible for all the other WPCs scattered across my patch of Berkshire, as well as you two. You've been shown around by Sergeant Hartwell here, haven't you? Good. You'll soon get the feel for the place and how we do things. And … what is that on your hands, WPC Baxter?"

Pattie jumped. She'd been daydreaming through Miss Robertshaw's opening spiel. She turned her hands over, looking for dirty marks.

"Sorry, Miss Robertshaw, I'm not sure what you mean?"

"This." Miss Robertshaw pointed to a tiny, delicate French manicure that I could barely see on Pattie's nails.

"The wearing of nail varnish is strictly prohibited, WPC Baxter. When we've finished here, I'll get you some acetone and you will take it off." She gave Pattie a penetrating stare.

We spent the rest of the morning with her, learning about our role in the station. It turned out that Pattie and I would work together infrequently, only when our shift patterns coincided, or on special patrol. There had to be a woman officer on duty at each shift and there weren't many of us to go round. While Miss Robertshaw could call on us at any time, we were also to take instruction from whichever sergeant or inspector needed our services, especially where women and children were involved.

Once Miss Robertshaw had left to check in on another WPC, Bob Hartwell took us on our first beat to get to know the "manor", as he called our patch.

"I'll hold your hands today, so to speak," he said. "And then, for the next couple of weeks you're on the men's beats with a buddy PC, just to show you the ropes."

Being Wokingham born and bred, I knew every inch of the town and most of the people in it. Pattie, coming from Newbury, didn't. We patrolled past Joel Park, where familiar figures I knew were out and about: the bank manager in his striped trousers, long black overcoat and distinctive Homburg hat walking his dog, Esme Cripps's now-teenage twin boys bumping up and down on a seesaw that was too small for them.

Every time we crossed roads, vehicles stopped to let us go. Pattie sashayed across with a big smile to the drivers, revelling in the attention.

"Jim keeps telling me I'm a girl who could stop traffic," she whispered. "Seems like I do."

A lorry driver waved us across. "Cor! You wait ages for one policewoman then two come along at once!" he called, went to say something else, then wound up his window when he saw Bob behind us.

Several people did a double take when they saw me in my uniform, some wanting to chat as they hadn't seen me since September. My switch from the solicitors' office to the station opposite warranted a mention in the local newspaper – *Law girl turns PC* – so they had read about it and wanted to wish me well.

"Come on, WPC Crockford, this is the police force, not Mothers' Union," grumbled Bob as we were stopped for the fifth time. "But granted, you do seem to know your public."

We stopped by a telephone box. In 1952, police patrol cars were fitted with two-way radios, but none of the beat constables had portable radios. Incredible as it seems now, the only way the station could get in touch with officers remotely was by ringing a phone box and expecting them to answer.

Bob explained how it worked. "Along the beat routes, officers 'make points' by stopping at designated boxes every half hour," he said. "They wait to see if the phone rings, and if it doesn't, they continue their beat to the next one and wait to see if that rings. They mustn't be late to each point."

"What happens if we're caught up dealing with something and can't make our point on time?" I asked.

"Well, the good news for you ladies is … beat points don't apply to you! Just us men. You can choose to patrol where you like unless instructed otherwise. You've actually got more freedom than we have."

"How come?" asked Pattie.

"We need your reassuring presence and sharp eyes around town, WPC Baxter. Feel free to wander round shops, stores and cafés, chatting to the public. Just not too much time sitting in coffee shops, eh?"

Pattie and I chuckled.

Bob continued, "To answer your question, a PC's failure to answer would prompt one of us to cycle or drive round and check on him. If he's dealing with something, fair enough. If he's just late, woe betide him. But if you ever hear a telephone ringing, and there's nobody near the box, answer it."

This system relied on the phone boxes not being vandalised, which they weren't in those days. People generally respected public property.

We returned to the station after our inaugural beat, in time for a tea break in the airy canteen. We attracted a lot of looks from officers we hadn't yet been introduced to and a wave from Henry Falconer. It was good to see a familiar face and he was actually quite nice-looking when he smiled. I started to feel as if I could fit in here.

"I'm going to be very kind and let you go home early today," said Bob. "But tomorrow, WPC Crockford, I'm putting you on early turn. You need to report for your shift at 5.45 a.m. WPC Baxter, you're on lates, so please be here at 13.45."

Pattie grinned broadly, resisting the temptation to punch the air; she wasn't an early bird, and finishing at 10 p.m. was no hardship for her. I would finish at 2 p.m. and have to find something to fill my time before supper at seven at Mrs Cunningham's.

As we walked down to the locker rooms, we reflected on our first day.

"Bloody hell, my brain's frazzled, Gwen – there's so much to remember. I don't think I'd be able to do that route again on my own."

"You will, Pattie. Wokingham's not a big place. You'll get to know it."

A bottle of industrial-looking acetone sat on top of Pattie's locker.

"If Miss Robertswhatsherface thinks I'm going to use that paint stripper on my nails she's got another think coming," said Pattie. "Bugger though, I thought I'd done them so nobody would notice."

"Our WPS doesn't miss a trick," I said.

It was dark and drizzly as we left, muffled into our winter coats; Pattie heading for the railway station, me towards Murdoch Road.

"Good luck for tomorrow," called Pattie. "I'll be willing you on at six in the morning from under my eiderdown. Oh wait, no I won't be, because I'll be *asleep*." She cackled as she tripped off to catch her train.

I smiled. "Thanks for that."

The next day, following inspection parade at 6 a.m., I marched (badly) out of the door with the other early turn officers for my first ever beat, shadowing the glum PC Willoughby. It was still dark and I wondered if this was what night duty felt like.

We "shook hands with all the doorknobs", as we called it, testing the locked shops' security, and noted down the registration number of a passing car. We had to record the numbers of all cars driving at night. Did this count as night?

"I think we can count this as the 'hours of darkness' even though it's our morning," mumbled PC Willoughby, so I noted it.

As the wintry sun came up, I caught my reflection in a dress shop window mirror. In the quiet street, and pretending to study the window locks, I couldn't stop staring at myself. A shiny chrome badge with its Berkshire stag emblem glinted on my cap and silver buttons and whistle chain adorned my jet-black tunic. I looked official. I even looked confident. I didn't appear nervous that someone was going to ask me something I knew nothing about, even though I was. No longer was I little Gwen from the typing pool, I was WPC Crockford. And it felt good.

PC Willoughby and I seemed to spend most of our beats moving on badly-parked cars and giving people directions. We admonished one woman for beating her dusty carpet in the street, contrary to The Town Police Clauses Act, Section 28, Clause 24 (I managed to learn this at Mill Meece after all, despite Pattie's and Jim's midnight shenanigans) but we didn't caution her as it seemed a bit mean.

Towards the end of my third week, I was able to go out alone on my free-form solo patrol. Just as I was beginning to worry that police work would be relentlessly routine, I dealt with my first proper incident. Patrolling past Farmers greengrocer's, I was aware of some sort of commotion ahead. A woman ran up to me.

"Officer! There's been an accident! Can you come?"

I ran with her to the junction of Peach Street and Easthampstead Road. A delivery van lay on its side in front of a coal truck with a dented bonnet and grille, steam rising. A group of men gathered round the van, jostling each other, trying to grab the driver crumpled in the bottom of the cab and haul him up through the door.

My first aid training from Mill Meece and a considerable amount of adrenaline kicked in: *Under no circumstances should you allow members of the public to move an accident victim, unless there is immediate danger to life. He may have sustained a spinal injury that could be made much worse by moving him, even resulting in paralysis.*

"Gentlemen, I need you to back off so I can assess the casualty," I ordered.

"It's all right, miss, we nearly got him out for you," said one man.

"Don't touch him!" I ordered in a louder and more desperate voice. "He may have spinal injuries."

"What about if the petrol catches fire and the whole thing goes up?" said a man with a cigarette hanging from his lips. "He'll be burned to a crisp!"

"You can put that out for a start," I said.

The man glared at me and tossed his cigarette away. The others continued rummaging in the cab. They knew best, apparently.

What to do? I wasn't prepared to shout or lose my temper, but I also wasn't prepared for that van driver to receive life-changing injuries, not from the accident, but from "rescuers".

I stepped back and assessed the van. The rear door had come open and I could lift it. Some of the men noticed what I was doing, came round the back and held it open while I crawled inside. The driver had been delivering precious commodities – eggs. A slippery, drippy mess of smashed whites, yolks and shells coated the whole of the van's interior. I gagged at the mucous smell. Inside, a portly man, his face a mess of blood and his trousers covered in egg had somehow ended up behind his driver's seat.

"Hello, can you hear me?" I called out.

"Hello, love." He groaned. "I'm in a bit of a pickle."

"I'm going to help you. Where does it hurt?"

"My shoulder. And across here." He indicated his chest. "I felt something go when they were pulling me."

"What's your name?"

"Ernie. Ernie Chambers."

Ernie tried, painfully, to pull himself up into a sitting position. I noticed he could move his legs. I was now less worried he had a spinal injury, but I still wasn't going to take a chance by moving him.

"Keep still, Ernie."

The woman who had originally alerted me appeared at the van door and passed me some bandages and a sling.

"There's an ambulance on its way, Constable," she said. "I stopped a policeman on a bicycle and got him to call one."

I thanked her.

Keeping Ernie talking and conscious, I bandaged his head wound and supported his arm in a raised sling. He was more comfortable holding his arm up, which made me think he'd broken his collarbone. I was about to ask for blankets and coats to keep him warm when I heard the dring of the ambulance bell.

An ambulance man's cheery face appeared at the door. "Cor, it's a bit of a mess in there, isn't it? We'll take over now, love."

I crawled through more egg, out of the van, and stood back as the ambulance crew extracted Ernie. Bob Hartwell, summoned by my absence at my designated point, directed traffic round the accident.

I remembered my next task was to find witnesses. I didn't have to search long. Two eager eyewitnesses gave me identical accounts:

"I saw the van, stopped at the halt sign. A Humber Pullman, number plate NGU 737, was behind him. The driver seemed impatient, overtook him into the main road and roared off. He made the coal lorry swerve and slam into the van, overturning it."

Back at the station in my slimy uniform, the inevitable joshing started.

"What happened to you?" Sergeant Lamb chuckled. "Tried to arrest some chickens?"

"She suspected fowl play," replied Bob.

"Why did the WPC cross the road . . .?"

And so on.

A few weeks later, I came in for late turn.

"An admirer's sent you a present, WPC Crockford," said Sarge.

"Oh? What is it?" I blushed under his twinkling gaze.

"Remember that Ernie Chambers from your road traffic accident?"

Ernie was a lucky man, coming out of that accident with only a broken collarbone and some stitches in his head. Traffic patrol found the driver of the Humber and charged him with careless driving. He claimed Ernie had stalled several times at the Halt sign and he was forced to drive round him. But he admitted, before the magistrate, being late for an appointment and taking a risk pulling out of the junction. He was fined a substantial five pounds.

"Mr Chambers wanted to say thank you and dropped these off for you." Sarge reached under the counter and presented me with a tray of a dozen eggs.

"You know I'm not supposed to take any kind of bribe or gift from members of the public, Sarge?"

"I won't tell if you don't." Sarge winked.

Mrs Cunningham would be pleased. I hadn't been able to eat an egg since Ernie's accident.

CHAPTER 6

From Accidents to Zebras:
all in a day's work

I'm not going to pretend that every day of my WPC years
brought a dramatic accident like Ernie's or a fascinating
investigation. Much police work in the 1950s was boring
and routine: typing reports, walking uneventful patrols
or standing around courtrooms. But when I think back
on the variety of things we dealt with, some incidents still
stand out.

Because Wokingham was a sleepy town with a substantial police presence, motorists were under constant
surveillance: there weren't many of them, by today's
standards, and our eyes were always drawn to a vehicle
going by. Nobody got away with worn tyres, a lost
registration plate or a broken headlight.

Pattie and I were convinced the justice system was
funded by halt sign fines, judging by the number of
convictions reported in the newspaper each week.
Halt signs were the predecessor of our modern red
octagonal STOP signs at junctions; even now you can
fail your driving test by not making a proper stop at
one with a solid white line, although it's highly unlikely
a police officer would jump out and catch you. But
in my day, some constables made a habit of hanging

around road junctions, even hiding in bushes, waiting for an easy catch of motorists who "failed to observe the halt sign".

I wasn't one of those officers, but one halt sign violation sticks in my memory. My patrol that day covered Bill Hill crossroads, a notorious accident black spot. I spotted a car powering towards the junction. The middle-aged male driver was staring straight at me, grinning.

He's approaching the main road far too fast, I thought.

He shot the halt sign and drove straight out into the main road without looking, in front of an approaching car. I could only gasp and watch. Everything switched into slow motion – the other car swerving, a horn blasting, tyres screeching, and I anticipated a terrible bang. Which didn't come. To my relief, the other car manoeuvred out of trouble at the last second and roared away, retaliatory horn still beeping.

"Whoah, whoah, whoah, STOP!" I shouted, flapping my hands at the first driver.

The man pulled over on the side of the main road. I marched round to his side. He looked me up and down through his open window, incredibly, still grinning.

"Excuse me, sir!" I coughed to make my voice less trembly. "You failed to stop at a halt sign and endangered another motorist."

"Did I?" The man chuckled. I wondered if there might be something wrong with him.

"May I ask the reason why you didn't stop?"

"I didn't see the halt sign because I was too busy looking at you," said the man, "It's unusual to see a lady policeman, especially one with such nice legs as yours."

I really didn't know what to say. I took out my pocketbook, determined now to charge him.

"What is your name?"

"Thomas Godfrey."

"Address?" He gave his address. "Thomas Godfrey, I am charging you with driving without due care and attention, and for failing to observe the halt sign," I said, mumbling vague sections of the Road Traffic Act because my recall seemed to be letting me down today. Luckily, he didn't notice and I noted his registration.

"That's really not on, officer. I didn't actually *cause* an accident," he wheedled. "You should be grateful that I'm complimenting you on your lovely legs. You've also got nice . . ."

"Mr Godfrey! Please stop there, before you say something you regret. You very nearly did cause an accident!"

He was silent at last.

"Look out for a summons in the next few days for your options about appearing before the magistrate. You can be on your way now." I stepped back onto the pavement.

Mr Godfrey sat in his car looking at me in the rear-view mirror for a few moments, then started the ignition at his leisure and moved off.

Unbelievable, I thought as I carried on with my beat. It was usually Pattie who distracted drivers.

Mr Godfrey didn't appear in person at the magistrates' court, choosing instead to send a letter itemising nine reasons why he didn't stop at the sign. I was item one, apparently, and the chairman could barely keep a straight face as I recounted the conversation, blushing.

"And item 10 will be a fine of £2," he ordered.

I was in the canteen, smiling at the newspaper report of my encounter with Mr Godfrey, when Pattie slumped into the chair next to me, slopping her tea.

"I see your halt sign weirdo and I raise you a weirder lorry one," she said.

"Do tell."

"I pulled a lorry over on Finchampstead Road because I didn't like the look of its tyres. Big bloke got out. I pointed out the wide patches of canvas showing on the tyres – no tread at all. Blow out waiting to happen." Pattie took a slurp of her tea. "You know what he said?"

"What?"

"Why don't you look for murderers?"

"Really?" We were both laughing. "How did you respond?"

"I said if you can tell me who has been murdered, I'll send someone to look for their murderer, but in the meantime, you can have a charge of driving a lorry with defective tyres. That shut him up."

While we almost universally detested everything about traffic duty, there was one aspect of the job nearly all of us enjoyed – dealing with animals. Having a station pound for stray dogs meant that we usually held at least one four-legged – sometimes three-legged – detainee and a steady stream of bobbies on their breaks visiting them, scraps of canteen sausage in hand. A skinny stray could be quite plump by the time its owner came to collect it.

The dogs had a quite remarkable effect. I noticed some officers would come in shaken from dealing with a fight or an unpleasant accident, and, after a few minutes fussing the strays, were calm and collected enough to get on with their day. I often saw Henry Falconer before or after his shift posting dog biscuits he'd bought from the pet shop through the kennel wire.

Not all our strays had owners to come and collect them and we only kept them for seven days. After that they had to be rehomed or the vet put them to sleep. Usually, word of mouth from officers who had become fond of the dogs was enough to find them new homes with friends or family.

Nearing his day of execution was "Foxy", a particularly unattractive, elderly, snaggle-toothed terrier cross that smelled and looked like a wonky fox, hence his nickname. Nobody's neighbour or auntie had come forward to adopt him and he was due at the vet's in the morning.

That afternoon, my late turn beat took me down Sturgess Road and ahead of me I saw someone in a trilby hat and overcoat, with a dog identical to Foxy, going door to door. My antennae twitching that he may be an unlicensed hawker, I called out, "Excuse me, sir."

The figure turned round. It was Sergeant Lamb, looking different in his civvies, on his afternoon off. I caught a whiff of the dog from three yards away.

"Are you taking Foxy for a last walk?" I asked, feeling a stab of pity.

"Well, sort of," replied Sarge. "Desperate times call for desperate measures, WPC Crockford. I'm going round asking if anyone wants him, saying otherwise he gets put to sleep in the morning."

"Well, a shaggy dog story and a bit of emotional

blackmail goes a long way, Sarge," I replied, not believing anyone would take a mangy, smelly old mutt from some random bloke knocking on their door.

I caught up with Sarge as I came off duty at 10 that night.

"Any luck finding a home for Foxy?"

"As a matter of fact, I did." Sarge beamed. "Doris Savin took him, saying she'd been thinking for ages about getting a puppy for her daughter. He's ideal for her Millie, what with her polio braces and all, because he's old and slow and won't pull her over."

The Savins gave Sarge regular updates about Foxy. He lived for another three years and died in his sleep in his basket at the foot of Millie's bed.

Because Wokingham was in a rural, farming area and various livestock markets were held regularly, we had to be well-versed in the law relating to farm animals and Ministry of Agriculture red tape and licences for moving them around. Foot and mouth disease was a serious problem in the early 1950s; there were 500 UK outbreaks in 1952 alone and we had to be constantly vigilant that it didn't take hold in Berkshire. I knew to look out for any cloven-footed animal – pig, sheep, goat or cow – that seemed lame, maybe drooling or slobbering, and check their hooves, tongue, mouth and nostrils for tell-tale blisters.

Swine fever was another notifiable disease. If I heard a pig so much as burp, I'd be straight over, checking it for swollen red eyes, discolouration on its ears and snout, and any vomiting or diarrhoea. We'd even been warned about the possibility of people contracting anthrax from animals and had to ask farmers about flu-like symptoms or skin ulcers. This often meant standing in the rain for half an hour, hearing about Farmer Fowler's lumbago or Cowman Gollop's unexplained rash. Happily, all my market dealings were with healthy animals and farm workers, usually with their paperwork in order.

Which is more than could be said for our wild rabbit population. Patrolling past Robert Mullins's farm one damp Wednesday, I noticed his meadow was full of slow-moving, seemingly sleepy rabbits. I called to him over the fence.

"Have you been growing narcotics again, Robert? Those rabbits don't seem in any hurry to run away."

"Never seen anything like it, miss," replied Robert, picking up a sluggish rabbit by its scruff and bringing it over. The poor creature hung limply from his fist. I couldn't even see its eyes, so red and swollen, and it seemed to have cysts elsewhere on its body.

"Foxes won't touch 'em, and even my lurcher, who'd normally rip 'em to shreds gives 'em a wide berth. I'm not happy about this. I've notified the council, not got a reply yet. Rabbits can't get foot and mouth, surely?"

"I don't believe they can," I said. "It's very strange. I'll ask around and get back to you."

"Appreciate it, miss. Now you might want to be on your way as I'm about to take my shotgun to these rabbits. I can't have no suffering here and there are things a lady shouldn't see."

The new rabbit disease soon got personal.

"You all right?" I asked an unusually glum Bob in the canteen.

"Ah, I had to leave my little Susan crying her heart out over Joey, her pet bunny, this morning. He died of some horrible illness that made his eyeballs stand out from his head, and they were all yellow, and he was obviously blind as he kept bumping into things."

I told Bob about the rabbits on Mullins's farm.

"We need to have a word with The EF about this," said Bob. "Something's not right." We went up to his office.

"Myxomatosis, that's what it is," declared Superintendent Barker, puffing on his pipe.

"Myxo ... what?"

"Rabbit virus from the Americas that they introduced into Australia to sort out the rabbit overpopulation problem there. Looks like it has somehow found its way here. Ministry of Agriculture says it should be allowed to take its course and eliminate the wild rabbits, because their destructive ways are costing British agriculture £50 million a year. Should be a godsend to farmers. Sorry about Joey, though, Bob."

It seemed strange to me that we'd had to probe for this information. Usually, the Ministry of Agriculture were quick to issue us with notifications about new animal diseases. I called in on Robert Mullins to tell him about myxomatosis.

"Seems a nasty way of controlling rabbits, miss," said Robert. "But, in truth, they ate a fair bit of my oat crop last year. Just the damn foxes and weasels to sort out now. Buggers won't leave my chickens alone."

Occasionally we came across wanton animal cruelty that upset us all. One of our probation officers, Terry

Fulford, ran in to report an attack on a nesting pair of Wokingham's much-loved swans.

"I was driving past Old Forest Meadows, looking out for the swans, as you do, with the handmade 'Slow – Swans In Road' signs, and I saw smoke rising from the side of the Emm Brook where they nest. I couldn't believe it! I saw the male swan, all distressed on the riverbank, running round in circles, plucking at his tail feathers, which were on fire.

"I stopped the car and looked down. I saw two boys – they can't have been more than 10 – standing round the swans' nest, which was burning. I could see a tiny cygnet and some eggs on the nest, engulfed in flames, and the female on the other bank, madly flapping her wings. One of the little sods was holding a kind of torch thing made of a stick with a rag wrapped round it and the other one was aiming a catapult at the female. I yelled at them and they ran off, laughing."

I drove to the Emm Brook with an RSPCA inspector. He stroked his beard and was silent for a while. Two forlorn swans swam round their charred nest.

"Would have been a bumper clutch this year too," he said. "Seven cygnets. Who would do something like this?"

Who indeed? Wokingham had its fair share of tearaway children, some crueller than others, it seemed.

Not all reports of incidents involving animals had such a tragic ending as the Emm Brook swans. I answered a telephone call from Mrs Falmer, an elderly and somewhat eccentric resident of a big house in Cranbourne. She often rang to report people who "looked funny" or vehicles she thought might belong to Russian spies.

"My dear, I have a strange horse at the bottom of my garden. I wouldn't mind, but it's eating my dahlias."

Here we go again, I thought.

"A strange horse, Mrs Falmer? Is there a farm nearby it could have wandered in from?"

"All the farms round me are cattle or arable. No gee-gees, my dear. Could you send someone round to get it out before it eats my entire flower border?"

"Yes, of course, Mrs Falmer." I sighed and put the telephone down.

"Have we got any riding tack, like a bridle, kicking around?" I asked Henry. "Potty Mrs F now wants a 'strange horse' removed from her garden."

"Does she now?" he replied, rolling his eyes. "There's some rope in the tool shed. I'll come with you."

Mrs Falmer took us down the stone path beside her manor house into the back garden.

"There he is!" she trilled, pointing a gnarled, arthritic finger at some dry, overgrown meadow at the end of her garden. At first, I could only make out the horse-like shape of its head. Then it moved.

"That's a zebra!" exclaimed Henry. "Cracking camouflage!"

"A zebra!" cried Mrs Falmer. "How on earth did that get in here?"

"I think I know exactly where it's come from," said Henry, "and I'm certainly not going to approach it and scare it. May I use your telephone?"

Ten minutes later, a Billy Smart's Circus van drew up outside Mrs Falmer's. Henry and I watched open-mouthed as several circus keepers rushed down the garden towards the zebra. Startled, it let out the most bizarre, high-pitched whinnying barks, like someone sawing metal, then leapt over a box hedge into the pasture beyond.

"Oh bloody hell," groaned Henry, "this is a police matter now it's headed for the road."

"Town Police Clauses Act, Section 28," I puffed, breaking into a run, "but it doesn't specifically mention zebras."

We tagged onto the chase, stumbling across the pasture, the zebra thundering like a racehorse towards the road and the council houses opposite. Cars slowed to a standstill and curtains twitched as people watched the undoubtedly entertaining spectacle of a zebra cantering into a cul-de-sac, with several sweating humans chasing it.

When we staggered up to the action, a keeper had managed to get a bridle onto the runaway and the zebra stood as peaceful as a lamb, some foam on its flanks the only evidence of its solo steeplechase. A small boy was offering it a carrot.

Henry and I returned to the station. The rotund figure of Billy Smart himself, instantly recognisable with his cigar and Stetson hat, stood in the lobby.

"Dreadfully sorry that Tepe led you on a wild zebra chase this afternoon, officers," apologised Billy. "She must have cut across the fields from our Winkfield site. Can I pay for any damage she caused?"

"Mrs Falmer might appreciate some replacement dahlias," I said, "but other than that, no harm done, Mr Smart."

74

"It's not only Slough[2] that's got a zebra crossing now," said Henry.

And we roared with laughter at his clever, topical quip.

---

2 The first ever zebra crossing, complete with Belisha beacons, appeared in Slough, Buckinghamshire, in 1951. And so did a joke that's been trotted out for the last 70 years.

CHAPTER 7

A burial in the churchyard

There's nothing that galvanises a community into action more than a report of a missing child.

In the back office with Bob and Henry, I was on the telephone trying to pacify an irate man complaining about something or other, when we heard commotion in the lobby. Henry stopped pecking at his typewriter keys. Usually, station noise like this was drunken misbehaviour and Sarge was generally able to subdue it within a minute or so. He wasn't managing to this time. A strange urgency made the two men exchange glances and stand up.

"Sounds like some hysterical woman giving Sarge grief," said Bob. "I'll go as Miss Crockford's on a call."

With only half an ear on my caller's complaint now – *what was it with everyone today?* – I heard a female voice shouting, "My boy's gone! Somebody needs to help me! Please!"

Bob opened the door and went straight out to the front desk.

I noticed Henry pause, his hand on the door knob. It was as if he was psyching himself up to face whatever was going on behind that door, making himself step outside. He took a deep breath and went into the lobby. I hurriedly finished my call and went out too.

Bob had managed to get a trembling woman, eyes staring like a wild animal, hands bleeding, hair dishevelled and escaping from a floral scarf, to sit down on one of the lobby seats. He managed to get her name – Niamh Valentine – and her address out of her, that her four-year-old son Harry had gone missing from her front garden and a description of him. Then she jumped up, shrieking that she couldn't waste any more time, she had to find her boy, and ran out of the station.

Sergeant Lamb was straight on the phone to all the points telling beat officers to look out for the missing child. No sooner had he put the phone down, it rang with the beat officers themselves reporting the disappearance to Sarge. Everyone who was available dropped what they were doing and headed out to search. As I left, Sarge was organising a boat to check the Emm Brook – the small river that ran through Wokingham.

In those first frantic hours searching for Harry, Niamh had become hysterical to the point of seriously harming herself. She had run across roads without looking, hammered at doors until her knuckles bled and at one point physically banged her head against a brick wall. Her behaviour unsettled the police and town's volunteer searchers who had turned out in their hundreds to look for the little boy. We worried that although we would probably find the little lad alive and unharmed, we would return him to a traumatised, injured and bleeding mother – not an ideal situation.

As I was about to turn into the King George V Playing Field to search the thickets in there, Sergeant Robertshaw pulled up beside me in her patrol car.

"Miss Crockford, can you come with me please? We need to take Mrs Valentine home, calm her down and keep her out of the way so we can get on with the job," she said. "She's doing herself, and the search, more harm than good."

I wondered how on earth we would persuade Niamh to leave the search and come with us. We drove round, and when we found her among a group of searchers in Holt Copse, Sergeant Robertshaw approached and spoke to her, her hand resting on her arm. To my surprise, Niamh calmly left the group and came and sat in the back seat of our car.

"You're so right, officer," mumbled Niamh. "If my Harry comes home by himself and I'm not there, he might go out looking for me and get himself into some real trouble."

Sergeant Robertshaw winked at me. That was the way to do it.

The Valentines' home had a cloying, organic smell of domestic neglect. The parlour rug felt sticky underfoot and thick dust covered a small oak sideboard. I felt itchy. Officers searched the whole house upstairs and down.

"You're not going to bloody well find him in there, are you?" cried Niamh as a constable rifled through her dressing table drawers. It felt horribly intrusive, but it had to be done.

"Niamh, love, I need you to tell me exactly what you remember from this morning," Miss Robertshaw said.

"But my boy … where's my boy?" cried Niamh, still not really focusing.

"Niamh – everybody is out looking for him: police, neighbours, local volunteers, farmers, all the squaddies from Arborfield garrison. We've even got the bloodhound from Buckinghamshire police coming down. We're combing the whole area. Between them, they know every nook and cranny to search. When they find him, they'll come and tell us."

Niamh gave a long sigh, then collected herself. Her eyes were a washed-out blue in the bloodshot whites and her nostrils red raw.

I scribbled frantically to keep up with Niamh's statement: *Got up about seven … left him to play with his toys … changed the sheets … Harry wet the bed last night … sometimes plays hopscotch with other kids in the street … usually other mums around to keep an eye … I can get on with everything else while he's occupied, shopping, cooking, washing, doing the housework, doing the garden … husband's in the Merchant Navy . . .*

"Could I have a glass of water, please?" asked Niamh.

"Of course, I'll get you some," I said.

I went into the tiny kitchen. A small dustbin overflowed with potato peelings, yellowing cabbage leaves and empty pilchard tins with a fat bluebottle buzzing round them. Dirty plates, cups and mugs filled the sink. An unwashed pan crusted with what looked like porridge sat on the stove next to a blackened stockpot full of grey sludge with chicken bones sticking out of it.

Filthy clothes were piled into a tin washtub by the coal hole. The small back garden belied Niamh's gardening claims, with foot-high grass, dandelion clocks and a stiff rope washing line green with algae.

This is hardly the home of someone who spends lots of time cooking and cleaning, I thought. Niamh was what Mum would call a slattern.

I found the least dirty glass in a cupboard, filled it with water from the sputtering tap and brought it for her. She continued with her statement and I continued taking notes.

. . . couldn't find Harry anywhere . . . ran up and down . . . hammered on doors . . . nobody had seen him. People came out to help me look . . . I ran into the police station . . .

Finally, Niamh curled herself tightly into the chair, forehead on knees and into herself. Sergeant Robertshaw signalled that it was time to give the interviewing a rest.

The long grey day turned into a long grey evening as people came and went. Bob Hartwell, making door-to-door enquiries, said the search would continue into the night. A neighbour, Iris, bustled in with milk, sandwiches, cake, clean cups and saucers and Fairy liquid. While she set to cleaning up the kitchen with gusto, we stepped outside into the drizzle for the cigarette break we had been craving. We closed the back door so we could talk.

"Are we all right letting Iris clean up the kitchen, Miss Robertshaw?" I asked. "She's doing her bit to prevent us all getting food poisoning, but she's not disturbing a crime scene, is she?"

"We don't know that there's actually been a crime,

Miss Crockford. If the worst happened, God forbid, we might take the house into consideration, but the real crime scene would be where we found the ... er ... body."

We both fell silent, looking down at the cracked concrete path, rolling our cigarettes contemplatively between our fingers.

"You haven't noticed anything untoward, have you?" she asked.

"Mrs Valentine talks about how busy she is with shopping, cooking and cleaning etcetera but the house is absolutely filthy and doesn't look as if it has been touched for months. What does she do all day? Do you think she's guilty of neglect?"

"Always innocent until proved guilty, Miss Crockford! No, I don't. Looking after a child is hard work for some mothers. Niamh is on her own with her husband away. I don't think right now would be the time to challenge her on her housekeeping standards. Just you wait until you come across a real child neglect case. You'll know the difference."

I blushed, feeling ticked off for making assumptions, and bad for being so judgemental about Niamh, when Miss Robertshaw displayed such surprising empathy. Perhaps I should learn to put myself in other people's shoes before I repeated my mother's automatic judgement trick. And what on earth would real child neglect look like?

We came back in, through to the gloomy parlour. Niamh was asleep beneath the feeble standard lamp, her head tipped back against the armchair wing and her body unfurled a little. Her mouth hung open and for

81

the first time that day her face was peaceful. It seemed unkind to wake her. Miss Robertshaw tiptoed out and drove off.

An hour or so later, there was a knock on the door. Henry Falconer stood in the drizzling rain, his police cloak dripping.

"What is it?" I whispered.

"We may have found something. Can you come?"

Leaving Iris, wide-eyed and desperate to know what was happening, with Niamh, I got into the patrol car.

"What's happening, Henry? What have they found?"

Henry pursed his lips solemnly.

"Oh God, they haven't . . .?"

"We received a call from a vicar in the next parish, Reverend Tucker. One of his parishioners noticed disturbed earth against the north wall of the churchyard.

"Can we investigate on consecrated ground?"

"Apparently so. Tucker spoke to the Archdeacon and in the light of Harry going missing, he got us permission to dig immediately."

We drew up outside a square-towered church, next to other police vehicles. Bob was extending a cordon to block Church Lane and keep onlookers away.

Ducking under another cordon rope, I could see floodlamps, and flashbulbs going off in the far corner of the churchyard, where some tarpaulin had been hastily erected to keep off the rain. Reverend Tucker, DI Dankworth and PC Higgs, spade in hand, stood back as Bennett the clues officer paced and photographed the area.

"Reckon you can go in and dig now, sir," Bennett said.

Higgs laid another tarpaulin on the ground and began to move soil onto it. As he piled it up, Bennett inspected it.

"Don't be surprised if you turn up some old bones," said Reverend Tucker. "The church has stood for 800 years and thousands of people are buried here. Mr Jarvis often comes across medieval or Tudor remains when he's digging a grave. Put anything you find in this flowerpot. I'll make sure they're reinterred properly."

Higgs took the proffered flowerpot and looked uncomfortable at the possibility of unearthing human bones as well as whatever might be freshly buried here now. He kept digging. One foot deep, nothing. Two feet deep, nothing. He slipped down into the hole to continue removing the soil. Soon, the sound of his spade on soil changed tone.

"Whoah! I've found something."

Higgs scraped the soil aside to reveal what looked like a Post Office mail sack. A flashbulb popped to record the find. He ran his hand over the sack and recoiled slightly.

"There's something in it – it feels solid and ... bony."

A chill ran through us all. Everybody had wanted to find something, now nobody wanted to find out what it was.

Higgs continued uncovering the sack. It was just the right size to contain a small child. He hauled it out onto the tarpaulin.

"Probably weighs about three stone?" he said.

The bag's draw cord was tied with a double bow. Bennett photographed it.

"Guess we'd better see what's in it," said Dankworth, stooping down to the neck of the bag. He cut the cord, avoiding the bow, opened the bag and shifted position. Now on his knees and elbows, he gestured for a torch.

Shining a light, he peered in. "Hmm," he said, reaching gingerly into the bag with his bare hand.

We stood as still as a tableau, silhouetted against the lights. Nobody dared breathe, all eyes focused on the bag. Dankworth slowly pulled out … a fresh red rose. It was a little squashed from being buried three feet under, but recognisable nonetheless. He handed it to Bennett. Nobody knew what to expect next.

He peered further into the bag.

"Blimey," he said. "Scissors, please."

Bennett got into position with his camera.

Dankworth snipped the bag, and with one swift movement of the scissors, slit it from end to end. He pulled back the sides. Bennett's flashbulb momentarily lit up a white, bulging eye, pointed teeth and a curled, black, hairy body. We recoiled as one, as if we had somehow summoned a demon from the underworld.

"Bloody hell, it's a dog!" exclaimed Henry.

Curled up in the sack was indeed a dog – a black, skinny Labrador type, elderly, its entire face grey. One large, milky eye was open and its lips were drawn back, revealing jagged yellow teeth. A large tumour on a forepaw suggested a reason for a last, heartbreaking trip to the vet. Its worn leather collar bore a brass tag that simply said "Eric".

We sighed, laughed, swore and muttered collectively with relief. We weren't dealing with a child murder – yet.

"Why would somebody bury a dog in a graveyard?" mused Higgs.

"Clearly his owner wanted him buried in consecrated ground," I replied, patiently. There was a touching poignancy that old Eric must have been such an adored companion that his owner gave him a DIY Christian burial.

"What are we going to do with its body?" asked Dankworth. "I couldn't take it to the rubbish tip."

"It's more than just a dog's body, isn't it?" said Reverend Tucker. "It's a gesture of love. Whoever buried him did so in faith. I suggest we put Eric back in the hole with his rose and rebury him. But keep this strictly between us, otherwise everyone will want their Tiddles or Bonzo buried with full honours and we can't set that precedent."

It took far less time to reinter Eric than dig him up. As we stood around, Reverend Tucker said a few words of blessing for Eric's owner in their time of loss and prayed that Harry Valentine be found safe and well, for attention must now turn back to finding that little boy.

"Tell everyone there's no evidence that anything untoward has occurred and blame badgers for digging around the compost heap," suggested Dankworth.

We drove to the police cordon, where Bob was still shooing away the interested and the nosy. Bob lifted the rope and looked at Henry quizzically. Henry wound down the window.

"Damn badgers, playing at being gravediggers again," he said.

"You mean it's not…"

"No, thank goodness … I'll tell you later."

We drove back to Niamh Valentine's house. I tapped on the door. Iris opened it, her eyes as wide as they had been when I left.

"Have you found my Harry?" Niamh jumped up from her armchair.

"No, Niamh. It was something that turned out to be nothing and not connected to Harry's disappearance in any way. I'm sorry I can't bring you some better news."

Niamh flopped back down in the armchair, equally relieved and bitterly disappointed.

"I'm about to go off shift just now but night duty are about to come on. We're back tomorrow. Are you going to be here alone?"

"I'll stay with her tonight, officers," said Iris. "My husband has dropped off some bedding. I'll sleep in one of the chairs – I could sleep on a washing line, me."

"If anything turns up during the night, the police will let you know immediately. We'll see you tomorrow. Please try to get some sleep," I said to Niamh, although how the mother of a missing child could sleep, I couldn't imagine.

The station mood was sombre the next day when I arrived for my shift. Harry Valentine had been missing for more than 24 hours, a worrying length of time for a child to be absent. I was in the women's office, about to begin typing Niamh's statement when the telephone rang. It was Sarge.

"WPC Crockford, could you get out here to the front desk, please?"

Robert Mullins, the giant of a farmer we all knew, was standing by the desk with a small child bundled up in a rough, hairy blanket and wearing Sarge's helmet.

"Is this what you're looking for?" Robert asked. The lad peered at me from under the helmet.

"Hello," I said. "What's your name?"

"Harry." I felt as if lead weights lifted themselves off my shoulders. I nodded at Robert.

"And what have you been doing?"

"I been playing houses with the cows. It got dark."

"Dog went nuts in the barn when I went in to get some fodder," explained Robert. "I couldn't see nothing at first but he wouldn't give it a rest. Found this lad in a little hidey-house he'd made among the hay bales. Must have been there all night, with the cows wandering in and out. He was warm, granted, but he didn't have any food or water."

"I drinked the cow water," said Harry. We all grimaced.

"There was I, out on a search party yesterday, and never thought to check my own barns first," said Robert, rolling his eyes.

I stooped down to Harry's level. "Was it fun playing in the barn with the cows?"

Harry smiled and nodded.

"Weren't you scared when it got dark?"

"I wanted Mummy. I didn't like the big doggie so I hided."

"The big doggie found you, didn't he? Shall we get you back to your mummy right now?"

Harry nodded happily and slipped his hand into mine, ready to go home.

Sergeant Robertshaw arrived a few moments later. She towered over Harry, who cringed away from her behind my skirt. She looked down at him.

"That's him. Fits the description to a tee. Who's been a very naughty boy giving us all a scare like that? You could have got yourself into all sorts of danger. Your mother has been worried sick. Now give Sergeant Lamb's helmet back and we'll take you home."

We drove to Niamh's house. I sat in the back with a silent Harry, still wrapped in the blanket, his face buried against my tunic. He perked up as we drew up outside his house.

"We're home now," I whispered. "Do you want to go and knock on the door and give Mummy the best surprise she's ever had?"

When she saw her son, Niamh's jaw dropped, she covered her mouth with her hands and began to sob.

"You've found him! You've found my Harry!" she cried as she hugged and hugged him as if she could never let him go. My own eyes started filling with tears and I turned away so Miss Robertshaw wouldn't notice.

Paperwork completed and Harry given a clean bill of health by Dr Wickes, we left the Valentine's and took the scenic route back to the station, past the churchyard where Eric the loved Labrador rested in peace among centuries of human bones.

"All's well that ends well," chirped Miss Robertshaw.

"For a horrible moment there, I thought we might be dealing with a child murder," I replied. "Thank God we weren't."

Tragically, it wouldn't be too long before Berkshire would be rocked to the core by a real child murder.

CHAPTER 8

Manhunt

29 April 1952

Today is going to be a good day, I thought as I walked to the station on the warmest, sunniest afternoon of the year so far. The sky was azure, the parks were crammed with daffodils, bluebells fringed the woodland edge and in the playgrounds, schoolchildren laughed and squealed in the sunshine on their dinner break. I was looking forward to my patrol today.

I ambled past the allotments, admiring their neatness, towards the telephone box. I heard it ringing from a distance. *Always pick up a ringing phone, Bob said*. I sprinted to the box and grabbed the receiver.

"WPC Crockford," I panted.

"We need everyone back here," barked Sarge. "Straffen's escaped from Broadmoor."

My tummy turned over. No further explanation was needed. The name John Straffen struck a chilling chord with everyone in Berkshire and probably the whole of 1950s Britain. Every parent's worst nightmare, he was an insane child killer who had abducted and murdered two little girls in Bath last summer. The first girl, six-year-old Brenda Goddard, was out picking wildflowers. Straffen enticed her into a copse, promising her better flowers, then strangled her. The second girl was nine-year-old Cicely Batstone, who he met in a cinema. Afterwards, Straffen took her to a different cinema to see another film, then on the bus to The Tumps, a wooded parkland on the outskirts of the city, where he strangled her as well.

Because of his mental incapacity, the jury at Taunton Assize Court returned their verdict of "insane and unfit to plead" and Straffen was transferred to Broadmoor Hospital just down the road in Crowthorne. Formerly a criminal lunatic asylum, Broadmoor became the Ministry of Health's responsibility, its inmates now treated as patients. I knew from my beat conversations that the residents around Broadmoor were uneasy; some were dismayed at the absence of an early warning system should dangerous patients escape, others were angry that such heinous criminals escaped the death penalty and apparently lived in luxury in the hospital.

With the entire shift amassed at the station, The EF, our superintendent, coordinated our response to this major incident. Bennett, working like a demon, produced multiple "Have You Seen This Man?" flyers of John Straffen gazing vacantly at the camera. We flapped the pictures dry as the ink was still wet.

Some officers went to search Crowthorne and around Broadmoor, while Bob and I were to patrol the wooded outskirts of Wokingham, raising the alarm and asking residents if they had seen anyone fitting Straffen's description.

We drove among the forests and ancient wood-lands between Wokingham and Crowthorne. Towering, papery silver birches on the edges gave a light, open aspect that led inwards to deeper, deciduous woods of spreading beeches and gnarled oaks. Deeper still were areas of impenetrable, densely-planted conifers. Although well-used footpaths and bridleways cut through the woodlands, there was far more forest off the well-trodden tracks, perfect for a fugitive to hide in. Straffen's escape made the deep woods seem sinister and hostile, despite the beautiful sunny afternoon.

"There's a caravan down there," said Bob, pointing to a rough track leading into some woods. "Belongs to a widower bloke called Rodney Carroll. Handyman by trade, old lag, been inside. He's supposed to be rebuilding the old derelict cottage."

We turned down the track. Smoke rose from between a gap in the trees. Some spiky, rusted farm machinery reached out of a patch of nettles like a giant claw. A tree stump with an axe buried in it and a washing line with two girls' dresses on it framed a lopsided, dirty white, mildewed caravan, its tatty awning flung back over the roof. Its single small leaded window and the glazed stable door were hung with thick, yellowing net curtains, making it impossible to see inside. A bicycle with a basket stood propped outside.

"Welcome to Butlin's," whispered Bob as he parked by a rusty barrel.

I knocked on the door. I heard some muffled muttering and scuffling that I wasn't sure came from inside or outside, then it went quiet again. A pair of magpies chattered and creaked among the silver birches above. Perhaps that was what I heard?

I was about to knock again when the top half of the door opened. A man appeared, his thick black wiry hair dishevelled and a just-lit cigarette hanging from his lips. He wore a grubby white vest and khaki moleskin trousers, held up by braces. He took a long drag on his cigarette, and I noticed with distaste that he had ACAB[3] tattooed on his knuckles. He slowly looked me up and down, his gaze settling a little too long on my bustline, then burst into a huge gap-toothed grin that made his tiny eyes disappear.

"Officers! To what do I owe this pleasure? Those kids haven't been getting themselves into any more trouble, have they?"

"Afternoon, Mr Carroll," replied Bob. "No, the kids aren't in any trouble. Well, no more than usual." He laughed. "In fact, it's because they get about playing all over town that we'd like to have a chat with them. I don't know if you've heard, but John Straffen jumped over the wall at Broadmoor this afternoon." Bob held out the identity photograph. "It's possible that they may have seen him."

"John who?" asked Carroll, squinting at the picture.

"John Straffen. The bloke who murdered two little girls in Bath last year?"

"That bastard? Should have hanged him when they had the chance," said Carroll. Then he yelled, "DORA! YOU GET IN HERE!"

Carroll's bellow made us jump. We turned around to see a girl of about five standing in the front yard,

3 All Coppers Are Bastards – a popular prison tattoo.

clutching a doll. She wore a yellow gingham dress, but had rolled the skirt up around her waist and was doing a gyrating dance, while laughing with delight. She was wearing no knickers.

Bob had no idea where to look and flushed pink.

"I said get in here," growled Carroll.

Dora continued to giggle and wiggle around in a circle, delighted at being the centre of attention and able to stop a conversation midflow.

"Oh, Dora," I said gently, "nobody wants to see your … your … tummy. Do you want to pull your skirt down?"

Dora had stopped dancing and was pulling down the dress when Carroll threw his cigarette aside, kicked open the bottom of the caravan door and with two huge steps reached Dora. He roughly yanked down her skirt then grabbed her by the arms and threw her up over his shoulder. She squealed and started crying.

"You don't do that in front of strangers! Get inside!" he shouted.

Carroll half-threw Dora into the caravan, and before he closed the door, I caught a glimpse of an older, pale-faced girl inside gathering up her screaming sister. The girl looked vaguely familiar.

"I am so sorry, officers," gushed Carroll. "I can't have one of mine behaving like that in front of you. I don't know what came over her. I am so embarrassed."

Bob, still blushing, could only utter, "Kids will be kids, I suppose."

I was unsure what to make of the daughter's and father's behaviours. There was an extremeness about both that rang alarm bells, but I also knew that police turning up made people react in uncharacteristic ways. Some children like to shock adults – the Ferals did all the time for devilment, after all. Dora had shocked her father and seemingly Bob too. Plenty of children played on the beach or in streams naked and nobody batted an eyelid, so what was it about this childish display that made the two men react?

"Are your other children here?" I asked.

"Bernie's in there with her – she don't go out much anyway," said Carroll. "Charlie and John are out somewhere. They don't usually come back before dusk, then only when they're hungry."

"You know what, I suggest we leave it for today." Bob's eyes were wide and pleading.

"You might find them down the gravel pits," said Carroll, retrieving his cigarette from the ground and relighting it. "They said they might go for a swim today as it's warm."

Back in the police car, Bob wiped his brow. "That went well."

"We need to find John and Charlie – I'm really not happy about them swimming in the gravel pits, especially with an escaped murderer at large."

"Let's go," he said.

I was relieved to be going there with Bob rather than on my own.

The gravel pits were a bleak, treeless, almost lunar landscape of extracted sand and shingle. The live workings, at one end of a series of deep artificial ribbon lakes, consisted of huge, chugging machinery that washed and processed the extracted sand and gravel.

The furthest pit, nearest to the road, was usually where the brave, the foolish and the unwary came to trespass and swim in the summer, curving as it did behind the huge extraction piles, out of sight of the workers. A single barbed-wire fence had long been trampled down, leading to a kind of artificial beach of extracted sand.

On a warm sunny day like today you could almost imagine you were on holiday in a bleaker part of the Lake District, but with a thrill seeker's frisson of illegality and real danger, as the land was privately owned and the water deep and cold.

From the road, we could see several dots splashing in the middle of the ink-blue water and another figure sitting on the sand. Scattered around were individual piles of clothing.

"I reckon that's them," said Bob.

We stepped over a Danger Keep Out sign that had long been trodden into the undergrowth. As we approached the group, the figure on the sand leapt up, waving urgently and shouting to the others, "Coppers! The coppers are here!"

The strongest swimmer reached the shore first and clambered out, stark naked, grabbing his pile of clothes and running behind a gravel mound. The clothed figure ran with him, hesitating, torn between escape and urging his pals to get away from the coppers.

Bob reached the shoreline from land just as the other three boys did from the water. I followed behind.

"You three, out and get dressed. You two . . ." Bob called, loud enough to be heard behind the mound, "get back over here!"

The three in the water sheepishly crawled up onto the shore towards their clothes, two cupping their hands over their privates to hide their embarrassment. The tallest boy, shameless, curled himself up straight with his hands on his waist, hips thrust slightly forward, and stared me out. I had been careful to look only at the boys' faces as they were scrambling away and this youth was now making piercing eye contact with me, daring me to drop my gaze lower. A smirk played at the corner of his mouth. I continued to lock gaze, desperate to look away, but desperate not to appear weak either.

"Come on, Johnny Weissmuller,[4] stop poncing about and get some clothes on," Bob said, breaking the deadlock, and the tall boy fumbled about putting his underpants and shirt on.

From behind the mound emerged an athletic, bespectacled lad who I instantly recognised as Roger Wickes, the doctor's son. He looked dejected, as if being caught by the police would herald the end of his awfully big adventure misbehaving with the Ferals, reconsigning him to his life of school, tea, homework, bath, bed until it was time for him to go to medical school.

The youngest clothed boy emerged with Roger. He had tousled, flaxen hair, a ripped striped shirt and carried a beaten-up brown leather pouch on a strap across his body. *Charlie Carroll?* I wondered.

I didn't recognise the two other scared-looking boys: one freckled lad with buck teeth kicked the sand around with a bare foot – he didn't seem to have any

---

4 A US competition swimmer and actor, who played Tarzan in the films of the 1930s and 1940s.

shoes. A younger one, whose quizzical, coal-black eyes and twitchy nervous grin made me think of mice, shifted from foot to foot in a pair of tatty brogues that were far too big for him.

And then there was the tall one. *This must be John Carroll*, I thought. I was sure I'd moved him on from Martin's Pool – Wokingham's outdoor lido – when a group of sunbathing girls complained that he kept staring at them over the fence. His now-drying wiry black hair was the giveaway that he was Rodney's son and he had slight gaps between his teeth, not quite as pronounced as his father's. The beginnings of a dark moustache shaded his upper lip and he even managed to swagger standing still, gazing around as if all this couldn't be a bigger waste of his time.

"Names?" asked Bob.

"Er … Roger Wickes."

"Charlie Carroll."

"Dennis Felton."

"Carl Felton."

"John Carroll."

"You do all know that you're trespassing on private land here, don't you?" I asked. There was a mixture of nodding and shaking heads.

"And you do know that it's incredibly dangerous to swim here?" I continued. "The water's deep and it's cold. You could get cramp or into difficulty and not make it back to the edge."

"Please, officer," ventured Roger, "it's why we swim in a group, so we can watch out for each other. I've read about hypothermia in one of my father's textbooks and I know what early stages to look out for so we can get out."

"Are you going to arrest us?" Mouse-faced Carl Felton looked up at Bob, pleading, "Our dad will go berserk."

"No, we're not. We just want to ask you if you've seen this man," I said, holding out Straffen's picture.

The Carrolls and Feltons shook their heads.

"He looks like that psycho man who killed those little girls last year," said Roger. "I read it in the newspaper."

"He is. It's John Straffen. He escaped from Broadmoor Hospital this afternoon. Have you seen anyone around today who looks like him? Tall, blond, in a blue suit?" I asked.

All the boys shook their heads, the younger ones looking frightened.

"I want to go home. I don't want to meet a psycho murderer man," said Carl, his bottom lip trembling.

"I think it's best you do. How are you all getting home anyway?" I asked. "You don't even have any shoes on," I added, pointing at Dennis's feet.

Somehow cramming all five boys and us into the police car, Bob and I set off to drop the Ferals home. At least they were cleaner after their dip in the gravel pit, although the car soon filled up with the musky fug of pubescent boys.

Sharing the front seat with Charlie, I asked him, "What's in your bag?"

Charlie clutched his leather pouch tighter to him.

"'E collects things," chimed in Dennis. "Bottle tops, coins, funny shaped stones."

Charlie unfastened the buckle and opened the bag, thrilled that somebody was taking an interest in his "treasures". He pulled out a tiny greenish bottle with bubbles in the thick glass, a Victorian penny, a freshwater mussel shell and what looked like an army-issue spent rifle bullet.

"It's for my museum," he said proudly. "One day when I grow up, I'm going to be a museum keeper."

We dropped the Carroll boys off on the track by the caravan – Charlie gave us a cheerful wave as we left – and the Feltons at the top of Rose Street, where the slum housing was. Roger hid on the back seat and begged to be dropped in a quiet road a few streets down from his house.

"What are we now, a bloody taxi service?" asked Bob as Roger slunk out of the police car.

We called back in at the station for our break about eight o'clock.

"They got that bugger Straffen!" said Sergeant Lamb at the front desk. "Just heard. Broadmoor staff and police caught up with him outside the Bramshill Hunt pub. Bit of a chase and a bit of a scuffle, but managed to get him back to the hospital. He was only out for four hours after all that."

"What a relief," I said. "That man has haunted my dreams for a year. How he could so casually kill those two little poppets in Bath, I'll never understand." I shuddered at the memory.

"Mine too. Thank goodness for that," Bob said. "We can sleep easy, knowing that maniac is back behind bars."

But little did we know as we slept easy that night a mother and a stepfather, Mr and Mrs Sims, in nearby Farley Hill were frantically searching for their little girl, five-year-old Linda Bowyer. She'd gone out to play on her bike around 4.30 p.m. By 8 p.m., Mrs Sims was getting worried about Linda and asked around her friends, but nobody had seen her. When her husband came home later, he drove to Eversley to see if Linda had gone to see her grandfather, but she wasn't there either.

Around midnight, police were alerted. As dawn broke, Linda's bicycle, then her body, were found by a police sergeant in a copse behind the grocer's shop, 200 yards from her home and a mile and a half from where Straffen had been caught near the Bramshill Hunt. Home Office pathologist Dr Donald Teare examined Linda's body and decided that she had died from strangulation. There was no evidence of sexual assault.

Straffen incriminated himself the next morning when detectives visited him in Broadmoor. Nobody had told him of Linda's death, but when asked if he got up to mischief while he was out, he replied, "I did not kill her," and when probed further, "I did not kill the little girl on the bicycle." He was tried at Winchester Assizes, sentenced to death and refused leave to appeal. A week before he was due to hang, he was reprieved. He would spend the next 55 years in prison.

The murder of little Linda Bowyer so close to home stayed with me for life. How unlucky was that child, playing on her bicycle on a beautiful spring evening, to bump into a serial child murderer during the only four hours he was free in 56 years. Years later, when I had my own young daughter, I kept her in as much as possible, and whenever she did go out to play, I worried the whole time that she would meet another Straffen. That kind of thing never leaves you.

CHAPTER 9

Juvenile delinquency
– how it began

Police work is like a cross between a gigantic jigsaw puzzle where you're only ever given some of the pieces – not necessarily from the same box – and a memory game: is that the car number plate we have to look out for (checks notebook)? Is that the same man seen running away from the break-in (he's not wearing a hat)? Putting names to the Ferals' faces at the gravel pits were the corner pieces of a complex puzzle of delinquency, youth crime and "care or protection" issues that started off small in 1952 and would develop throughout my time in uniform.

Their mischief was a bit of a joke to begin with. Members of the public dropped in to report their more creative pranks. Pattie and I sometimes eavesdropped, trying not to laugh as Sarge diligently took notes:

"So there we was, minding our own business, sitting waiting for the 3A bus when I saw something moving out of the corner of my eye. Somebody – hiding on top of the bus shelter – was lowering a rotting pig's head down on a piece of string and jiggling it about, then pulling it back up again. It was disgusting! All fly-blown and oozing, with its dead eyes, tongue lolling out and jagged teeth. It stank to high heaven! My little Gerald was sick all over his shoes."

"And can you describe the perpetrators?"

"They jumped down off of the bus shelter and ran away, dragging that … that horrible thing with them. Three scruffy-looking kids. I only saw their backs."

Miss Marsh, the town librarian, was next in. "We've put up with the childish booby traps in the library for long enough," she complained.

"Booby traps, Madam?"

"Whoopie cushions underneath the armchair seat by the enquiries desk. Poor old Mrs Pinnegar sat on one today. Even people in the reference section looked up. She kept apologising, I kept reassuring her it wasn't her . . . at least I didn't think it was . . . she got a bit distressed. Then, we found dried beetles in the card index drawers, and a dead shrew on top of the Featured Book of the Week."

"Whoopie cushions, eh?" replied Sarge. "I'll get WPC Crockford to call into the library on her beat."

Sure enough, I found an instantly recognisable gaggle of four giggling boys – Roger Wickes, Charlie Carroll and the Felton brothers – crowded round a study carrel in the library's medical reference section. Spotting me, Dennis Felton slammed shut the book they were poring over and tried to stuff it under his jumper, but it fell on the floor, flopping open naturally at pages 66 and 67. It was *The Illustrated Handbook of Midwifery*, one of the most thumbed books in the reference library.

"Biology homework?" I asked, picking it up, trying to ignore the double-page spread illustration titled *Female External Genitalia*.

Carl and Dennis nudged each other, sniggering.

"I'm doing arithmetic," said Roger. "In here, Mother can't hover over me telling me long division wasn't done like this in her day."

Charlie had in front of him a pile of picture books about old coins, crockery and bones from the History and Archaeology section.

"I like it in here 'cos it's warm," he said.

"And what are you two studying?" I asked the Feltons. They shuffled uneasily and I'm sure Carl murmured "fannies" under his breath. "I've had reports that somebody keeps putting whoopie cushions under that chair and leaving dead things around to scare people. You wouldn't know anything about this, would you?"

Four heads shook.

"What's in your satchel, Roger?"

Roger opened it to show me a selection of maths books, school notebooks and a ruler.

"And your bag, Charlie?"

Charlie shook out his usual eclectic collection of shells, coins and pieces of broken pottery. The Feltons didn't have bags.

"Turn out your pockets please, boys."

Out came catapults, a mouse skull, a box of matches, some desiccated hornets and a whoopie cushion.

"It wasn't us! He made us do it!" The Feltons pointed at Roger, who blinked with wide-eyed innocence.

I called Miss Marsh over.

"Out!" she said. "You two are barred from the library for a month. Consider yourselves very lucky that I'm not asking the WPC to press charges."

I couldn't think of any crime they'd committed to press charges anyway. And although I was unable to prove it, I suspected that Roger and Charlie set the clueless Feltons up as patsies for their entertainment, to get the blame.

Barred from the hallowed hall of learning that was Wokingham Library, it was probably the Feltons who devised an even less sophisticated form of entertainment. Suzette was in her dressing gown and fluffy yellow slippers one afternoon, still groggy from her daytime sleep after the nightshift. I'd just got in from my early turn and we were sharing a pot of tea in the kitchen. The ship's bell jangled.

"I'll go," she said. "Might be a parcel from home."

Next thing, I heard Suzette shouting, "Gwen! Something's on fire here!"

I grabbed Mrs Cunningham's broom and ran to the front door. A smoking newspaper parcel, small flames coming out of it, sat on the doorstep. Before I could stop her, Suzette instinctively stamped on it to put out the flames. But as she stamped, something spattered all over her beautiful slippers – slimy green dung from a fresh cowpat wrapped inside.

I pushed the smouldering package off the doorstep with the broom, ran to the gate and looked up and down Murdoch Road. Some indistinct, childlike figures retreated into the distance.

"Oh no, your slippers are ruined, Suzette," I cried.

She sighed. "Well, that's taking Knockdown Ginger[5] to a whole new level."

While the Ferals' japes bordered on the criminal, sometimes we'd get a report of real youth crime that required female officers. One Friday afternoon, Sergeant Robertshaw sent us up to the CID office to see Inspector Dankworth.

"Ladies, we've received a report from the manager of WHSmith. He's discovered discrepancies in the takings between April and now, and thinks one of the young Saturday shop assistants has got her fingers in the till. He's asked us if we can do some surveillance. I think it's a classic case of the assistant ringing up less than the value of the goods and pocketing the difference, and we'll need you to go undercover tomorrow. Can you come in first thing in civvies?"

The next morning, ahead of me, Pattie clacked into the back office on high-heeled white slingbacks. She'd really gone to town on her disguise, in a sleeveless high-collared navy-and-white dress that plunged down the front to a tightly-cinched waist, accentuating her generous bosom and curves. Over her arm she carried a white cashmere cardigan and a white Italian leather handbag. Her thick blonde hair, liberated from its usual array of pins and clips, flowed around her shoulders.

A couple of the officers wolf-whistled. Beaming, she struck a catwalk pose and theatrically threw her cardigan over her shoulder, giving chuckling Sergeant Lamb a wink.

---

5 The game of knocking on someone's door then running away before they opened it. Also known as the GPO parcel service.

"Cor – this is a sight for sore eyes," said Bob. "What's all this in aid of?"

"Stake out. You'll find out soon enough." Pattie laughed, pointing at him like Marilyn Monroe.

I shuffled in behind her. I wore a tweed overcoat two sizes too big that I'd borrowed from Suzette and some scuffed burgundy leather lace-up brogues. I'd tied a brown headscarf over my curly hair with a knot under my chin and put on some pink lipstick, badly. Looking in the mirror, I hardly recognised myself – I looked 40 years older and rather frumpy. I scrubbed down into a pensioner persona rather too convincingly for my liking. Like Pattie, I looked, and felt, a completely different person out of my police uniform. No wolf-whistles heralded my entrance, just some puzzled looks.

"Well, good morning, officers," I creaked in my best tremulous old lady voice. "Which nice young policeman is going to help me across the road?"

Everybody burst out laughing as they realised it was me. Henry Falconer, who was wearing his traffic gauntlets, offered me his arm and flamboyantly stopped imaginary traffic as he guided me, shuffling unsteadily, across an imaginary street, acting a helping-an-old-lady-across-the-road scenario. It was an uplifting start to the shift. We'd been short on laughs recently and the chuckling took a while to subside. Henry was uncharacteristically smiling well into the briefing.

On the way out, I pinched Pattie's bare, tanned arm. "Goodness, Pats, you look like Diana Dors. If you're trying to go incognito, you're going to attract a lot of attention."

"There's method in my madness, Gwen," she said, tapping the side of her nose. "If I doll myself up, other customers will be looking at me and the shop girl might take advantage of attention being focused away from her. You blend into the background looking frumpy and watch for any theft."

"Story of my life." I laughed. "It's a good idea, though, Pattie. Let's see if it works."

Approaching WHSmith separately, I shuffled along Market Place in character while Pattie trotted gaily in to peruse the magazines and stationery supplies. After a few minutes, I followed her. I clocked two female shop assistants, both about 13 years old. One with her back to me rearranging typewriter supplies was pale and slender with a long mousy plait and another at the till had freckles and a mop of ginger curls.

I loitered at a carousel of greetings cards by the till, pretending to choose a birthday card for a husband. A woman bought some typewriter ribbons and a packet of carbon paper. She gave the correct money to the ginger-haired girl, and the correct money went in the till. A man bought a *John Bull* magazine and some chewing gum. Again, the correct money went in the till. Other purchases took place, none of which was fraudulent.

As I moved slowly around the shop, I caught Pattie's eye and gave a little shake of my head to indicate that the ginger-haired girl wasn't embezzling the till – yet.

We didn't know how long we could stay in WHSmith without drawing attention to ourselves.

After 10 minutes, the girl with the ginger curls left the till and spoke to the other assistant who had been busying herself at the back of the shop. I heard her say that she needed to pop down to the storeroom – could she look after the till?

I did a subtle double take as the other assistant approached. I recognised her. It was Bernie Carroll, the eldest girl from the caravan. Now I knew why I thought her face was familiar when Bob and I visited the Carrolls; I often popped into WHSmith for a newspaper or a bottle of ink.

Pattie and I exchanged glances. Now might be the time to strike. Pattie grabbed a third magazine in addition to the two she was holding. Together they came to a total of nine shillings. She gave Bernie a handful of coins.

"Can I give you these? I need to dash to an appointment. I think nine bob is right," she said, fanning out the magazines so Bernie could see the cover prices.

"Yes, that's fine, thank you," replied Bernie.

I nonchalantly moved back into position by the card carousel, trying to make it look as if I had finally decided on a birthday card for my non-existent husband.

Pattie sashayed out of the shop, her hair flowing, and she was absolutely right – people turned to look at her as she left. Everyone except me. I watched Bernie Carroll ring up five shillings on the till and drop four into her skirt pocket.

I chose the cheapest birthday card and gave Bernie thruppence ha'penny. Bernie rang up the money and dropped all the coppers into the till. She barely gave me a glance, let alone recognised me as the police officer who came calling at her home.

I left WHSmith with the redundant birthday card and a heavy feeling. We would have to arrest Bernie Carroll, she would lose her job and we would close the door on any trust we had built up with the Carrolls as a "problem family".

Back at the station, Pattie had already changed out of her glamorous civvies and was pinning her hair back up. We reported to the CID office.

"Sir, you were right. WPC Baxter bought some magazines and I witnessed the shop girl short-change the till, bold as brass," I said.

"All right. Well done both of you. I'll telephone the manager, get him to check the till and the stock, and once he has confirmed there's money missing, we need to arrest her."

"There's another thing, sir. I recognised the shop assistant as one of Rodney Carroll's children. Bernie, I think he said her name was. She was in the caravan when we called there hunting for Straffen."

"Carroll? Well, that explains a lot."

"Perhaps Bernie's stealing to feed the family. None of the children look particularly well fed."

"Much as you would love to excuse every waif and stray, Crockford," said Dankworth, "we're dealing with a crime here – embezzlement. I'll ring Mr Dickinson the manager now. Be ready to make an arrest."

An hour later, we were back at WHSmith. On Dankworth's advice, Mr Dickinson had cashed up the takings and tasked Bernie Carroll with tidying the magazine shelves. The ginger-haired girl had been sent home early.

Bernie Carroll stared at us as we walked into the shop in uniform, colour draining from her cheeks. She looked puzzled, as if we were oddly familiar, but she couldn't quite place us. Mr Dickinson nodded at us.

I approached Bernie.

"Miss, we have reason to believe you have been fraudulently taking money legally belonging to WHSmith. Please would you turn out your pockets."

Bernie rummaged in her skirt pockets, beads of perspiration forming on her forehead. I crossed my fingers that she hadn't hidden the money somewhere else to collect later.

Bernie pulled out four shillings. "It's grocery money. Dad gave it me to do some shopping on the way home."

"I'm suggesting that this money should have gone in the till this afternoon," I said.

"I'm four bob down today, Bernie," added Mr Dickinson, "as I have been several times when you've been working since April."

"It's that Molly," said Bernie. "She's always turning up with new shoes or nail varnish. It's her what's stealing out of the till, not me."

"I'm afraid I watched you take that money today, Bernie," I said.

Bernie's mouth dropped open. "You never!"

"You remember the blonde lady who bought three magazines and gave you nine bob?"

112

"Vaguely . . ."

"I watched you ring up five bob and put four in your pocket."

"What? How? I didn't see you in here earlier?"

"I was in plain clothes in a headscarf and a brown overcoat, standing behind the cards carousel."

Bernie's eyes flicked from side to side as she tried to recall. "Oh, that miserable old bag?" I flinched at her description. "That's not fair, creeping around spying on people."

"I'm afraid we have a duty to investigate a theft report by whatever means we think fit and plain clothes surveillance is one of the ways we do it," I replied.

"You're all sneaks!" cried Bernie.

"Bernadette Carroll, I'm going to have to ask you to come back to the station for further questioning with our inspector. You are not obliged to say anything, but anything you say may be given in evidence."

"And I'm formally terminating your employment," chipped in Mr Dickinson.

We escorted Bernie, weeping, back to the station.

"Please don't call my dad. I'll tell you everything but please don't call him," pleaded Bernie.

In the interview room with Dankworth, Bernie sat cross-legged and cross-armed, glaring at the floor. Rodney Carroll sat beside her, his massive square frame dwarfing his petite daughter, his usual wide toothy grin replaced with a brooding frown.

"Yes, I took money out of the till, but never more than 2s.6d at a time, honest," stated Bernie.

"But I saw you, Bernie, and you didn't have any sixpences in your pocket," I replied.

"I'm sorry, but we have no choice but to charge you with embezzlement, contrary to section 17 of the Larceny Act 1916," said Dankworth. "Mr Carroll, you'll have to accompany Bernie to the juvenile court."

Bernie burst into tears again.

Carroll chipped in, "Since I haven't been working, officers, it's been difficult making ends meet. We rely on Bernie's wages to put food on the table for the little 'uns. If she can't work . . ." He took out a cigarette and lit it. Something about him both irritated me and made my skin crawl.

"Well, you'll have to look harder to get yourself a job then, Mr Carroll," snapped Dankworth. "Save all this for the court."

Sarge formally charged Bernie, his eyebrow raising at the name Carroll, and filled in the necessary paperwork. The Carrolls left the station. Through the window I saw Rodney give Bernie's shoulder a rough shove. Perhaps a walk home might dissipate some of his anger. I felt a sick feeling in the pit of my stomach when I thought about what might happen behind the closed caravan door when they got home.

Down in the locker room, Pattie was leafing through her *Film Star* magazines from WHSmith, paid for on police expenses.

"That was a bit of a result, wasn't it? A successful stake-out and arrest, and a heap of free mags too! Ooh, I love Gregory Peck, don't you?" she cooed, holding up a whole-page photo of the admittedly gorgeous Mr Peck.

"You can read these after me if you like. Did you get anything?"

I held up my card: *With love to my darling husband on his 50th birthday.*

Pattie burst out laughing.

I flicked the card onto the top shelf of my locker.

CHAPTER 10

Hilda Bloom, probation officer

Although the quirky Arts and Crafts building we worked in was called Wokingham Police Station, it housed what was in effect a small law enforcement village. The police station itself shared premises with the probation office and the magistrates' courtroom, making collaboration between the various agencies fairly straightforward.

Bernie Carroll was assigned to Hilda Bloom as her probation officer. Pattie and I would get to know Hilda well over the next few years as the lines between the police and probation service were far more blurred than they are now. We shared what Hilda called "gender-defined work roles" – our remit was dealing mainly with women and children because we *were* women and we were even referred to as "the gentle arm of the law". The "rough arm of the law" generally left us to get on with our "female issues", so we worked with Hilda, applying our collective discretion and common sense to cases, without too much male interference.

I had a lot of time for Hilda. Of German-Jewish heritage, and always dressed in tweed, she was a bit of an icon; one of those effortlessly strong, decisive women that I aspired to be. We would huddle together at a corner table in the police canteen, deep in ethical conversations about offenders, trying to balance welfare with punishment to give the best outcome for them, while also considering their victims.

Fascinated by her, I was at first a little afraid to ask Hilda how a German ended up in Wokingham in case she thought me nosy. One particularly slow afternoon, I bit the bullet and asked. She was remarkably forthcoming.

"My family got out of Berlin and to England in the early 1930s through the foresight of my father, Samuel Blum, who was a university professor, like my mother. He realised before many others that things could only get much, much worse for our Jewish community as Hitler rose to power. My parents had to make the decision – it was heartbreaking, Gwen, to leave friends and family and sail to England. Most of them perished in the camps."

Hilda paused for a moment and I hoped I hadn't upset her. But then she continued.

"We were happily settled in west London and anglicised our name to Bloom. When the war broke out in 1939, we were twice as scared as everyone else: if Hitler invaded, we Jews would be at the top of any extermination list. We were also afraid that the British government would intern us as enemy aliens. Having to register as German nationals with our local police station was uncomfortably like having to register as Jews in Berlin. Happily, most of us Jewish refugees were Category Cs – 'exempt from internment and restriction' – which meant we could get on with our lives unhindered. And, as you know, Hitler didn't invade.

"Out of the blue one wartime day, my parents announced that we were moving to a small town in Buckinghamshire, called Bletchley. I remember Mutti saying we would be safer from the bombs away from the city, and she and Vati got themselves some admin jobs. We found a cosy little house and I enrolled at the local school with my own house key to let myself in. Off would go Vati and Mutti on their bicycles to work in a huge old house in the town.

"Sometimes there was so much admin that one of them had to work late, or into the night. *Poor Mutti and Vati*, I thought, their jobs were so long and so boring that they didn't want to talk about them when they got home – to me or even each other.[6] Instead, they focused on my schoolwork and studies, encouraging me to read, play the violin and discuss ideas, making me ... how do you say ... precocious, with knowledge beyond my years that academic parents' only children often have. I was a little spoiled, educationally."

"I guess your experience must have given you your sense of social justice?" I asked.

"*Ja*! I felt exhilarated that we had come through a world war and a social revolution, with the National Health Service and the welfare state. I had a strong need to give something back, but what, I wasn't sure.

---

6 It was only decades later, when Bletchley Park in Buckinghamshire was restored and its work declassified that the penny dropped. Perhaps Hilda's parents worked there?

I might have done nursing, but I couldn't stand the sight of blood. I went to the London School of Economics to study economics – boring! – and sociology and social psychology – interesting! After, I somehow fell into social work, training with Paddington and Kensington Family Services. My first real job was at East London Juvenile Court as a probation officer, which was fascinating, not bureaucratic, and busy. But I like the countryside, so when I heard about this job in your pretty Wokingham, I applied."

Pretty Wokingham. I had never really thought of my hometown like that before. I rather envied Hilda going to university and gaining Big London experience. Why would anyone swap that for provincial Wokingham?

One Wednesday, Hilda knocked on the door of the women's office. "Gwen, they are painting the probation offices. The smell is awful. Can I use the little office to interview Bernie Carroll? She's one of yours anyway."

"Yes, of course, Hilda. There's just me in at the moment."

At Bernie's allotted time, Hilda brought her through the main women's office into a small side one. Bernie kept her eyes on the floor, ignoring me completely.

Hilda shut the door. I forgot to mention that the wood and frosted glass partition between the offices stopped 18 inches short of the ceiling. I heard every word of the interview.

Hilda cheerily introduced herself and asked her name. Bernie said nothing.

"You're not being helpful, are you? Do you want to end up in an Approved School?"[7] she asked in her mannered way. "I'm afraid that's the reality if you don't let me help you. I'm going to ask you some questions and I'm asking them for your own good – to help you."

"Why do you talk funny?" asked Bernie.

"Because I came here from Germany before the war. I'm one of the good guys, honestly."

I knew that a substantial number of post-war Germanophobes expected Hilda to explain herself, and to thwart them, she practised speaking like a BBC announcer to dilute her accent. I imagined the Carrolls didn't read newspapers, listen to the wireless or take much notice in school, so the wider implications of the war probably never filtered through to the children. Germans bad, Churchill good was all the analysis the Carroll children had, if that.

"Anyway, this is not about me, it's about you," continued Hilda. "Tell me about yourself."

"Don't know what to say, really."

"What made you steal the money from WHSmith?"

Silence. This wasn't going to be an easy interview.

"Are you happy at home?"

"S'pose so."

"And you all live in a caravan?"

"Yeah."

"Do you get on with your brothers and sisters?"

"Yep."

---

7 A residential institution where courts could send young people, usually for offences committed, but also if they were "beyond parental control".

"What about your mother and father?"

"Mum's dead. We live with Dad."

"Oh, I'm sorry."

"Sorry that we live with Dad?"

"I'm sorry that your mother died. Should I be sorry that you live with your dad?"

Silence.

"What does your dad do? Does he work?"

"He does odd jobs from time to time. Bit short of work just now."

I heard a pencil scribbling.

"Are you on your own most of the time? Who does the cleaning and cooking?"

"Yeah, most of the time. I cook and clean when I'm home and when we've got food in."

"And what happens when you haven't?"

"We walk into Wokingham and get some chips or summat. Dad sometimes brings some home on his bike."

"Now, Bernie, did you get on all right with the people you worked for at WHSmith?"

"Mr Dickinson was OK, I guess. Until the bastard fired me."

"Why did you steal from them?"

Silence.

"Do you understand what it's like to have someone steal money from you? You must have known it's wrong and how bad people would feel?"

"But it's not really people, is it? It's WHSmith's. Seeing all them people comin' in every day with money to waste on magazines, chocolates and cards, well, I thought it was only fair that some of that should come my way. So I borrowed it. But only 2s.6d at a time."

"You borrowed it? So you really intended to pay it back?"

"Yes'm."

"And no one asked you to do it?"

"No'm. I did it off my own bat. Dad was furious when he found out what I done. You're just tryin' to get me to dob him in, ain't you?"

"Bernie, I'm not a policewoman. I'm here to advise, assist and befriend you."

"Yeah, but you're on the coppers' side, ain't you? I don't need no friendship."

"The only thing I'm interested in is what happened, so I can help the court to deal with *you* appropriately. Tell me, if you didn't get sent to an Approved School, would you be tempted to do it again?"

"No'm. But that money would've been a help to us, what with Dad's work being irregular an' all. I didn't think I'd get caught, or I'd lose my job or end up in here. Never crossed my mind."

"Look, how about I ask the court to look at probation for you, rather than an Approved School? Do you know what that is?"

"Probation? Yeah, think so. I'd be up and down like a fiddler's elbow to Wokingham having to see you all the time."

"There's more to it than that, Bernie. Over the next couple of years, I'll be here to help you stay out of trouble. But I must warn you now – if you mess around and get into trouble with the law again, you'll be brought straight back to court. They'll punish you for your WHSmith theft as if you'd only just committed it, understand?"

"Yeah."

"So, do you reckon you could make a go of this?"

"Yeah, think I could."

"All right. I'll have a word with the chairman and see what I can do. I'll see you again before you go to court."

Bernie had a wan smile on her face as Hilda showed her out. She still blanked me.

"What are you going to do with her?" I asked when Hilda returned.

"I'm inclined to give her a chance, you know. Recommend her for probation. Her home life sounds chaotic. Not sure the dad is entirely focused on the children's welfare and upbringing. Am I right in thinking they all live in a caravan?"

"Yes, I've been there. Only outside, mind. I dread to think what the inside is like. The father gives me the creeps. When's she coming up before the juvenile court?"

"Next week. I think I need to do a home visit before that, ideally tomorrow. Thursday's a lean day for families like this, if the father has even managed to get a week's work. It'll give me an idea of worst-case scenario. Do you want to come with me?" she asked.

"Am I allowed?"

"I don't see why not. See it as part of your training. I'll clear it with Miss Robertshaw."

Hilda drove me in her green Morris Minor along the country lanes. We wondered what we were going to find inside the caravan.

"People always surprise me," she said. "I've visited the most unprepossessing slum house in Rose Street, and although sparse, it was neat, clean and tidy, with a jam jar of wildflowers pride of place on a trestle table. Whereas one sprawling Victorian semi was full of rubbish and animal faeces, not cleaned for months."

We drove down the track. The lopsided, mildewed caravan was barely visible behind a wall of five-feet nettles, hogweed and willowherb that had relished the wet weather. There was no bicycle propped up outside, although there was a tin bath. We caught a whiff of stale urine and excrement.

"Nice place they've got here," she said.

Hilda knocked on the door. The thick lace curtain twitched and Dora's small face appeared.

"Hello, we've come to see Bernie. Is she here?"

The small face disappeared and after a few seconds Bernie opened the door, grey rings beneath her eyes.

"Hello, Bernie. Is it all right if we come in?"

"Yeah, s'pose so." She curled her lip slightly at me.

As we climbed the step into the caravan, it wobbled on its metal legs. I wondered if the whole thing would topple over.

The air inside smelt musty and greasy, heightening the claustrophobic feeling from the dark varnished wood used to kit out the whole caravan. Dora sat at the table on a faux velvet banquette opposite Charlie. They seemed to be playing a game with cockle shells, skulls of birds and small mammals, and some broken clay pipes. Bernie sat down beside him.

"Who are these little people?" Hilda asked Bernie.

"My name's Dora," the little girl replied, confidently.

"And I'm Charlie. Do you want to look at my museum?"

Bernie rolled her eyes.

"I'm Hilda. I'm a probation officer and I'm helping to look after Bernie. I think you know WPC Crockford here. Yes, your museum is, er, lovely. I just need to have a look around your caravan."

"You're a nosy lady." Dora giggled and I noticed that she went to pull her skirt up. Bernie batted her hand away and shushed her.

We did a 360-degree glance around the caravan, taking in the small two-ringed Calor gas stove with a whistle kettle perched on it, the Belfast sink beneath a flip-up marble-effect surface and an open unit with a cutlery box, five chipped plates and five green egg cups in it. An enamel water jug, teapot, saucepan, frying pan and a harlequin selection of chipped cups and glasses lined up on a shelf above the sink.

"Where do you get your water?"

"There's a standpipe outside. Used to supply the cottage when it was liveable in," replied Bernie, pointing through the window. We could see the walls and some broken rafters of a derelict building beyond.

"How do you heat it?"

"We boil the kettle and mix it with cold water to make a warm bath. In winter, we bring the tin bath in."

The Carrolls' bathtime ritual was really no worse than most Wokingham families – including mine – had done through wartime, and some still did.

A double bed with a faded, threadbare hexagonal patchwork quilt took up the right-hand side of the caravan, a canvas Z-bed folded at its foot.

"Where do you all sleep?" she asked.

"Me an' Bernie sleep in the big bed," offered Dora. A rail with a thick tapestry curtain bunched up at the bed-head end hung across their sleeping area.

At least the girls can draw the curtain across for privacy, I thought.

"Charlie and John, they sleep on these," she continued, pointing to the banquettes they were sitting on, some blankets and pillows at the ends.

"Daddy has the fold-up in the miggle."

It seemed a reasonable arrangement, and no different from caravans many people stayed in on holiday, although, to be fair, this was a permanent residence.

"And how do you, er, go to the lavatory?"

Charlie and Dora started giggling and pointed to chamber pots under the double bed.

"Only for pee pees." Dora laughed. "We go poo poos in the woods."

"And wipe our bums on leaves," added Charlie, collapsing into hysterical laughter.

Even Bernie cracked a smile. "Don't tell fibs," she said. "There's an outside lavvie in a shed by the old cottage."

Dora scratched at her matted hair. I glanced into it and saw what I was expecting – grey insects scuttling about. Head lice. They probably all had them. I desperately wanted to scratch my own head.

"I see. And where's your daddy and John now?"

"Dad's on a job and John's gone out with his friends after school."

"Do you know what time your dad will be back?"

"Hmm – any time. Usually before it gets dark, though."

"What food do you have for tonight?"

Bernie opened a cupboard under the sink unit. In it was a loaf of bread, two tins of Heinz baked beans and two eggs.

"Well, thank you, Bernie. I think we've seen enough now," said Hilda. "It was nice meeting you, Dora and Charlie."

Dora and Charlie looked at each other and giggled again.

As Bernie saw us out of the door, Hilda said, "Oh, by the way, there may be a job going at the local stables. It would be mucking out and grooming the horses, but at least you'd get paid for it. Interested?"

Bernie nodded and expressed as much interest as she ever did in anything.

"I'll be in touch," said Hilda as we walked to her car. The caravan door had already closed.

Was this a real child neglect case that Sergeant Robertshaw told me I would recognise? I wondered. I asked Hilda on the way back.

"The caravan kitchen was one of the better-equipped ones I've seen," she said. "And it was reasonably clean. It's a little cramped for five people and the toilet and washing facilities are basic. The youngest has nits, which probably means they all have . . ." Hilda scratched her head and so did I.

"The food's not inadequate," she continued, "Compared with the bare cupboards in some of the slums around Paddington where I trained, it was positively a feast. Charlie and Dora are fine left with Bernie until their father comes back. It's all relative, though, isn't it? The Carrolls are better off than my Paddington families, while the Paddington slums would be palaces for those poor souls in the Warsaw ghetto . . ." She was silent for a moment. "Sorry, Gwen, I can get a little carried away overthinking human misery."

The country needs more Hilda Blooms, I thought. She even made me feel grateful that I grew up in Seaford Road, much as I complained about it. And I still wasn't sure I'd seen the worst of child neglect.

CHAPTER 11

Post-mortems

Sergeant Lamb used to send probationary PCs on errands.

"WPC Crockford – could you do me a favour, love?" he asked on a slow day.

"Anything's better than typing up this two-on-a-bike report, Sarge," I replied.

"Could you pop this envelope over to Crowthorne CID for me? It came in just after Dankworth left and he needs it."

"Of course, Sarge," I replied, stubbing out my cigarette and blowing the smoke out of the corner of my mouth.

Sarge handed me an overstuffed foolscap manila envelope secured with a brass split pin.

"What is it?" I asked.

"Under no circumstances are you to look at what's in it, WPC Crockford. It's not for your eyes. Just deliver it to Crowthorne and make sure Dankworth gets it. There's a train in half an hour. Ta."

I headed out of Wokingham station in an empty train carriage, the envelope on my lap. I kept glancing at it. What could be in it that was so bad I wasn't supposed to see? I stared out of the window, then I found myself staring at the envelope again. When someone says you mustn't look at something, what's the first thing you do?

On no account must I look at the contents. I mustn't look. Who would know if I looked? It's not sealed, it's fastened with a split pin. No one would know . . .

"Oh sod it," I muttered. *I'll be wondering from now until Doomsday what I'm not supposed to see.* I unfastened the split pin.

Inside was typed paperwork from what looked like a closed case: a post-mortem report, some witness statements, some expert statements – and a smaller 5 x 7 manila envelope. I glanced around. There was no one in the carriage to see me, so I furtively scan-read the documents:

> **Post-mortem report**: *stripped naked ... petticoat around neck ... trussed ... electric flex ... string ... strangled ... sexual assault ... cigarette butt between thigh and abdomen ... stomach contents indicate ... within an hour of the victim's last meal...*

> **Home Office analyst's report**: *electric flex ... tarred string ... same types as found in accused's house.*

> **Report from Imperial Tobacco**: *cigarette butt from body identical to cigarette taken from accused . . .*

Then I pulled out the small envelope. That wasn't sealed either. Poking about inside, I drew out some black-and-white scene of crime photographs. True to the post-mortem report, I saw an unclothed young woman lying on some gravel, with a petticoat around her neck. I winced as I saw how the electric flex and tarred string had been used to truss her in such a way that any shred of dignity had gone.

Underneath was a close-up photograph of her bruised face. I jumped with shock. Two pale eyes stared straight at me, the whites completely blackened, the mouth open and slack. The only way I could process this horror was by clicking my mind back into the Forensics Week lecture by a Home Office pathologist that we attended at training school.

"So this is what petechiae look like when they're at home," I tried to rationalise under my breath. *Haemorrhages under the skin and of the blood vessels in the eyes, caused by strangulation,* I heard the lecturer's voice say in my head. It had all sounded so cold and clinical, as did the reports in the package. Yet here was a woman, not much younger than me, whose terrifying last moments – unable to move, brutalised by her attacker, a hot cigarette butt dropped between her belly and thigh – must have been beyond nightmarish.

My mind raced as I sought some way of coming to terms with the horror. How frightened and alone must this poor woman have felt? Could her terror have somehow anaesthetised any of the pain? I had heard stories of escaping prisoners of war realising they were gravely injured only when they reached a place of safety and hoped that the same natural body chemicals may have been merciful to this unfortunate girl.

Realising that I was allowing personal feelings to crack my professional carapace, I pushed the other photos, presumably shots of the body from different angles and post-mortem pictures, back into the envelope and closed it. I reached for my cigarettes just as the train drew into Crowthorne station. *Serves me right for being nosy*, I thought. *I was told not to look.*

After dropping the package with CID, I took the next train back to Wokingham, feeling a little subdued. As I collected a folder of reports from the front desk for typing, Sarge smiled at me.

"All right, WPC Crockford?"

I gave him what I thought was a bright, cheery smile.

"Yes thanks, Sarge, all safely dropped off for DI Dankworth. I'll get onto these reports just now."

I settled into my chair in the back office, lit another cigarette and drew the smoke deeply into my lungs as I threaded paper and carbon paper into the typewriter. I could feel Sarge's eyes boring into me, but I resisted looking up. He knew I'd opened the envelope. I would only find out years later that it was a test. Of course everyone looked in the envelope. It was the precursor to the next rite of passage for a police officer – attending a post-mortem.

At the end of a strange week, Pattie, Higgs and I found ourselves at the public mortuary to experience our first post-mortem. Pattie was uncharacteristically quiet, chewing her thumbnail. My legs felt slightly unsteady. Sweat beaded on Higgs's forehead, but his silly grin was still there.

"Don't worry, ladies, I'm here to catch you if you keel over," he smarmed.

Although I'd seen the dead body of an elderly lady at training school, this was the first time I experienced a functional mortuary's forensic smell of disinfectant, chemicals and rubber, and the clanging of metal trolleys and cadaver drawers. It wasn't the last. I would attend many more post-mortems throughout my police career, but it's always the first one that stays with you – their name, their story and how they died.

As we trailed along the corridor behind pathologist Dr Sladen and his stocky assistant Hackett, the telephone rang.

"Go into that autopsy room there," he said, taking the call. "I'll be along in a moment."

We entered a grimy, white-tiled room, lit by two bare lightbulbs hanging from the ceiling. Our eyes were drawn to a smallish form, covered by a sheet on the comparatively huge autopsy table. Bunioned feet stuck out of the end, a label tied to one big toe.

"Th ... there's a real dead person under there?" ventured Pattie, her complexion greenish under the light.

"Ticky ticky ticky ticky!" Higgs giggled, tickling the ball of a cold, purplish foot. "If that doesn't wake 'em up, they're definitely dead."

Pattie and I looked at him in sheer disbelief. Before we could say anything, Dr Sladen and Hackett swept into the room.

"First post-mortem is it, ladies and gent?" Sladen asked.

We nodded, wide-eyed.

"You're lucky with this lady as she died only yesterday. Sometimes police officers get road traffic accident victims or people who've been dead for several days as their first PM. Those can be a bit rough for first timers. Although, be warned, this dear soul did allegedly hang herself."

The room started to spin slightly. I had an inkling I knew who was going to be under the sheet, as bad news spread round Wokingham fast. Hackett pulled off the sheet to prove me right, revealing the dead, naked body of Marjorie Curtis, the sister of one of my Seaford Road neighbours.

"Frank Curtis's sister has only gone and topped herself," Mum had informed me only the day before when I'd bumped into her in Timothy Whites. "And we all thought she was just being a hypochondriac."

Poor Marjorie. She was always in and out of the doctor's surgery. I couldn't believe she was on the slab in front of me, but it wasn't really Marjorie, just the shell she'd left behind.

Dr Sladen began the external examination of the body, dictating to Hackett, who was scribbling furiously all the while. I didn't feel it was right to stare at Marjorie's body, so I focused on her closed eyes and how peaceful she looked.

"As you can see, there are circular marks on the neck forming two grooves, consistent with the double piece of clothes line that she allegedly used to hang herself with," he said, and we all looked closely. He took several flash photographs. "See how her hands, forearms, feet and lower legs are this dark reddy-purple colour?"

We nodded.

"Livor mortis. Once the heart stops beating, gravity takes over and blood pools in the lowest extremities.

This lady's livor mortis is consistent with hanging." He picked up a scalpel. "We're going in now. You'll find there's surprisingly little blood."

He made a Y-shaped incision from the top of Marjorie's shoulders, round and under her breasts, then down to the top of her pubis, exposing her internal organs. He then crunched off Marjorie's ribcage using what looked like garden loppers.

"Just like cutting out stubborn pieces of privet hedge," he chirped, revealing the chest cavity.

The room was filling with a metallic, meaty smell, but Pattie and I were now so fascinated seeing how neatly packed Marjorie's heart, lungs, liver and intestines were that we'd stopped noticing it. As Dr Sladen removed each organ for examination, he sliced it up and pointed out the features. We even managed to ignore the cheesy smell of the stomach contents as he tipped them into an enamel dish, because the digestive tract was so interesting.

"Ooh, is that the gall bladder?" asked Pattie, peering closely.

"Yes, smell this." Dr Sladen drained some bile out of it and we were hit with a sour, acidic stench.

"Blimey! Is this what smelling salts are made from?" cried Pattie, her eyes watering.

"Probably one of the human body's worst smells," said Dr Sladen, as he carried on cutting.

"Looks like she was developing a bowel tumour here," he commented, slicing a firm mass with a long knife and puncturing the large intestine. The odour of excreta joined the other organic smells in the room.

Higgs was still standing by Marjorie's feet, but out of the corner of my eye I noticed him swaying. As if in slow motion, he crumpled gracefully into a heap on the floor.

Dr Sladen barely lifted his gaze from Marjorie's colon. "Man down, Hackett. Could you do the honours, please?"

Hackett wordlessly put down his clipboard. I helped him drag a groaning, semi-conscious Higgs out of the autopsy room and onto a chair in the corridor where a mortuary attendant gave him a glass of water.

When I returned, Dr Sladen was revving a small circular bone saw. "Shame. He didn't even get as far as me taking the top of the cranium off . . ."

Heading back to the station with a silent, whey-faced Higgs, Pattie and I were hyped, chattering over each other about our most and least favourite bits of the post-mortem. It was honestly the most fascinating thing I had ever seen. I also felt an immense sense of gratitude to dear Marjorie for her contribution to our learning. Gasping for a cup of tea, we went straight to the canteen to decompress. Higgs slunk off to the gents.

"Aye, Aye! How'd it go? Anybody throw up?" called Bob.

He and Henry were sitting at a table by the window. Pattie pointed to Higgs's retreating figure and mimicked a faint.

"There's always one." Bob laughed. "Henry, you remember our first post-mortem? We really drew the short straw with that bloater, didn't we?"

"Bloater?" I asked.

"Body fished out of the river that's been in there a while. Someone drowns and sinks then the foetid gases build up and lift the body back up to the surface. Ours was fished out of the gravel pit. What was it the pathologist said, Henry?"

"Something about it being jolly good luck for us that the body was pulled out of the gravel pit and not the river," replied Henry. "No fish to nibble bits off, apparently, which was somehow better. He told us to brace ourselves for the gas release."

"That pathologist was not wrong, you know," continued Bob. "The release of gas and bodily fluids as he cut through the bloke's abdomen and digestive organs filled that room with wave after wave of noxious stench." He grimaced.

"Ooh, I know what you mean," said Pattie. "It's sort of chemically, meaty, earthy, isn't it?"

"And pond-slimy, in our case."

"You were the last man standing, weren't you, Henry?" said Bob. "Guess you'd seen enough decomposing bodies for this one not to bother you so much."

Henry said nothing, but reached for his cigarettes. He offered them to me and Pattie.

"The smell stays with you for days," Bob said. "A corpse's stench gets right into your nasal membranes and sits there, like some sort of slow-release stinkbomb. It's unmistakable."

On the way out, I had a chat with Sarge, the station's all-knowing oracle.

"What do we know about Marjorie Curtis?" I asked. "I heard she committed suicide."

"Was that who . . .?"

"Yep. She was a housekeeper for one of her brothers in Langborough Road. Her other brother was my neighbour."

"Ah, I see. Night shift got a call from her brother at 5 a.m. He'd gone out to their outhouse to find her hanged from a crossbeam using a length of washing line. There was a metal bucket nearby that she'd probably used to stand on."

At Marjorie's inquest, a doctor and a district nurse revealed that before her death she had high blood pressure, thyroid problems and failing eyesight, as well as "mental worry". The coroner read out her suicide note. In it, she expressed fear that she was about to be sent to hospital to have her eyes removed, thanked her brothers for their kindness and apologised for leaving them. The coroner returned a verdict of "Suicide whilst the balance of her mind was disturbed".

When I arrived back at Murdoch Road, Suzette was in the living room, crocheting.

"How was it, Gwen?" she called. I'd told her I was nervous about attending the post-mortem that morning and I couldn't divulge whose it was.

"You know what, Suz, it wasn't bad at all. In fact, it was actually fascinating how the human body all fits together. I won't worry about going to another PM."

"At least your patient won't holler when you stick a needle in, or puke on your shoes." She chuckled. I didn't mention Marjorie's stomach contents.

"Give me the living over the dead any day," she said. I'd begun to feel the same, having had a relentless death theme going on all day.

"So what's been going on in the world of Suzette today then?" I asked, settling into an armchair.

"I was in casualty. A boy with a saucepan jammed on his head, the usual dog bites, a couple of workmen fell off ladders, a baby fell out of her pram but was all right – a nice undemanding day, all told."

We chatted until seven o'clock when Mrs Cunningham tinkled the dinner bell for us to go into the dining room. Some well-boiled potatoes and diced carrots sat in a serving dish on the table.

"Here you are, my hardworking girlies," she chirruped, bringing in two plates. "Lovely liver and bacon in gravy! Got to keep your iron levels up."

Suzette tucked in with gusto, but I couldn't manage the rubbery liver with its tough, gristly tubes and the gravy that looked like intestinal contents.

"Not hungry, Gwen?" asked Suzette with a sympathetic smile.

"I never thought I'd hear myself say this, but today of all days I'd have preferred one of Mrs C's 80 per cent swede stews."

CHAPTER 12

The baby in the basin

On a chilly November afternoon, Miss Robertshaw and I were filing reports in the women's office when the telephone rang. She picked up the receiver.

"Wokingham police station, women's office. Sergeant Robertshaw speaking ... yes ... I see ... a baby, you say? Yes, we'll be right there . . ."

My ears pricked up at the mention of the word "baby", immediately jumping to a worst-case scenario conclusion. My career would expose me to so much infant and child mortality that for the rest of my life I believed children were probably far more vulnerable and fragile than they in fact are.

"Get your coat on, Miss Crockford. Somebody's abandoned a baby in the women's cloakroom at the Town Hall."

"Is the baby all right?"

"Yelling its head off, apparently. It would seem so."

I breathed a sigh of relief.

It was a five-minute quick march from the station to Market Place and Wokingham's Neo-Gothic town hall, where a clerk met us. We heard mewling cries before we even reached the women's cloakroom. A tall, elegant woman in a powder blue overcoat stood by the washbasins, jiggling a bundle wrapped in a navy flannelette shawl.

"I came in to use the Ladies and I saw him in the washbasin," said the woman. "He was crying and quite blue around the mouth, but he stopped immediately when I picked him up and cuddled him against me. I waited a while in case his mother came back, but she didn't. He's only just started crying again."

"And you are?" asked Miss Robertshaw.

The woman smiled. "Mrs Madeleine Kirby. I would shake hands but they are rather full at the moment."

I stood waiting for Miss Robertshaw to make a move towards the baby, but she didn't.

"May I see him?" I asked.

Mrs Kirby opened the shawl and the baby's grey eyes gazed unblinkingly towards my face. His mother had dressed him well in new clothes – a coatee, frock, mittens and bootees. He stopped crying and made a little gurgling sound.

"Right, we need to get it straight to the hospital and warmed up," said Miss Robertshaw, as she went to take the baby from Mrs Kirby at arm's length. She struggled to keep hold of him: his heavy head flopped backwards and he threw his hands up in a startle response, like a baby monkey. He started screaming.

Mrs Kirby grimaced. "You need to put your hand under his head . . ."

"Oh, you take it, WPC Crockford!" Miss Robertshaw thrust the baby at me.

I instinctively held him upright and close, his chin on

my shoulder, rocking from side to side until he stopped crying. Then he was sick all down my back.

Ever-efficient Sarge had organised two cars – one to drive Miss Robertshaw and Mrs Kirby to the station to take her witness statement, and one to whisk me and the baby to hospital. He had also telephoned ahead to warn the medical staff. A reception party awaited us and I was delighted to see Suzette, her arms full of blankets, waving at me from the main entrance, accompanied by a doctor and a staff nurse called Penelope.

"We've been expecting this little man, haven't we, sweetie?" cooed Penelope, sweeping the baby into the crook of her arm and swaddling him in Suzette's blankets.

"We'll have to call him something until we find his mother," she said. "How about Bobby?"

"We'll need to give Bobby a full examination first," said the doctor. He turned to me. "Will you be in attendance as well?"

I'd expected to drop the baby and leave; attending was probably above my rank, but I couldn't pass up the opportunity to observe a foundling's medical examination. Anyway, Miss Robertshaw hadn't seemed at all unhappy to leave the hands-on baby stuff to me.

"Absolutely. All part of the investigation," I said, with no idea whether it was or not.

We trooped into a stuffily warm side room off the children's ward. Penelope laid Bobby on an examination table, where he kicked and wriggled, fascinated by the lights and the new faces. She undressed him down to his towelling nappy and I checked his clothes for any notes or labels that might identify him. There were none and all his clothes were hand-knitted.

"How old do you think he is, Doctor?" I asked.

"He's a good-sized lad, but his umbilical stump hasn't quite dropped off yet. I reckon he's about 10 days old," he said.

The doctor shone a torch into Bobby's eyes and listened to his heart with a stethoscope. He held him upright to see how his legs and joints moved.

"What are those red marks on the back of his neck?" I asked, pleased with myself that I may have picked up some signs of abuse.

"Stork bites," said Penelope.

For a split second, I believed her. Mum had told me, Barbara and Ron that the stork had arrived overnight, bringing our baby sister Jean.

"They're birthmarks," she explained. "We just call them that. Rather sweet, isn't it? They fade within a few weeks."

"Let's get a fresh nappy for this little lad and I'll check for undescended testes," said the doctor. Suzette whisked away his wet nappy, folded a clean terry towelling square and placed it under Bobby. The doctor peered down.

"Don't forget to hold down his . . ." said Suzette.

Too late. A surprisingly powerful golden arc of wee caught the doctor squarely in the face, splashing his glasses. The nurses rolled their eyes and I laughed out loud.

"They get me every time." The doctor chuckled, wiping his glasses on his handkerchief. "He appears to be a healthy, well-cared-for baby boy," he continued as he went to leave. "He'll need a good feed, a long sleep and of course his mother, if you can find her, officer."

There was a knock on the door and Penelope was called away. Suzette pinned Bobby into his fresh nappy, pulled some rubber pants over it and dressed him in a clean sleepsuit. She dandled him effortlessly in front of her face, supporting his head and bottom, his eyes and hers wide with delight, before kissing him on the forehead and bundling him into a blanket.

Penelope returned.

"Seems news travels fast. There's a journalist from *The Wokingham Courier* in reception wants a photo of Bobby for this week's edition. Says it might help his mother come forward."

Bobby was drifting off to sleep in Suzette's arms as we walked into reception. Conrad Jardine, the *Courier*'s grizzled reporter, stood there, notepad in hand and a camera slung around his neck. He read out a reasonably accurate account of how Bobby was found – he must have chatted to the town hall clerk.

"Now, all I need to get is a photograph of the little chap for the front page."

Suzette stepped forward and held up Bobby so that his face, albeit sleeping, could be clearly seen.

"Thanks, love, but could you pass him over to the staff nurse for the photo?"

"But I've only just got him off to sleep," replied Suzette.

"It's just that staff nurse Penelope looks ... well ... more official."

Penelope took the bundle from Suzette who stood there, blinking. Bobby opened his eyes.

"Conrad, both Penelope *and* Suzette have been looking after this baby," I said. "You need them both in the photo."

"Very well then, squeeze up together, look adoringly at the baby and say cheese," he huffed.

The flashbulb popped. The two nurses blinked. Bobby jumped at the pop and the flash and started screaming. Conrad Jardine left with his photo. And when the story came out on the front page of Friday's *Courier*, there was a photo of Penelope with Bobby. Suzette had been cropped out.

Back at the station, an all-hands-on-deck investigation was underway to find Bobby's mother.

"A witness said, 'I saw a young woman with distinctive dark curly hair feeding a baby matching the description on the bench outside the town hall at lunchtime,'" read Henry from his pocketbook.

"None of the bus conductors saw a woman with a baby matching the description on their bus," reported Higgs.

We didn't have to search for long. The next day, a petite young woman with black ringleted hair rang the bell on the station front desk.

"My name is Lily Lewis and it's me who left my baby in the town hall cloakroom."

Miss Robertshaw and I led Lily Lewis into our interview room.

"How is my little Anthony?" she asked.

"Well, apart from being nicknamed Bobby, he's very well and being looked after beautifully in Wokingham Hospital," said Miss Robertshaw.

Lily started crying. I handed her my handkerchief.

"Let's start at the beginning, shall we?" began Miss Robertshaw. "When was Anthony born?"

"First of November."

"And where did you have him?"

"At home. He just sort of popped out. My nan had delivered babies before and knew what to do."

"So, you didn't go to hospital to get you and him checked out?"

"No."

"How old are you?"

"Nineteen."

"You're not wearing a wedding ring. Do I take it you're not married to Anthony's father?"

"That's right."

"And who is Anthony's father?"

"Leslie Bradley."

"And does he know that you've had his baby?"

"Oh, yes. It's complicated, because Les is married. He and his wife want to adopt Anthony but I don't want them to have him. I'd rather put him up for adoption."

"Why's that, Lily?"

"I just don't think he would be a good dad."

"I see." Miss Robertshaw took a deep breath. "Now tell me what happened yesterday, November the tenth, Lily."

"I walked into Wokingham from Barkham. I strapped Anthony onto me with a bedsheet under my coat. I was

146

planning to leave him on the doorstep of All Saints Church, because nuns take babies in, don't they?"

Lily was getting her religious denominations muddled up as there were no nuns attached to staid old C of E All Saints, but I felt her intentions were sincere.

"But it was so cold and I thought it might be a while before anyone came along and found him. At least the cloakroom in the town hall was warmer and people are in and out all day. I gave him a last feed on the bench outside, then tucked him under my coat, went into the women's cloakroom and put him in the washbasin. Then I walked home again."

Lily started sobbing again.

"What did you tell your mum and nan, Lily?"

"They'd been nagging on at me to get him adopted so I told them I'd taken him to the social services. Not that I know where social services even is."

"And you meant to leave him in the washbasin? You didn't just put him in there intending to come back and collect him?"

"No. I wanted someone to find him and take care of him."

Miss Robertshaw and I looked at each other. Lily was no monster. In fact, I admired her. She'd been honest and candid coming forward to the station with her account, but she had committed an offence. If only she'd known where she could have accessed services to help her.

Miss Robertshaw had a slight catch in her voice when she said, "Lily Lewis, I am charging you with abandoning a child in a manner likely to cause it unnecessary suffering . . ."

"I never intended to make my baby suffer!" Lily wailed.

"I know. It's just what us police have to say, Lily," I tried to reassure her, feeling my eyeballs prickling.

I accompanied Lily to the magistrates' court the next morning. She sobbed in the dock as Beeton, our uniform inspector, prosecuting, outlined the details of her case to the panel, just as she'd told us.

"I'm going to adjourn this case for 14 days for psychiatric and probation reports," said the chairman, "and I am ordering the child to be taken into the care of Berkshire County Council."

"Thank God Les isn't going to get his hands on him." Lily sniffed, wiping her tear-soaked cheeks on her sleeve, as I escorted her to the lobby and her waiting mum and nan.

I had no idea who Lily's psychiatrist would be, but I knew she would be in safe, humane hands with Hilda Bloom preparing her probation reports. The paint smell had long gone from the probation office so I would be unable to eavesdrop on Hilda's and Lily's conversations in our small police office. Not that I really needed to eavesdrop – Hilda would tell me anything about my cases. I only had to ask.

I met up with Hilda in the canteen.

"How are you getting on with Lily Lewis?" I asked.

"She is not a bad girl. I don't believe she has a wicked bone in her body. She has just been very silly having an affair with a married man and unfortunately getting pregnant. I believe she panicked and left Anthony in the

148

town hall cloakroom, but she chose a place where at least he would be warm and soon found."

"She could get up to six months in prison for abandonment?"

"Ach, I can do better than that for her. I think she needs to get away from her mother, grandmother and those Bradleys, and learn some skills and routine so she can move on from all this. I hope the chairman buys my recommendations."

I was on court duty the day Lily Lewis appeared before Wokingham Magistrates for sentencing. Lily smiled at me and Hilda gave me a wink. Lily stood ramrod stiff before the chairman began his spiel.

He took off his spectacles and stared straight at her. "Miss Lewis, I assume you appreciate that the punishment for abandoning a child in a manner likely to cause it unnecessary suffering given by this court can be six months' imprisonment?"

Lily nodded, the colour draining from her face and her bottom lip trembling.

"The law says that that is to be the punishment unless there is some other suitable course we can take. That is why we asked for these probation and psychiatric reports."

Lily's shoulders sank a little.

The chairman continued, "Thanks to these reports, you will be placed on probation for three years, one of which will be a year's residency at St Cuthbert's Salvation Army Training Home."

Hilda nodded sagely.

"You should approach your training feeling grateful, Miss Lewis. The people there are taking you in spite of your criminal record and will do their best to turn you into a decent citizen and a woman who will behave as normal women do."

I watched Hilda screw up her nose at the chairman's pompous words. But at least Lily Lewis wasn't going to prison.

CHAPTER 13

Man down

Police in the 1950s were a close-knit family. Sure, we tutted at incompetence, pomposity and unfairness, but when the chips were down, we'd always take care of our own. Much as PC Higgs only had to walk into the room, grinning, to make my hackles rise in irritation, I wouldn't want to see him attacked, injured or worse. I would do my utmost to get him out of harm's way if I had to.

The death of a police officer, particularly in the line of duty, rips through the morale of a force, making everyone question whether the job is worth it. Yet everyone returns to the job with renewed determination that the bad guys can't be allowed to win and to honour a colleague's ultimate sacrifice.

I didn't experience the murder or manslaughter of a close colleague during my police career, but one night we came close to losing one of our best officers.

I was on late duty, with just 40 minutes left of my shift, walking down Broad Street to check the shop windows. Ahead of me, sitting precariously on a ground-floor windowsill, gazing at the pavement, was a statuesque, well-dressed woman in expensive red high heels, a poppy-red mackintosh and a burgundy circle hat.

Red hat, no drawers. Mum's scathing saying popped into my head. I wondered if this woman might be a prostitute, not that Wokingham could be considered a hotbed of the vice trade. She was swaying slightly, about to fall off. As I approached her, a strong smell of alcohol wafted towards me.

"Hello, are you all right?" I asked.

"I's a fine," slurred the lady in red.

"What's your name?"

"Ishabel. Ishabel Brown-Watson."

"Have you been drinking, Ish … I mean Isabel?"

"Jussa lirrle bit."

"What are you doing out here by yourself?"

"I feel ill. Anive had a upshetting day."

"Where do you live?"

"I'm shtaying at the Beeches Hotel."

"On your own?"

"Yesh."

"Would you like to get down from the windowsill and stand up for me?" This was a classic test to see how drunk somebody was.

Isabel tried to step down from the sill but fell forward and I wasn't quick enough or strong enough to catch her. She landed on her knees and hands, tearing her stockings, and her circle hat rolled into the road.

"Bladdy hell. Shorry, oshifer," she mumbled, before heaving and throwing up all over the pavement, and my shoes. *More vomit. Why does everyone throw up on me?* I took a deep breath, forcing myself to look away from the sick.

"I'm sho shorry."

The Beeches Hotel was a couple of miles outside Wokingham. There was no way Isabel was in any fit state to get back there. The police station was a 10-minute stagger, and the safest place for her would be in one of our cells while she sobered up. Cooperative and unfortunate as Isabel was, I would have to arrest her for being drunk in a public place and at least she wasn't being disorderly. I would also be obliged to stay in the station all night on matron duty[8] – a real pain, especially as I had the day off tomorrow, but I had no option.

I retrieved her hat from the road. Pulling herself up on the windowsill and with my help, Isabel stood up unsteadily and managed to put one foot in front of the other by holding onto walls and leaning on my arm. Throwing up a couple more times into a flower tub and a rubbish bin, we arrived at the police station, Isabel's cheeks stained with run mascara.

Sergeant Lamb was on night shift desk duty that night. I was glad to see him rather than one of the gruffer night duty sergeants.

"Got a rather tired and emotional guest for the Blue Lamp Hotel tonight, Sarge," I said.

Sarge looked a bit grey and had an uncharacteristically serious expression on his face. Wordlessly, he took his form pad.

"Name?"

---

8 Historically, the first women the police employed were called "matrons" to guard and look after female detainees and children, often overnight. Us WPCs did that job now and we still called it "matron duty".

I watched him as he took down Isabel Brown-Watson's address and the details of the charge. His hand was shaking slightly.

"Isabel Brown-Watson, you are charged with being found drunk in a public place, namely Broad Street, Wokingham at 10.20 p.m. ... contrary to the Licensing Act of 1872 Section 12."

Isabel swayed and looked as if she might throw up again. I grabbed a wastepaper basket. Instead, she gave a ladylike belch.

"When charged, the prisoner gave no reply," he continued.

"You all right, Sarge?" I mouthed.

"I'll tell you in a minute."

That sounded ominous.

I accompanied unsteady Isabel to the cells and got her settled in for the night. I brought a beaker of water and a couple of extra blankets for her as it could get quite cold in there, even in the summer. If she needed anything, I explained, she could press a button that would light up our electric cell alert box in the front office.

Isabel had sobered up somewhat and was starting to get argumentative, questioning why she was in a police cell with little more than a low wooden bed, a bucket and a headache. I'd had enough of her for one night and needed to talk to Sarge, so I slammed the cell door, leaving her hammering and shouting.

That's all we need, I thought as I came back from the cells.

Sarge had his head in his hands.

"What's up?"

154

"There's been a road traffic accident," said Sarge. "Henry Falconer. At the crossroads coming out of Reading. Sounds like a bad one."

My tummy turned over. "Oh Lord. Is he all right?"

"We don't know, love. Bob and some of our boys are over there now with Reading Borough Police. From what I understand, Henry's Austin was hit by a flatbed truck that didn't stop at the Halt sign. It spun the Austin round, flipped it over several times and it ended up in a ditch. Henry got thrown out onto the road. They've arrested the truck driver and his mate, and they smelled of booze. Seems like a cut-and-dried drunk-driving case to me. Poor Henry. I hope they throw the book at the buggers."

I felt sick for the second time that evening. Henry seemed a complicated, private man, but he could be funny and kind. There was nobody I'd rather chase a zebra with than him and the station dynamic wouldn't be the same without him.

Any thoughts of my comfy bed were abandoned as I now had to stay on station premises with Isabel, who hammered intermittently on her cell door. I sat at the front desk with Sarge, puffing on cigarettes under the "Strictly No Smoking" sign.

"I'm supposed to have given these things up because of this wretched cough," said Sarge, "and we shouldn't really be smoking in the public area of the station."

I shrugged. "Seriously, what members of the public are going to walk in at this time of night and see us?"

"You could call it special circumstances, I suppose," he replied, taking a deep drag and closing his eyes with pure pleasure.

I wasn't used to seeing Sarge upset. We probably didn't appreciate him enough, taking his comforting, fatherly presence at the station for granted. When he retired in the not-so-distant future, he was going to leave a big hole in the fabric of Wokingham station.

"Cigarettes, eh? What haven't they seen us through?" mused Sarge, contemplating its glowing end. "I remember one of my men in the trenches looking over the parapet just at the wrong time and a Bosch bullet took half his mouth off. Once we'd staunched the bleeding, we stuck a cigarette in the other half to try to make him feel better."

"Did it?" I asked, feeling that Sarge bringing up his Great War memories might not be particularly helpful at this time.

"Poor sod. But, couple more inches and he'd have been dead. The nicotine calmed him down a bit and they managed to get him out to the base hospital and home."

"That truck must've been coming to the junction at one hell of a speed for Henry not to react and get out of the way," I said, changing the subject. "He's one of Wokingham's best drivers."

"Yeah," replied Sarge. "I remember reading his traffic test report – you know that one where they have to drive from London to Brighton at top speed where they can, mainly on the wrong side of the road *and* give a commentary?"

"I do. It sounds absolutely terrifying."

Sarge smiled. "Smart Henry got 100 per cent."

"Who's supporting his wife just now?" I asked. "Has someone been to see her?"

"He hasn't got a wife, love." Sarge stubbed out his cigarette. "Of course you probably don't know this, as it was all before your time. Henry joined the constabulary after the war. I heard rumours – don't take this as Gospel – that he did have a fiancée, but she died in the Blitz."

That explained a lot. Although Henry would join in with station banter, I sensed he had ingrained melancholy brooding just under the surface. Now I knew why.

"That's terrible. And now this. Just how much sadness and bad luck can one man take, Sarge?"

"I don't think the poor bloke had a good war either. I noticed the Italy Star on his medal ribbons and all I got out of him was that he was in the Italian mountains with the US Fifth Army in '44. Some say that muddy, bloody, miserable campaign was as bad as some of the trench warfare in the Great War. I would probably beg to differ . . ."

"And now this."

We both sat in silence contemplating what a rotten hand of luck Henry had been dealt. He was a good policeman, able in a crisis. Berkshire had a chronic shortage of officers anyway and to lose one this capable would be a blow.

To occupy myself, I checked the cell alert box and sure enough, the Cell Number Three light was illuminated. Clearly, Isabel had sobered up enough to find her call button. I looked through the cell door peephole and was relieved to see she'd fallen asleep, on her side, under the blankets and was breathing heavily. In fact, she was snoring, so I knew she was all right. I went back into the office to type up my report for her appearance before the magistrate next morning.

Bob came in at 1.30 a.m. He wasn't supposed to be on nights at all, but the accident happened towards the end of his two-ten shift and he had volunteered to go. I pressed a mug of hot tea into his hands.

"Jesus," he said, slumping down on the lobby seat. "If Henry survives that, it'll be a miracle. I've never seen such a mess."

"What happened?"

"I was first on scene, but the ambulance men got there soon after me. Henry was lying on the road, his face covered with blood, trying to keep himself conscious through swearing and sheer bloody-mindedness – you know what he's like. He must have been dazed as he kept asking me where his rifle was. Looks like he's got a compound fracture of the femur – nice bone sticking out, some damaged ribs and some head injuries. They pumped him with morphia and took him off to casualty at the Royal Berks – so you know it's serious when they get taken there."

"Do you think he'll be all right, Bob?" I asked.

"Depends how bad his internal and head injuries are. It could go either way."

As the night shift came to an end, grim-faced officers filed in for the early shift briefing. I waited for Pattie to arrive and handed over the Isabel Brown-Watson case and my report to her. She was trying hard not to cry.

"You'll need to accompany Miss Brown-Watson to the magistrates' court this morning for her 'drunk in a public place' hearing, present my statement and then see that she gets back to the hotel all right."

But Pattie was barely listening. "Do you think he's going to die, Gwen?" she asked.

"I really hope not, Pattie. They took him to the Royal Berks so he's in good hands."

Isabel Brown-Watson was nursing a furious hangover, with sore grazed knees and dried vomit down the front of her poppy red raincoat. She was much nicer when she was drunk.

"I shall be making an official complaint about being detained against my will, completely ignored all night and the damage to my attire. I have connections, you know," she threatened as a shredded Pattie patiently explained what would happen when they arrived at the magistrates' court.

Good luck with that, I thought.

"You on lates today, Gwen?" asked Pattie a little later.

"No – I've actually got the day off, but I'm now going to be sleeping for most of it, thanks to Miss Red Hat No Drawers there." I tutted.

"Fancy meeting up for a coffee this evening? I need a bit of cheering up. I'm going to pop over to the Royal Berks when I finish shift to see if there's any news on Henry."

"Yes – why not? You probably won't be able to see him, though – it sounded bad."

"I can just try on the off-chance."

"Shall we say Pat's Café at six o'clock?" I asked. "I'll need to get back now and try to sleep at some point today

– not sure how successfully – it's been quite a night. You can tell me how Henry is and how Miss Hoity Toity here gets on with the magistrate."

I woke up, groggy, about 3.30 p.m. I had slept fitfully, not helped by Mrs Cunningham running the vacuum cleaner up and down the stairs. I'd drifted in and out of strange dreams about red hats and raincoats and crashing vehicles and Sarge smoking cigarettes, and a river of vomit flowing down Broad Street. A shot of caffeine was just what I needed and I looked forward to catching up with Pattie.

Pattie was already sitting at a gingham-covered table in Pat's Café, nursing a strawberry ice cream soda when I arrived at six o'clock. I ordered a cup of black coffee and sat down. Pattie offered me a cigarette and lit it for me.

"Did you go?" I asked her. "How was he?'

"Oh, Gwen. They let me have a peek at him through the intensive care unit door. He managed to give me a smile, but they haven't even washed the blood off his face. He's had an operation to put a massive pin in his leg to hold the bones together. The leg is up in traction and he's got just a plaster on his nose. But he's alive and they're mending him. I saw the chief super coming out; the truck driver tried to resist arrest apparently and the Reading Borough boys gave him hell. Drunk as a skunk."

"Oh, thank goodness it's not as bad as Bob thought. And Sarge was right about the drunk driving."

We chewed over the events of the night again.

"I wonder if he'd passed out before he got to the junction?" said Pattie. "And anyway, how do you know if you're too drunk to drive? Some people can drink all night and be fine, whereas others are almost falling over on a couple of Babychams."

"Somebody needs to come up with a way of measuring the amount of drink people have had," I said. "I don't think it's enough to get drivers to walk in a straight line, or just smell their breath and make a judgement. And there needs to be a limit. Four pints, perhaps?"

"Can you imagine the uproar that would cause?" said Pattie. "All those men driving to the pub or parties – how would they get home? And the pub trade would be furious because people would drink less."

"Talking of drunks, how did the lovely Isabel Brown-Watson get on before the magistrate?" I asked.

"Oh, she pleaded guilty after all that fuss. Claimed she'd been ill, had had an upsetting day and had drunk a bottle of wine to make herself feel better."

"A whole bottle? No wonder she was sick."

"The chairman was funny. He said, 'I suggest in future you try a different medicine,' and fined her five bob."

"Too right," I said. "Seeing what havoc drunks cause, I've got even less tolerance for them than I had before."

Meeting in the café had cheered both of us up. It looked as if we weren't going to lose Henry after all and my appetite had returned.

"Do you fancy tea here, Pattie? They've got scampi and chips on the specials board and I'm ravenous."

Mrs Cunningham's regular Thursday tea was salad: usually two limp slices of ham, lettuce, tomato, cucumber, a couple of radishes if she was feeling extra generous and a squirt of Heinz salad cream. A starter of scampi and chips to fill me up before a Mrs C salad was some sort of recompense for a ruined day off.

"Yeah, go on, then," said Pattie, calling the waitress over. "Chips are always the answer."

CHAPTER 14

Night patrol

I enjoyed being out and about during the day. We generally patrolled alone, occasionally crossing paths with our fellow officers. We weren't supposed to stand around chatting to the PCs unless we were liaising on an incident, and technically, we could be put on report for "gossiping on duty" if Inspector Beeton caught us as he did the rounds on his bike. Paradoxically, police training gave us acute observation skills, which meant we could spot a senior officer a mile off, so we would all stop for chinwags, scanning the horizon for superiors all the while.

One intersection point was the Victorian marble drinking trough outside the town hall, not far from Market Place's beat point telephone box. As few draught horses slurped there any more, it had been converted into a water fountain for a welcome drink on a hot day. Before his accident, Henry and I would keep an eye out for Inspector Beeton there, joking in American accents that we weren't gossiping, we were "sharing intel".

Us WPCs worked two shifts – earlies and lates. We didn't do the 10 p.m. to 6 a.m. "nights" that the PCs did. Earlies could start at any time between 6 a.m. and

9 a.m. and finish in the afternoons, and lates could start at 3 p.m. or 4 p.m. and go on until 11 p.m. or 12 a.m.[9] Once a week, we did the almost universally detested "split shifts", which were two lots of four hours with a gap in the middle. Split shifts meant we didn't get a paid meal break – we worked a full eight hours rather than seven and a quarter hours.

Earlies were a combination of walking around as a reassuring presence, giving directions to shoppers, scrutinising motorists and occasionally chasing a shop-lifter. They were sociable times too: because I'd grown up in Wokingham, I was rarely more than 10 feet away from a friendly face.

Lates were different. I would occasionally help male colleagues calm down a few drunken pub scuffles spilling out onto the street after closing time, but towards midnight, the town became eerily quiet as residents retired to bed. There would be little sound save for the occasional nocturnal robin – some people said it was a nightingale – burbling away by the streetlight.

Patrolling past the town hall building, with the fire station beneath its Gothic arches, I would get cheery, emergency-services-together waves from the night shift firemen. Along the commercial streets, checking that all was well in the twinkling glass-fronted shops, and down the alleyways, shaking handles and padlocks to make

---

9 There was a gender pay gap between WPCs and PCs. Women were paid 10 per cent less than men because they worked slightly fewer hours and no nights. At one point, women officers were asked to vote on pay equality. The majority voted against it as few were willing to work nights.

sure everything was secure, the only footsteps echoing were my own. To my eternal annoyance, the sudden bloodcurdling yowls of cats fighting over the dustbins behind the Ship Hotel always made me jump.

The streetlights would cast moving fingerlike shadows across the shiny wet pavements as tree branches wagged in the breeze, creating creeping shapes up the rendered walls. I felt more unnerved by these streetlight shadows than I had ever done walking around Wokingham during the wartime blackout. The blacked-out town had somehow felt safer as eyes quickly and naturally adapted to night vision and there were few spooky shadows, apart from on moonlit nights. There was little to fear, apart from the obvious airborne squadrons of homicidal Nazis that could appear over the horizon at any moment to drop bombs on us luckless inhabitants.

"As we're a man short with Henry in hospital, could you check out the Emm Brook riverbanks tonight, WPC Crockford?" asked Bob. *Oh great, patrolling alone*[10] *near water*, I thought. Truth was, I couldn't swim and although I never mentioned it to anyone, I was phobic about being near water.

When I was eight, one of my brother's idiot friends, who should have known better, threw me into Martin's Pool to see what would happen. I never forgot that feeling of rushing blue water closing over my head as I sank in the deep end, disorientated and thrashing,

10 Incredible as it sounds nowadays, we could patrol alone on late duty. It was unthinkable that anyone would attack a police officer. Years later, it saddened me when it became necessary for police to patrol in pairs.

my vision blurred and the sounds of other bathers muffled as if I had a pillow round my head and equally suffocating. Just as I could hold my breath no longer and was about to give up and gulp water, I felt myself being hauled to the surface by a lifeguard's strong hands. Gasping, choking and coughing, I clung to my saviour with all four limbs like a little primate, too traumatised to release my grip.

Swimming and lifesaving training expectations for police officers were patchy across the constabulary. Sandgate, near Folkestone in Kent, where Henry and Bob trained, included them in the curriculum, using The Leas freezing outdoor swimming pool by the shingle beach. Mill Meece (much to my relief at the time) didn't. We were supposed to learn in our own free time, but I never did. That lack of skill would, however, come to bite me roundly on the backside later.

"Keep your eyes peeled for Ron the Roach," said Bob. "There's every chance he'll break out again tonight. You've got the best chance of bumping into him if you include the riverbanks."

Ron the Roach was one of our "regulars" – a senile elderly gentleman whose skills at breaking out of his residential home matched those of the Great Escapers from Stalag Luft III POW camp. Nearly every other night we received a call that he had gone walkabout and we'd have to find him on his wanderings. His passion in his younger days was fishing – hence the nickname – and he had a habit of heading towards the river wearing just his pyjama bottoms, if he even remembered to put those on, which he often didn't.

So I headed for the fields along the banks of the Emm Brook river on a still, damp summer night, a sliver of crescent moon the only occasional light in the dark cloudy sky. Although I carried a powerful police issue torch, old wartime habits die hard and I preferred to let my eyes adapt to the darkness. I felt that torchlight was a bigger danger than the darkness; it gave away, rather than concealed, my position to any scallywags potentially hiding in the bushes tracking my illuminated movements.

The river's sluggish water glowered and glistened as it flowed beside the tussocky meadow. I was relieved to see that the well-trodden riverside path was a good 20 feet from the greasy-looking surface, although the stark, pollarded willows stretching twiggy fingers out across the misty water made me shiver a little. To add to my discomfort, a tawny owl shrieked twice from somewhere in the copses on the other side.

I'm not scared, I told myself. *I'm definitely not scared. Not at all. Realistically, who's stupid enough to be out here by the river at 11 o'clock at night? Apart from me. I'm stupid enough to be here. Although I'm not stupid. I've been sent out here by Bob. Bob is the stupid one. Although he's not. He's been asked to look out for Ron the Roach wandering about in his pyjamas, who's not stupid either as he's a master escaper and hates his care home and . . .*

Too many panicky thoughts started to take over my mind. I stopped, took a deep breath and reached into my breast pocket for my cigarettes and a box of matches. Lighting up and inhaling deeply, I felt the nicotine rush through my bloodstream, making me feel a little braver.

Right, let's get this stretch over with and I can cross over the footbridge, back into town and get a cup of tea in the canteen, I told myself.

I set off with nicotine-fuelled resolve along the soggy grass track as a second tawny owl screeched a response to its mate in the copse. I soon fell into a semblance of the comfortingly military step we'd learned at training school, even managing to swing opposite arm to opposite leg in time, which I'd never managed on Mill Meece's parade ground. *Brave little soldier*, I told myself, then felt a bit foolish at the childish analogy and threw my cigarette butt away in irritation. Shump, shump, shump, shump went my police issue shoes through the wet grass.

The footbridge will appear round a couple of bends in the river, I reassured myself. Keeping my eyes straight ahead, wishing I could bump into wandering, pyjama-clad Ron the Roach so at least another human could accompany me in this eerie, watery place, I marched on.

After a while, I convinced myself I could see ahead of me and in the distance, a pale figure moving about on the riverbank. I didn't believe the lurid tales of the Wokingham ghosts – the wandering white lady in Billing Avenue; the little boy who died of influenza, looking out of the upstairs window in the Duke's Head pub; Molly Mogg, the beautiful barmaid at the Rose Inn who died a spinster, or various ghostly horsemen ranging from headless to dwarves – until now. *Don't be so ridiculous*, I told myself.

I then became aware of a shuffling, dragging sound that was out of step with my own marching feet: shump, shump, shump, shuuuuuuuump. Shump, shump,

shump, shuuuuuuuump. It was accompanied by what I imagined to be a chomping, crunching sound.

I cast a quick look-but-don't-want-to-see glance over my shoulder. I could make out nothing but the dark shapes of the tussocks and the copses behind me, and silence. I set off again, still aware of something moving that wasn't me. I quickened my pace, rounded the first bend, and set my course resolutely in the direction of the pale figure.

As it came into sight, I noticed that the unmanaged copse further up had grown out towards the river, leaving just a small gap to squeeze past by the water's edge. Dead wood and dormant brambles reached out across the path towards the water and in the darkness it was difficult to see them well enough to step over them without getting tangled up. I was forced to stop and consider my move as the owls shrieked to each other once again.

Shuuuuuuuump, shuuuuuuuump, shuuuuuuuump, shuuuuuuuump.

There was definitely something moving behind me now. Something, or somethings, breathed deeply and hoarsely, snorting even. I froze in panic. Ahead of me was an unfamiliar, tangled mass of brambles with probably a ghost beyond. To my right were the greasy dark depths of the slow-moving river, which seemed to morph into the maniacally laughing face of my brother's mate before he flung me in Martin's Pool. To my left were those two bloody owls and behind me . . . what creature from hell was creeping up on me?

The shuuuumping had stopped and I was aware of

169

steamy, blood-temperature warmth and long, deep, rasping breaths enveloping me in a crescent of vapour and methane. I knew that my solid torch was not only a light, but a cosh as well – I could hit something with it if need be.

I slowly reached into my tunic pocket for the torch, flicked it on and swung round, panning the light into the darkness. Eight glowing yellow eyes recoiled from the beam and for a split second I thought I was facing some giant demonic spider. Two of the creatures snorted and mooed in fright, making me stifle my own shriek so as not to alert the figure ahead. Four little black Dexter bullocks backed off, scared, but still filled with bovine curiosity at this strange human who roamed their water meadow by night.

I wasn't particularly brave around large animals, although now I knew that these were earthly creatures my thumping heart steadied a little. My experiences with police dogs at training school had taught me to stand still when faced with a creature that had the potential to cause damage. The curious little Dexters inched forward, ears back in friendliness.

Pulling myself together, I manoeuvred myself away from the river's edge, allowing one little bullock to stand between me and the river. For me, the black water was more frightening than the black cattle. I felt strangely safe, now surrounded by my pretty little bovine bodyguards, with their warm breath and trusting eyes. Now my torch was on, I lit my way across the brambles and back onto the grassy track towards the pale figure. The Dexters nonchalantly ambled behind me.

The figure was tucked in behind some bulrushes, sitting down on the edge of the river with their legs in the water. As I approached, shining my torch, I saw that they were wearing a hair net and a full-length white nightdress. The bottom of it was soaking. It was difficult to tell their age. I couldn't chase Billing Avenue's ghostly white lady out of my mind, but then rationalised that ghosts probably didn't wear hair nets.

"Hello! Who goes there?" I called out shakily, slightly embarrassed that I'd blurted out a line from a 1940s war film.

"It's me," responded a quavering female voice.

"Who are you?" I asked.

"I'm not here," replied the damp figure through chattering teeth.

"You clearly are!" I said. "What on earth are you doing out here? Whoever you are, you must be freezing in just a nightie." I unbuttoned my tunic and put it round her shoulders.

The Dexters had formed a semicircle round the two of us, at a respectful distance.

"I'm 83, you know. You scared me."

"Believe me, I scared myself. These bullocks scared me, and you scared me. In fact, you're still scaring me. You're not out here doing anything silly are you, love?"

"I'm waiting for Ron."

"How do you know Ron?"

"He's my boyfriend. We go paddling together. He sometimes swims. In the nud."

Well, that would explain Ron the Roach's incessant jail breaks, the saucy old dog, I thought.

"What's your name, darling?"

"It's Elsie."

"Where do you live, Elsie?"

"Just behind the Dog and Duck."

"You don't live on your own, do you?"

"No, with me son."

"Well, we need to get you back home in the warm and dry. Walk with me to the phone box and I'll telephone for a car to take us to your home." I helped Elsie stand up and I was relieved to see she had some slippers nearby and hadn't walked on the brambly ground with her bare feet.

With our little entourage of Dexters, we rounded the bend in the river, Elsie leaning on my arm. We picked our way over the cattle grid and crossed the footbridge, leaving the bullocks behind, tossing their heads in farewell. We stepped into the pale cream lights of the town's outskirts and it was my turn to shiver in just my shirtsleeves.

Elsie stood despondently beside me by the telephone kiosk as I rang the station. I lifted the receiver, put in two pennies and dialled the number. On the second ring, the night desk sergeant answered and I shouted "TK7! TK7!" before replacing the receiver. This was to let him know that I was calling from Telephone Kiosk 7; the sergeant would then look down his list of beat point telephone numbers and ring TK7 back. I pressed a button to retrieve my pennies – we never paid for our phone calls if we could help it – and waited for his return call. The telephone jangled, its sound cutting through the dark night. I picked it up.

"Hello, Sarge. I didn't find Ron the Roach, but I did find a lady called Elsie who purports to be his girlfriend and she needs a lift home. Could you send a car to TK7?"

While I was talking to the sergeant, I was astonished to see a small, white-haired, completely naked figure hobbling quickly and single-mindedly towards the footbridge and the river beyond.

"Coooeee! Ron! It's me, Elsie!" called my nightie-clad charge, suddenly lively.

"Better make that two cars as quick as you like, please, Sarge," I barked into the phone. "You'll never guess who we've just seen . . ."

I dropped Elsie back to her astonished son, who apparently had no idea she crept out on night-time assignations with Ron. The next day when I saw Pattie, I recounted the night's bizarre events.

"What on earth was the old man wearing?" she asked, knowing full well the answer.

"I'm not entirely sure," I replied, "but it certainly needed ironing."

CHAPTER 15

Dyke, bike or all right

I didn't have to learn to drive from scratch, but Pattie did. I had a few refresher lessons with a retired police driving instructor to iron out some civilian bad habits, followed by an exhilarating screech round the skid pan. I would then be free to drive a police car, or even the Black Maria van if necessary, after my probationary period. Pattie, however, had never sat in a driver's seat before joining the force and it was taking her months to learn to drive, with several failed tests. She periodically left the station for her driving lessons in an old black Ford Prefect with a bell on the roof, with instructor Sergeant Joe Simpson.

Pattie would trip in after her lessons, flushed and giggly, and sometimes with a paper bag of baked goodies.

"I still can't get this double declutching[11] thing right, Gwen," she said. "I crunched the gears twice today. It was my turn to buy the buns. Here, have a teacake."

---

11 Double declutching was a tricky technique we had to use in old cars before the invention of synchromesh. Instead of simply shifting from one gear to the next, we had to take our foot off the accelerator, press down the clutch, slip the gears into neutral and let the clutch out. We'd wait for the engine revs to change, press the clutch down, shift into the next gear, then lift the clutch quickly. If you did it wrong, there would be a horrible crunching sound.

"What's this in aid of?" I asked.

"Well, Joe and I have this thing. If I get through a lesson without making a mistake, he buys the buns when we stop at a bakery, and if I make a mistake, I have to buy them. He's ever so nice." Pattie's cheeks flushed a little pinker.

I wasn't surprised she returned from her lessons hot and bothered. Former train driver Sergeant Joe Simpson, six feet tall, thick blond hair, geometrical cheekbones and a dimple in his chin was a poster boy for the Berkshire Constabulary – and he knew it. He was mainly based at Wantage, but dropped into the canteen after Pattie's lessons to see his mates Higgs and Jones – another young PC I didn't much care for – and some raucous macho banter.

I had tucked myself into an alcove table with a cup of tea and a pile of statements to sort when I heard the loud, blokey voices of Simpson and his cronies as they swaggered into the canteen.

"Three mugs of your finest Darjeeling, Joan darlin', and make it snappy," called Simpson to our ancient, doddery tea lady, clicking his fingers before sitting down. I couldn't imagine Sergeant Lamb, Bob, Henry or any of us for that matter expecting our Joan to wait tables. We always collected our drinks from the counter. Joan obediently wobbled towards them with three teas on a tray.

"Thanks, love. Can we have some sugar as well?" asked Simpson.

Joan wobbled back to the counter.

Joan shouldn't have to table-serve anyone. I thought

about saying something there and then, but my nosiness got the better of me and I decided to sit quietly in the alcove, unnoticed, and listen to their conversation.

"Good lesson today then, Joe? Lots of gearstick action?" Higgs sniggered.

"Ah, highlight of my week, having that little filly Baxter all over my crutch ... I mean clutch," boasted Simpson.

"Phwoar, she's a bit of all right, isn't she?" added Jones.

"She certainly was today, know what I mean?" said Simpson. "You ought to have a pop at her yourself, Jonesie, station bike like that, even an ugly bugger like you could get lucky."

I couldn't believe what I was hearing. I remembered a conversation I'd had at training school with Lottie, a feisty, worldly-wise EastEnder from a police family, who would end up in The Met.

"Me dad says there are three types of policewomen – dyke, bike or all right."

"I'm sorry, I don't understand," I'd said. These were new words for me.

"Dyke ... lezza ... you know, lesbian. Bike ... station bike because everyone can ride them. And all right? Well, I suppose that's when you're neither easy or a lezza," Lottie had explained in her inimitably blunt way. "You gotta be careful you don't get yourself a station reputation, otherwise nobody takes you seriously."

Miss Robertshaw strode through the door and the braying trio shut up immediately. As she glanced around the canteen, Simpson, Jones and Higgs gave each other meaningful looks. They switched to their usual conversation about car engine parts and anecdotes about breaking wind.

"Ah, there you are, Miss Crockford," she said, looking into the alcove. The three men stared in my direction.

Damn, she's blown my cover.

"Are those statements ready? I've got another job for you just now."

"Yes, Miss Robertshaw, I was just about to come back to the office," I said, standing up. I made a point of taking my cup and saucer back to Joan at the counter.

As we left the canteen, I was sure I could feel male eyes boring into my back, or more likely, my backside. I wondered which of Lottie's three categories Miss Robertshaw and I were being placed in.

A couple of weeks later, towards the end of an early shift, Pattie and Higgs had brought in a local tramp named Georgie Lawes. Sarge was preparing his charge sheet and Pattie was looking daggers at Higgs, grinding her teeth.

"So you had lunch at the Olive Branch café, knowing full well you couldn't pay for any of it?" Sarge asked Georgie.

"That's right, Sergeant. Double egg and chips, bread and marge, two cups of tea, and it was lovely," said Georgie.

"And when you said you couldn't pay, Mr Kowalski, the café owner, called the police?"

"Yes."

"And you resisted arrest?"

"Well, I just wanted to finish me tea, and I would have come quietly with your officers, but this young whipper-snapper here . . ." he pointed to Higgs ". . . got me in an armlock, arrested me and brought me in here."

Sarge read him the charges.

"Take Mr Lawes to the cells, PC Higgs."

"Oh, thank you, thank you, sir," said Georgie. "I'll get a warm night's sleep."

On the way out at 2 p.m., Pattie, looking a little peaky, pinched my elbow.

"Are you in this afternoon?" she asked. "Can I come round and see you about three?"

"Yes, of course, Pattie, I'm in. You all right?"

Pattie nodded, but bit her lip and hurried out of the station. She seemed anything but all right.

Today was ideal for Pattie to come round – Mrs Cunningham was out at a bridge afternoon and then going on to a cocktail party, so we had the house to ourselves. Two plates of something brown sat steaming over saucepans on the stove – Suzette's and my supper.

The ship's bell jangled. I showed Pattie to the living room, where I'd just brought in a pot of tea, and we sank into the overstuffed button-back chairs.

"What's going on, Pattie? You all right?"

Pattie glowered. "It's that bloody Higgs. He didn't need to be so mean to that poor tramp Georgie today, and quite honestly, Mr Kowalski could have just given him his lunch as a nice gesture. I mean, how much does egg, chips and tea cost?"

"How was Higgs mean?"

"When Georgie said he wanted to finish his cup of tea before he moved, Higgs grabbed him and he started struggling and then he put him – quite unnecessarily – in an arm lock and Mr Kowalski was shouting, "Arrest him, he's a thief!" Everyone was looking at us and Higgs dragged him kicking and screaming out of the door. I felt ashamed of my police uniform to be part of it."

"Hmm . . . Technically it's theft if Georgie didn't intend to pay and he could have come quietly rather than struggling. Higgs needs to stop crashing in like the proverbial bull and learn a softly, softly approach. But you're right, it could have all been avoided if Mr Kowalski had just let it go and chalked it up as charity. What is it Hilda always says – 'the view from the moral high ground is always the best one'?"

Pattie smiled.

"And knowing Sarge, he'll be taking a parcel of fish and chips down to Georgie this evening – paid for out of his own pocket," I added.

"I love Sarge," Pattie was getting a bit teary, "and I miss Henry. They're nice men, not like Higgs, or that Jones or ... or ... Joe Simpson . . ."

"I thought you liked Joe Simpson? You always look pretty happy after a driving lesson?"

Pattie burst into tears and hid her face in her hands. She sobbed, her shoulders heaving up and down.

"Oh no, what's happened?" I pulled a tissue out of a lacy box and handed it to her.

"Me and Joe, we would kind of get carried away after our driving lesson and you know . . ."

I think I knew what she meant. "I thought you were still seeing Jim?"

"Well, I am, some weekends," Pattie replied.

"Ah, OK." It was hard to keep up with Pattie's love life.

"Then that creep PC Jones asks me if I want to go round the back of the maintenance sheds with him and I says to him, 'What kind of girl do you think I am?' and he says that Joe says I'm a girl who likes to have a good time, how about it?"

Oh dear. All this was ringing true with the conversation I overheard in the canteen. I didn't want to upset Pattie further by repeating it.

"OK, so I hope you told Jones to sling his hook," I said, "and next time you see Simpson you call him a cad and refuse to have anything to do with him other than your last few driving lessons. You must be ready to take your test by now?"

Tears were still pouring down Pattie's face. "I did. But there's something else, Gwen."

"Go on . . ."

"I think I'm in the family way. I haven't come on for two months now – is that normal?"

The walls of the chintzy room seemed to close in on us. I couldn't think of anything to say. My churchy upbringing had instilled in me that a pregnancy outside marriage was the very worst thing that could happen to a woman. There was no sex education, or information available for unmarried women, so girls like Pattie who chose to have premarital relations had little idea about "safe" times of the month or contraception.

Pattie's announcement took me right back to when I was 14. I discovered I was bleeding, and after spending a miserable day trying to stop it, plucked up the courage to ask Mum if she could get me a doctor's appointment. Mum's reaction was to give me a packet of brick-like looped cotton pads with some sort of belt arrangement that cut into my waist and a single piece of advice:

"Now you are to go nowhere near any boys."

What did that mean? The men in the sawmill office? My brother? What did bleeding down there have anything to do with boys?

I barely slept that night. My tummy hurt and the uncomfortable pad and belt chafed. In the morning, after Dad had left for work, I burst into tears at the breakfast table in front of my puzzled brother and sisters.

"I can't bear this, Mum."

She pulled me into the scullery away from the others and hissed, "You're a woman now and you've got to put up with woman things. Don't tell your brother or sisters."

And that was all she ever said on the matter. Looped towels appeared magically each month in my dressing-table drawer.

Eventually, I found out the cause of the bleeding from kindly Mrs Woods, the sawmill office tea lady.

"You're looking a bit peaky, love – are you all right?" she asked.

"No, I've got something terribly wrong 'down there'. It keeps bleeding," I blurted, fighting back tears.

Mrs Woods put her arm around me in a kindly embrace. "You poor girl, you really don't know what's happening, do you?" And she explained everything – the "birds and the bees" as she called it. I was incredulous that something as horrible as this could be normal.

"Unfortunately," concluded Mrs Woods, "all us girlies have to put up with it. It's like the doggies when they have their seasons."

Relieved that I wasn't going to die after all, I still couldn't understand how babies were conceived in such a bloody union. What man would want to go anywhere near this mess? Why had the human race not died out centuries ago? (Even sagely Mrs Woods got this bit wrong, of course.)

A year or so later, Mum assembled me and my two sisters – not my brother – in the parlour for an announcement. Wagging a finger, she proclaimed, "I don't want you three bringing trouble into this house. No trouble, see. If any of you bring trouble here, you'll never darken my doorstep again."

The three of us, saucer-eyed with terror and not daring to speak, nodded in agreement, even though we had absolutely no idea what this trouble was we weren't supposed to bring. Thanks once again to Mrs Woods, I finally discovered what "trouble" was – it seemed to be a continuation of the birds and bees thing.

"It's only trouble if you let it be – these young girls who get themselves in the family way need help and support, not punishment and being thrown out of home," she said, a woman ahead of her time.

By the time I had finished my police training, not only did I know all about the biological and physical interactions that resulted in "trouble" and babies being born inside wedlock, I was also familiar with the illegal ones: men doing it with men, prostitutes soliciting men on the streets, men forcing it on women, men doing it with their sisters, children or even animals ... Mum would have collapsed in one of her funny turns if she'd known half of what went on in the wider world.

Pulling myself from my past back to the present predicament, I asked Pattie, "So you think you're pregnant and you're not sure who the father is, Jim or Joe?"

"It's definitely Joe's. Jim always uses a French letter. Joe refuses to because he says it feels like playing the piano with your gloves on."

"Oh, Pattie. What are you going to do?"

"There's not much I can do, is there? Lose my job and my freedom that I've fought so hard to get. Jim won't want to have any more to do with me. Joe will run a mile, I know it. I'll have the baby, probably have to give it up for adoption, then I'll end up as a shop assistant or something like that."

She started to sob again and I poured more tea.

Blowing her nose, Pattie added, "Although I've heard there's a woman in Reading who could sort me out. A friend of a friend went to her, allegedly. Ten minutes with a knitting needle and a douche bag and it could be all over."

I felt a tingle at the base of my spine. "Good Lord, Pattie, you know as well as I do that's illegal! And incredibly dangerous as well! You were in Sex Crime Week lectures with me. You mustn't even contemplate it."

"Yeah, but it's me we're talking about now." Pattie looked utterly crestfallen.

"Look, Suzette's due back from her shift at the hospital any time soon. I'll have a word with her and see if she can come up with a solution."

Pattie stretched out on the chaise longue and closed her eyes.

I heard Suzette's key in the lock and intercepted her in the kitchen. Whispering, I outlined Pattie's situation while her eyes grew wider and wider.

"Mercy," she said. "I've nursed women who went to backstreet abortionists. Some had perforated wombs and bowels, haemorrhages, terrible infections, septic shock, just dreadful. I'll have a chat with her."

Suzette switched mode from my best friend to professional nurse in an eye blink. She asked Pattie about her monthly cycle, when she had had intercourse – I stifled a sharp intake of breath at the frequency – and pressed around her tummy.

"You're a little swollen, but I can't be sure."

"I'm so grateful that you're going to be able to help me," said Pattie.

"Well, I can only do my best," said Suzette.

"So when I take this stuff you're going to get me, how long will it take to work?"

"What stuff?"

184

"Something from the hospital that'll get rid of it? A tincture or something?"

"Wherever did you get that idea from?"

"Gwen said ... I thought . . ."

"There's nothing I would get from the hospital! Abortifacients don't work. And even if they did, that would make me a backstreet abortionist!"

"No, no, Pattie, I never meant anything like that," I said. "I meant Suzette would be able to give you medical advice and she knows about the adoption process too."

"How the hell would we square that with the job? I couldn't hide the bump and then disappear for a month! I'm half-convinced Miss Robertshaw has already clocked my bloated belly and come to her own conclusions." Pattie slumped back onto the chaise longue.

"Look, Pattie," said Suzette, "just because you've missed one period and the next one is late doesn't necessarily mean you are pregnant. Have you felt sick?"

"Apart from after talking to that Jones creep, no."

"Have you felt more tired than normal?"

"No, not really."

"Are you needing to wee more often?"

"I'm always in and out of the Ladies, me. No, no more than usual."

"Are you more sensitive to smells?"

"Georgie Lawes smelled rank, but then that's probably just Georgie Lawes."

"Sore breasts?"

"Nope."

"Hmm. Apart from the missed period, you don't seem to have any other pregnancy signs, Pattie," said Suzette.

"You might be worrying about something too much, or burning the candle at both ends, and it's delayed your period."

Pattie burning the candle at both ends? Never . . . I thought.

"All I can suggest is try to relax – hard, I know – and have warm baths – they can make you come on. Other than that, it's a waiting game, I'm afraid."

We showed a marginally more cheerful Pattie out, hugging her as she left to catch Timothy Whites before closing to buy herself some scented bath cubes.

"What do you think, Suz?" I asked.

"Fifty-fifty. She could be, but equally she might not be. We'll have to wait and see."

CHAPTER 16

A new Elizabethan Age

June 1953

Henry Falconer spent two months in the Royal Berkshire Hospital having his broken bones repaired before he was well enough to be transferred to Wokingham Hospital for a month's physiotherapy and rehabilitation. There was a real possibility that he might not walk again and the specialist physio team at Wokingham was his best chance.

It was the day before Queen Elizabeth's coronation on 2 June 1953 and I had the day off. I was going to visit Henry and popped into the library to pick up a copy of the Featured Book of The Week (no dead shrew on top of it this time) that I thought he might like – John Masters' latest novel, *The Lotus and the Wind*. When I last visited, I'd noticed he was halfway through Masters' *Night Runners of Bengal*. With little else to do for the last 12 weeks, Henry had become a voracious reader.

I followed the corridor to the men's orthopaedic ward, passing Suzette hurrying along in the opposite direction with a urine bottle in her hand.

"Hello, Gwen, are you looking for that PC Falconer? He's just come back from the physio suite," she said.

I checked in at the nurses' station and waited, wrinkling my nose at that distinctive hospital smell of antiseptic, ether and bedpans. Some worried-looking parents sat at the bedside of a pale young boy with a cage keeping the blankets off his legs and another bed had drawn curtains round it. I saw Henry at the far end of the ward, being settled back into bed by an attractive physiotherapist. He was smiling at her and she was laughing uproariously at everything he said, patting his arm.

"You can go and see him now Cynthia's finished with him," said the nurse.

Cynthia looked up at me mid-laugh as I approached Henry's bed and her smile froze. "You seem to have a visitor, Henry," she said. "I'll leave you in peace now." She gave me a tight smile as I said hello and went to busy herself elsewhere.

"Hello, Gwen, come and sit down," said Henry, smiling, pulling himself up on his pillows slightly. Henry always stood up when a lady entered the room and this was the best he could do in these circumstances.

"Hello, Henry, please don't try to move on my behalf. How are you?" I asked, settling myself on the hard chair.

"I'm still on the intensive physiotherapy programme. I can't move my toes and my foot drops. They're not sure if I've got permanent nerve damage."

"Do you know how much longer you'll be in here?"

"They're talking today about letting me out on Saturday, as a matter of fact. I'll need to be on crutches, but at least I can get home."

"That's fantastic news! A shame you're going to miss the coronation celebrations."

"They're wheeling in one of those television things for us to watch it on, apparently. But if I wasn't in here, I'd have been up London with Bob and Higgs to assist the Met with crowd control in The Mall. Being that close to history being made would have been nice, but hey ho." He sighed.

I took *The Lotus and the Wind* out of my handbag and gave it to him.

"Ah, this is great, thank you," he said. "I don't think you can go far wrong with a John Masters. What are you reading at the moment?"

"*The Day of the Triffids*," I said. "Thought I'd go for some modern science fiction that could actually happen."

"Triffids, eh? I reckon my garden's full of those, not having been there for months. What's green and three feet long?"

"I don't know."

"My grass, probably."

We laughed. Cynthia looked up to see what all the hilarity was about and called over to tell us that visiting time was ending soon.

"Bob pops in and gives everything a water a couple of times a week," I said. "Don't worry about it, just concentrate on getting back on your feet. It's not often you get time to laze about in bed reading all day, so enjoy it." I found myself giving Henry a wink.

"I really must insist visiting time is over now," called Cynthia, irritation in her voice.

"See you soon, Henry."

"Yes, thanks for popping in, Gwen. I'm going to start your book now."

I smiled at Cynthia on my way out. She didn't smile back.

But I had an idea.

I walked past Market Place, where a joyless Coronation Eve open-air church service was taking place beneath a threatening black sky. Townsfolk and local dignitaries: the mayor, judges and gown-clad members of the council and corporations – including Basil Gill and Mum in a flowery hat, I noticed – sat solemnly on bottom-numbing wooden chairs as a vicar droned on about duty and patriotism. *Oh, Wokingham, you really know how to party*, I thought, hoping tomorrow's celebrations might be a bit more fun. Then the heavens opened, the deluge sending the dignitaries scurrying for cover.

Everyone was excited about Queen Elizabeth II's coronation day on Tuesday, 2 June. Pattie and I were on special patrol together to police Wokingham's week of celebrations, while our male colleagues were in London and we didn't expect any trouble. The place buzzed with delight that there would be a new, young queen on the throne. There was to be plenty of tea and cake, and people reminisced fondly about her father, King George VI, recalling where they were when they heard his voice over the wireless gravely addressing the nation on the outbreak of war in 1939.

I was in the locker rooms with Pattie, getting spruced up for our beat, when I heard a loud cry from inside the WC cubicle.

"Yes! Oh, thank Christ for that! Thank God!"

"You OK, Pattie?"

"I've only just gone and properly come on, haven't I? Well, hoo-bloody-ray for that."

"Phew, Pattie. What a relief."

"Yeah, phew indeed. Have you got a spare sannie? I deliberately didn't bring one because if I did, it wouldn't start."

Classic Pattie logic, I thought as I passed one of my looped bricks over the top of the cubicle.

We left the station in a good mood to wander around town.

"Bit bloody cold and windy, isn't it, Gwen?" Pattie brr-ed. "I bet it's going to pee down later."

"Feels like November," I said.

"Where is everybody?"

The streets were deserted. Just us. The only sounds to break the silence were our footsteps, the rustling of paper decorations and the angry flapping of bunting and flags in the strong wind. In a shop window in Peach Street stood a full-size model of Her Majesty in full regalia, holding an orb and sceptre, gazing out at nobody.

We soon discovered the reason for the empty streets. Through windows into living rooms we could see the backs of people's heads as they crowded round small glowing white squares showing moving grey shapes.

"Well, that's the way to make yourself popular," said Pattie. "Get one of those television box things and everyone comes round."

Where houses had no television, the wireless broadcast sounds of London's cheering crowds, thumping of marching military bands and Wynford

Vaughan-Thomas's cut-glass BBC commentary drifted out through open windows.

The next day was considerably cheerier. It was Children's Day and the fancy dress parade. School children, delighted to have a Wednesday off from the drudgery of rote-learning times tables and spellings, had raided their dressing-up boxes and parents' wardrobes. Every other girl seemed to have come as Britannia, helmets fashioned from tin foil and dustpan brushes, with cardboard shields and tridents. Others dressed as pillar boxes, cricketers, farmers, guardsmen, cowboys and Indians, nurses, pirates, princes and princesses; even, inexplicably, Tutankhamun. With Pattie and me as their unofficial police escort, the children marched in a blaze of colour, chatter and giggling down Denmark Street to Langborough Road recreation ground, to marquees set up for their coronation tea party.

In other parts of Wokingham during the week, people had hauled all kinds of tables, from wallpaper platforms to cast-iron garden tables, into the streets, creating jagged spines down the middle of each road, patchworked with colour from everybody's tablecloths. Eclectic seats – from dark oak carved Jacobean hall chairs to utilitarian wooden stools and garden benches – were placed along the snaking tables, an open-air museum of furniture through the ages. Life-size crowns, painstakingly handcrafted from papier mâché and scraps of red velvet sat on the tables. Someone had brought out their dusty aspidistra in a beaten brass pot and put it in the middle of one table.

Moss Firth, the flat-capped garage mechanic, wobbled by on his pride and joy, a restored penny-farthing bicycle that he wheeled out for every fair, fete and civic celebration. Children, used only to their tricycles, shrieked with delight as Mr Firth lifted them onto the high seat above the enormous spoked front wheel and wheeled them around.

"So high you could touch the sky," he said to every child, every time.

Mothers with babies in prams passed by. Esme Cripps's freckled twin boys, now lanky adolescents in too-tight Scout uniforms, skulked behind their mother, finding everything a bit too childish. Doris Savin walked arm-in-arm with her daughter Millie, stumbling in her polio braces, with Foxy, the death row dog, arthritically limping along beside them.

"Good to see Foxy's still going," I commented.

"He's like a puppy some days," said Doris. "Isn't all this bunting lovely? But tell you what, it's gonna take a while to get used to having a queen, after a king, ain't it? Vivat vagina and all that."

I sensed Pattie choking back a giggle.

Children sat on the mismatched seats while their parents stood around gossiping and drinking tea from green cups and saucers. Everyone filled their paper plates with spam sandwiches, jelly and ice cream and chunks of Victoria sponge. Paper cups with crowns on them were constantly refilled with orange squash and fizzy pop. The butcher walked up and down with a tea tray, handing out freshly baked sausage rolls. The edges of his fingernails were still stained with the blood of a lamb he'd portioned up that morning, but nobody seemed to mind. Sausage rolls were too much of a treat to refuse on hygiene grounds. All the children received a coronation mug to take home as a souvenir of their day spent waving flags and eating far too much cake.

Smaller coronation celebrations continued all that week, culminating in a grand finale on Saturday, which was to be an ox roast and fireworks in Market Place. At midnight on Friday, the mayor would ceremoniously light a fire, helpfully stoked by local firemen, to roast an entire ox ready for everyone to have some beef in a bun the next afternoon.

At the station, I was chatting to Bob, Pattie and Inspector Beeton.

"You know Henry's being discharged from hospital on Saturday?" I said. "How about we do a garden tidy up for him and a welcome home party?"

"It's a shame he missed all the parties and he's going to miss the ox roast on Saturday," said Beeton.

Pattie's eyes lit up. "Why doesn't one of us get take-away beef rolls for everyone from the ox roast and bring them back to Henry's house? That way, we'll all be able to have some?"

With Henry's discharge from hospital imminent, each shift took an hour out of their own time to work on his garden. Sergeant Lamb cut the hedges. I mowed the little lawn – it wasn't quite three feet high – with Henry's push-along mower. Higgs weeded the vegetable patch, although he had little clue what were weeds and what weren't, pulling up a whole row of carrot tops. I dug out the topless carrots and took them home to make a carrot cake. Pattie's shift tidied the garden shed, swept the path and tended to the flower beds.

On the afternoon of Henry's discharge, I nipped next door to borrow his key and some extra crockery. I'd also borrowed one of Joan's big kettles and a large teapot from the station canteen. We brought out carrot cake and Victoria sponges we'd made at home, tipped packets of crisps into bowls and Pattie created her exotic pièce de résistance: cubes of tinned pineapple and Cheddar cheese skewered onto cocktail sticks and stuck into a potato.

"Now that's posh," I said.

"I had it at a wedding reception once."

Pattie nipped out to the ox roast and returned with paper bags of generously-filled, fragrant hot beef rolls. I put the oven on low to keep them warm.

"I chatted up the army catering boys who were serving the meat – they gave us a bit extra." She giggled.

"Nice! The chaps will start arriving any minute, then Bob will come along with Henry."

Henry's colleagues who were not on shift or essential duties started turning up at the house and even our superintendent, The EF, ventured out. Everyone commented on the tidy, pretty garden and the mouth-watering beefy smell wafting from the kitchen. Pattie kept watch at the window for Bob's car.

"They're here!" she called and everybody hid behind the dining room door.

We watched as Bob parked and opened the passenger door for Henry. I bristled as a third, unexpected passenger – Cynthia the physio – skipped out of the back seat and fussed about lifting Henry out of the car and onto his crutches, making a great show of helping him up the garden path.

Although he was concentrating on putting one crutch in front of the other, Henry noticed how lovely his garden looked and his tired, grey face became pinker and brighter. He stopped to point something out to Cynthia, who cocked her head to one side at him, beaming. After what seemed like an age, Henry got himself into the kitchen.

We flung the dining room door open and everybody shouted, "WELCOME HOME!" before ushering Henry into the dining room and onto a chair at the head of his table. Not a man of many words at the best of times, he was speechless and could only smile.

I hurriedly took a tea plate and put a hot beef roll on it for Henry before Cynthia could get in first. Pattie poured him a cup of tea while he regained his composure.

"I'm absolutely overwhelmed," Henry said. "It's so good to be home, I can't tell you, even though I've been well-looked after in hospital." He glanced at smug, grinning Cynthia.

"Thank you so much for all this. And clearly the gardening elves have been at work while I've been in hospital."

"Some gardening elves who can't tell the difference between weeds and carrots," said Sergeant Lamb. Higgs blushed and we all laughed.

"Still, we got a nice carrot cake out of it," I said and everyone cheered.

The rest of the afternoon passed in a pleasant multi-rank hubbub of catching up on police business, chatting about the coronation celebrations, gardening and as much about the hospital stay that Henry could talk about with Cynthia being ever-present. She wore a fixed grin as she tried to show interest in the procedural conversations and in-jokes that police have when they get together. Higgs sidled up to her and tried to engage her in conversation, but she gave him monosyllabic answers until he moved away again.

When the party was winding down, we cleared away and washed up, returning the crockery next door. Henry was clearly tiring now. It was time to leave. Bob and Cynthia helped him stand up to say goodbye to his guests, on his absolute insistence; everyone else tried to insist he stayed sitting down. We helped him manoeuvre into an armchair in his sitting room to await the arrival of his mother and sister on the London train.

"Thank you so much for everything," said Henry. "I really can't express how much I appreciate what you've done."

"You concentrate on getting yourself better and back to work," I replied. "We all miss you at the station."

Bob gave Cynthia a lift back to the hospital and Pattie and I headed to the station carrying Joan's kettle and teapot. In Market Place, the roast ox had been picked clean and the only queue now was the dog owners, buying bones.

Although Wokingham's coronation celebrations had got off to a slow start, they were fun of sorts. After the last small piles of rubbish were swept from Market Place, a strange atmosphere of anticlimax hung over the town, not helped by cool, gloomy weather and dramatic, angry thunderstorms. Even the Hit Parade's number one single couldn't be about bubblegum or popcorn or jiving the night away. The dirgy 'I Believe' droned out of wirelesses in every café, workshop and kitchen: Frankie Laine growling about dark nights, glowing candles and babies crying.

Figuring I couldn't feel flatter than I already did, I popped in to Seaford Road.

Dad opened the door. "Ah, come in, Gwennie," he said. "Your mother's only just gone out shopping."

Good timing, I thought, relieved that I could have Dad all to myself for a change, without Mum listening and making barbed remarks.

"How's work going, Dad?" I asked, over a cup of tea.

"I think your mother's gradually getting used to having a husband who works at the sewerage plant," he said.

"But you're a plumbing engineer! Without you, the whole of Wokingham would be knee-deep in sh . . ."

We both laughed.

"Try telling her that, love. Her husband, dealing with other people's excreta, well really! She can't quite bring herself to elaborate on my job. She still calls me a plumber and then finds herself having to fend off requests for me to replace taps and mend boilers."

Typical Mum, I thought. We chatted police shop for a while.

"Want some tomatoes?" he asked, indicating a boxful of small, greenish fruits. His late summer tomatoes were legendary: huge, beautiful and flavoursome. I often took a couple of pounds of them home for Mrs Cunningham to have with our lettuce and cucumber. Both she and Suzette declared them the most delicious tomatoes they had ever tasted.

"Yes, please. But I can't see any plants outside."

"All right then, Detective," Dad chuckled, "I'll confess. They come from the sewage works. The plants grow, warm and sheltered, in the big skips of paper and rag waste. There's so much nitrogen and sun that they love it and produce huge tomatoes."

"How did the seeds get in there?" I asked.

"You know that tomato seeds pass undigested through the body and out the other end? Shall we just say that these tomatoes have, er, self-seeded?"

My appetite for them was waning, but I appreciated his wartime waste-nothing resourcefulness.

"Ah, all right. I just hope you wash them well."

Dad was giggling. "You know, sometimes I find yellow tomatoes. Those must have originated in the posh houses up Farley Hill, where they pay a fortune for those new-fangled varieties in Farmer's greengrocer's."

I was about to leave when through the window, I could see Mum struggling through the front gate with baskets of shopping. I hurried out to help her.

"Finally remembered you've got a mother and father, then?" she said, stomping up the steps.

I stayed for another cup of tea, listening to Mum complaining about how the butcher had tried to short-change her, the lack of letters from my brother in Korea, where he was doing his National Service, and how her back was playing up again.

As I was leaving, Dad handed me a paper bag of tomatoes.

"Don't give her too many, Wally, that little stall with the honesty box you get them from hasn't got an endless supply," Mum said.

Dad winked at me on the way out.

Back at Mrs Cunningham's, we had fried tomatoes on toast (I insisted we cooked them) and poached eggs for dinner. Suzette and I slumped listlessly in the living room afterwards, looking at the grey drizzly evening outside. Suzette picked up the newspaper and we contemplated the front page: the trial at the Old Bailey of serial murderer John Christie, former resident of 10 Rillington Place.

"Surely somebody who killed at least eight women, including his wife, and hid the bodies in his own house and garden must be completely insane?" asked Suzette. "After all, that Straffen man didn't hang because he was of unsound mind."

"I'm not so sure, Suz," I replied. 'Everyone at the station thinks he's a cold-hearted psychopath who knew exactly what he was doing. I think they'll find him guilty and hang him." I felt queasy thinking about 10 Rillington Place.

"Is it just me, Suz, or is everybody feeling a bit off-colour?" I added. "I thought a nice coronation would cheer everybody up, but it kind of came and went and not a lot has changed. Coronation Day itself was strange. Pattie and I felt we were patrolling a ghost town, everybody indoors staring at tiny screens, rather than out in the streets celebrating."

"You mean the telly box thing? I looked at it for a bit in the hospital but I couldn't see much. I prefer the wireless, me." Suzette leafed through the classified advertisements.

I sighed.

"You know what we need, Gwen?"

"What?"

Suzette pointed to an advertisement for a week in a caravan on Jersey: "A holiday."

CHAPTER 17

Jersey

"This should cheer us up." Suzette grinned as we stood by the steps at Blackbushe Airport about to board the little Dakota for St Helier airport.

"Supposed to be hot and sunny in Jersey. Not quite Bridgetown, but warmer than Wokingham."

I managed a smile. Although I was nervous about the flight, it felt good to be getting away from the oppressive, stuck-in-limbo atmosphere of our hometown, Mum's incessant moaning and Cynthia. Even that wretched 'I Believe' song followed us into the airport building, playing over the tannoy, as if it couldn't bear to let us go away on holiday without taking at least a little misery with us. The newspaper stands were covered with headlines like *Slayer Christie Dies On Gallows*.

"They hanged him then?" asked Suzette.

"Christie? Yes, heard it on the wireless this morning," I said. "Foregone conclusion, really. Three doctors appointed by the Home Secretary found him of sound enough mind to be executed."

"I wonder what will happen to 10 Rillington Place now?" asked Suzette.

"They'll probably bulldoze it and build some new houses. Notting Hill's a slum. Full of multi-occupied derelict houses, rubbish and rats. It's ripe for regeneration, especially now."

"Tell me about it." Suzette shuddered. "I stayed in Notting Hill when I first came over from Barbados. They can bulldoze the lot as far as I'm concerned. I wouldn't want to live on a piece of land where all that went on, new build or not."

"London's an old place," I replied. "I bet there's not a single plot of land where someone hasn't been stabbed, raped or massacred in the last thousand years. Rillington Place is just one of many."

"Well, I'm glad I live in Wokingham," said Suzette.

We strapped ourselves into our seats and sat in pensive silence. It was the first time either of us had flown and our palms were sticky as the little propeller plane lifted off and headed over the Channel towards Jersey.

Suzette had booked us a static caravan in a tiny park a short bus ride out of St Helier. As we checked in, an unsmiling woman looked Suzette up and down and said something under her breath to another woman, who looked up and stared at us.

"We have a booking under the name McDaniel," said Suzette, handing her the confirmation letter.

"You're in number three, about halfway down on the left. Enjoy your stay," replied Mrs Unsmiling, handing the key to me. I handed it to Suzette. As we left, I heard sniggering behind us.

We reached number three, a sky blue two-berth caravan with pots of geraniums beside the front door and pretty lace curtains with butterflies on them at the windows. Outside was a table with a stripy umbrella and two fold-up chairs, perfect for alfresco dining. Suzette unlocked the door and that familiar holiday home smell of furniture polish, someone else's soap and mustiness rushed out. The caravan was delightful – a fully-fitted kitchen, two comfortable little bedrooms, even a tiny bathroom of sorts and a living room. Perhaps this holiday would be the tonic we needed.

We spent most of our mornings at the beach, Suzette tutting as pale holidaying families turned pinker and pinker as the week went on. One badly sunburnt family kept staring at her as she applied suntan lotion liberally all over herself and made me do the same. Finally, the nurse in her could stand it no longer and she marched over to the family to lecture them on the dangers of sunburn and heatstroke and lend them her suntan cream. Later, the dad brought ice creams over to us to say thank you.

When we weren't on the beach, we wandered round the shops and arcades, stopping for fish and chips and pots of winkles. On the seafront, a man in a sparkly mock-Turkish costume and a Box Brownie camera hanging round his neck was parading a sad-looking, muzzled bear on a chain.

"Lovely lady! African princess!" he called to us. "You want beautiful photos with bear? I make him stand. Only two bob!"

We hesitated. The bear, despite its muzzle, was adorable and the man was pushy.

"Don't afraid!" he said. "Is OK, bear has had teeth removed. Is safe."

For a second, the bear and I looked at each other. I

felt a leaden feeling of compassion wash over me and my eyes prickled with pity. I pulled Suzette away.

Towards the end of the week, we decided to cook a special meal using up all our ration coupons. We wandered round the shops and stalls in St Helier. Suzette bought a small chicken, an onion, garlic, a marrow, cayenne pepper, mixed spice – because nobody had heard of allspice – Worcestershire sauce and a shrivelled lime. She dived into a dingy-looking off-licence and emerged triumphant with dusty bottles of Mount Gay dark rum and grenadine.

"I found the nectars of home! I'll make us real Barbadian rum punch tonight, Gwennie – you won't know what's hit you!" Suzette pulled up what looked like weeds from the roadside. "Wild thyme and marjoram," she said, rolling them between her hands and sniffing deeply. "Perfect for my chicken."

I marvelled at her foraging abilities.

When we got back to the caravan, Suzette expertly jointed the chicken with a tiny blunt knife and made a fragrant, spicy paste. She rubbed it into the chicken and left it to sit in a bowl under a tea towel.

"Can't say this is authentic, but it's the best I can do without my usual spices. It'll taste good, that's for sure."

I laid the table, then put my feet up, reading while Suzette made a large jug of rum punch: dissolving sugar for syrup, coaxing juice from the lime and measuring out rum. Later, with the spicy chicken baking, she cubed the marrow and fried it in butter with the garlic.

Even with inauthentic ingredients, Caribbean cooking smells wafted round the caravan site. One passing family commented, "Mmmm, that smells delicious," and a man with a knotted hankie on his head muttered, "Foreign muck," to his wife.

"Got you a little aperitif," said Suzette, handing me a tumbler of rust-coloured punch. I sipped it and although it tasted of liquified boiled sweets, it had one heck of an alcoholic kick.

I liked it, and as I began to relax, the punch loosened my tongue. "What's that physio like who works on the male orthopaedic ward?"

"Cynthia?" Suzette asked. "She's a flirt. I think she's got her eye on PC Falconer. She hangs on his every word when he's in for his daily physio. I heard her saying they should go out for dinner sometime."

I took another gulp of my punch. "It's going to be a while before he can walk, let alone go out for dinner, surely," I said.

"You like this man, it's plain to see."

Suzette doesn't miss anything, I thought.

"Oh, he's just a friend and colleague," I said, unconvincingly.

Suzette laughed and went back into the caravan to bring out her jerk chicken and marrow. She served me a generous, sticky portion. It was the first dish with any real spice that I had ever tasted and soon my tongue was burning and my eyes watering. I reached for a glass of water but it made no difference.

"I was going to say this is one of my blander efforts," said Suzette, tucking in enthusiastically. "I suspect that cayenne has been sitting in the shop since 1948."

A combination of rum punch, chilli heat, Jersey sunshine and Suzette's absurd humour had me giggling. My mirth spread to Suzette and we were soon in uncontrollable hysterics, struggling to breathe, like that first evening at Mrs Cunningham's.

Suzette scraped the spices off my chicken, then cut it up and mashed it into some marrow.

"Just like weaning a baby." She cackled, waving a spoon of the mush in front of my red, perspiring face. I nearly fell off the chair in spasms of laughter.

"Have another one of these." Suzette poured out another generous tumbler of rum punch. I could manage the chicken now. It was delicious and even the subsiding mouth burn wasn't unpleasant. The punch helped it go down nicely.

Dabbing our eyes and catching our breath, our hysteria subsided. I was having fun here with Suzette, away from the grey tedium of provincial Wokingham life. I drained my glass and reached for my cigarettes.

"How about your love life, Suzette?"

"No chance of that, Gwen. I've got a useless husband back home in Bridgetown."

This was a surprise. I had no idea Suzette was married. She didn't wear a wedding ring, never talked about a family and she seemed too young, somehow.

"I've got a son too. Colin. He's eight years old now. Lives with my mama. She's bringing him up."

This was an even bigger surprise.

"You've got a son? Oh, Suzette, you must miss him dreadfully! You didn't say?"

"To be fair, I don't speak about them because I miss Colin like crazy and it's better I just get on with my job, my opportunity, as many shifts as I can, earning money and sending it home so he gets a decent start in life. He's a good boy and my mama writes weekly, telling me how he's doing at school and all."

I often saw airmail letters addressed to Suzette with Barbados stamps on them sitting on Mrs Cunningham's hall table.

Suzette rummaged in her handbag and pulled out a photograph of a smiling little boy in shorts on a sandy beach. He was adorable.

"Oh, he's gorgeous!" I said. "He looks so much like you. I had no idea, Suzette. I thought you were single like me and it didn't cross my mind to ask. Are you going to go back and see them?"

"I'm saving to get my boy to come over here with me."

"What about his dad – does he see him?"

"When he can be bothered, or he wants a meal off my mama. Useless man, and not the most faithful. I don't miss him one bit." Suzette briefly stared into the middle distance. "But what about you, Gwennie? Slim, good-looking lady like you, pillar of the community, and in a uniform? Don't English men like uniforms?"

"When I see what Pattie gets up to, and with whom, I'm not sure I can deal with all that," I replied. Suzette rolled her eyes affectionately at the mention of Pattie. "I've worked so hard to become a policewoman I'm not sure I want to get married in a hurry and throw it all away."

"But if you got married, would you have to leave the police?"

"Not necessarily. The marriage bar forcing us to resign when we got married was removed in 1946, but there's an expectation that we should give up our jobs to look after our husbands, particularly if they're policemen too."

"That's too bad," said Suzette.

"So it's a stark choice. Get married and give up an interesting job, or stay in an interesting job and become a lonely, embittered spinster like our sergeant, Miss Robertshaw."

Suzette gave a throaty chuckle. "What makes you think Miss Robertshaw is lonely?"

"Well, she's a spinster, and she's quite grumpy, and she doesn't like children . . ."

"Just because she's a spinster, Gwen, doesn't mean she's lonely or unhappy. You know she shares a house with Miss Montgomery, headmistress of that posh girls' school?"

I knew, but hadn't really given it much thought. After all, I shared with Suzette and Mrs Cunningham. I nodded.

"Well, I see them around town together a lot – shopping, in restaurants, at the train station on the London-bound platform. The way they look at each other ... I don't think Miss Robertshaw is lonely . . ."

Despite my rum punch fog, the penny dropped. If Suzette was saying what I thought she was, Miss Robertshaw had found a way to have it all in this uptight, post-war world – a career, a relationship and no social or professional expectations. And of course, she and Miss Montgomery would be breaking no laws: lesbian relationships have never been illegal. It would be a very different situation between two policemen.[12] No doubt Sergeant Joe Simpson and his cronies had put Miss Robertshaw in one of the "dyke, bike or all right" policewomen categories, but I'd heard no rumours about her. I felt I understood her a little more.

We drained the punch jug. Suzette got up and went into the caravan, returning with the half-empty bottle of rum. She poured shots into our glasses.

"And what about your job, Gwen? Do you love it?"

"Recently, I've had rather too many pig licences to check, school crossings to patrol and wandering elderly people to find. What do I expect, policing sleepy Wokingham for the Berkshire Constabulary? If I were in the Metropolitan Police, I could be finding runaways, infiltrating illegal gambling dens and catching rapists."

"I think you enjoy the hands-dirty end of policing, Gwen. You were buzzing after that post-mortem, and dressing up like an old lady to catch the WHSmith girl, and bringing in that little baby found in the washroom."

Suzette had hit the nail on the head. I was astounded at her insight. She continued, "The issue is you are

---

12 Homosexuality was only decriminalised in England and Wales in 1967, when the Sexual Offences Act permitted private acts between men over the age of 21. Before 1967, gay men could be convicted of buggery or gross indecency and sentenced to up to two years in prison. Homosexuality was decriminalised in Scotland in 1980 and in Northern Ireland in 1982.

among the first women to do your job. In effect, you're a pioneer. The men in charge don't fully appreciate your capabilities – yet. They think because you're a woman, you can only deal with women and children, as if it's the cosy side of policing."

"Have *you* thought of joining the police, Suz? Your observation and psychology skills are a cut above most of the detectives!"

Suzette laughed. "No, I'm very happy with nursing. But I can tell you, from the National Health Service front line, that women and children work is difficult, tough and sometimes heartbreaking, but it can also be the most rewarding. Anyone who thinks it's a soft option needs to spend a week doing it!"

She was right. Although I'd only really had walk-on parts in our bigger cases: Straffen, Bernie Carroll, Lily Lewis's abandoned baby, I felt a pull towards family work precisely because the reality was anything but cosy. I wasn't sure if the Berkshire Constabulary would deliver the complex cases I really craved and in my rum-addled state I contemplated writing to Lottie and asking if The Met had any vacancies ... but then, I'd miss Pattie, Suzette, Henry, even Miss Robertshaw . . .

We'd talked enough about me.

"Anyway, what about your job, Suz? How are you finding being a nurse in England? You're as much of a pioneer as me, probably more so. You've left your son and family and home in a warm climate to come to drizzly England."

"The nursing itself is not so pioneering – there's set ways to stick a needle in a vein, make perfect hospital corners, read a drugs chart, or change a dressing. Us nurses are traditionally women[13] and we're not struggling to make our way in a man's job like you are. If anything, I feel sorry for a man who wants to be a nurse, if that's ever going to be a thing." Suzette laughed. "And some people like me, some people don't . . ."

"How could anyone not like you, Suz?" *I really, really love you, you're my best friend*, I thought. I was at that stage of inebriation.

"Nobody in hospital wants to be there, and some are scared and in pain, and sometimes losing their minds. They're at a low point in their lives. So I laugh a lot, I smile a lot, I do my job well. I make sure nobody's got a beef with me. I say, just be kind. Always kind."

"I think we're both pioneers," I said, raising my rum glass unsteadily. "To the pioneers!" And we clinked glasses.

As I got up to go into the caravan, I tripped on the step and only just managed to crawl into the bathroom. Suzette heard me throwing up and immediately clicked into nurse mode, checking I was all right, rubbing my back and handing me tissues when the retching stopped. She told me later that she helped me into my bed, loosened my skirt, took off my shoes and tucked me in, making sure I was lying on my side.

The next morning, I felt absolutely appalling. My mouth was dry, my head throbbed and my knee ached where I had caught it falling up the caravan step. I couldn't even face a cigarette.

---

13 In the early 1950s, around 7 per cent of general nurses were male. Today, nearly 70 years later, just 11 per cent of all nurses are men.

I lay in bed, mortified. *What a dreadful friend I am. Suzette had to deal with me being sick and I'd left her to do the all the washing up,* I thought. I emerged from my bedroom. Suzette was cheerfully flicking a tea towel round the final bits of drying up. The caravan was spotless, including the bathroom.

"Lord, I'm so sorry, Suz. I completely underestimated your rum punch and got a bit carried away gazing at my navel. I hope I wasn't too embarrassing and didn't make too much of a mess. I usually only drink Babycham."

"I'm a nurse, and I've seen much worse," Suzette trilled. "You matched me with the punch and the neat rum there, Gwennie. Not bad for an English girl." She laughed.

"Why did I do it? Never again." I groaned.

"You needed to loosen up, girl, and it did the trick. There's a pot of tea, so get some down you. Then I want you to drink this."

She handed me a small glass of rum diluted with lemonade.

"More rum?" I asked, incredulous.

"Hair of the dog. You'll feel better in no time."

I didn't. Despite the tea, hair of the dog and a Disprin, I still felt sick and oddly shaky. It was our last day, with our flight leaving St Helier that afternoon. We'd both been looking forward to a souvenir shopping trip but it was the last thing I felt like doing. Suzette breezed around the crowded shops and stalls, picking out presents to send home for Colin and her mother. I followed behind, trying to think through the hangover fog what would please Mum. *Nothing, probably.*

213

Suzette chose a Mickey Mouse tin bucket and spade and a tea towel with a map of Jersey on it and I picked out pretty, iridescent shell necklaces for Mum and my sisters.

As we went to pay, the grinning shopkeeper whispered, "Psst ... do you want some postcards for your menfolk back home?"

We looked at each other. I had no "menfolk" apart from my dad and brother, and Suzette had only her "useless husband" who she was disinclined to buy anything for. Going into police mode, I braced myself for possible illegal pornography. During Sex Crime Week in training, we'd been shown Victorian postcards of naked men and women in all sorts of funny positions. The male eyes in the room had been more focused on the reaction of us women trainees than the postcards' penetrative goings-on.

"What sort of postcards?" I asked, warily.

The man reached under the counter and brought out a selection featuring cartoons of exaggeratedly rotund, bosomy characters in seaside settings being leered at by men, some inexplicably in suits and bowler hats. One showed a man with an enormous belly standing on a beach, shading a child who was making a sandcastle underneath him. "I wish I could see my little Willy" read the caption.

Suzette started chuckling, then her laughter built to loud guffaws. Customers stopped to stare, some tutting, some amused. I joined in, and soon we were both whooping and giggling over the cards, like the Ferals finding a tattered copy of *Frolic* magazine under a hedge.

We paid for our presents and cards – I bought Pattie one of an obese policeman in a red one-piece swimming costume saying, "I should like a swim but I don't want to get my truncheon wet" – and headed for the airport. Arriving back at Mrs Cunningham's, we hugged each other on the landing, before going to our rooms and agreed we'd had a wonderful holiday.

Be careful what you wish for, they say. I'd worried that my job had become a tad pedestrian. I was glad I'd had a holiday, because my police career was about to get a whole lot more interesting.

CHAPTER 18

You don't mess with the WI

Pattie and I sat in the window of the Galleon Tea Rooms during our break one day, eating toasted teacakes and watching the world of Wokingham go by.

"Pattie, have you noticed a lot of the youngsters these days seem to be dressing like their grandfathers?" I said. "Look – there's one."

We watched as a pimply lad of about 16 sauntered past. He wore pleated wool trousers, a waistcoat (bottom button undone, of course), a thin black tie and a velvet-collared tweed jacket that went halfway to his knees. His hair was cut short at the sides, but was rolled and greased into a thick quiff on top. He looked smart and about 50.

"Edwardian boys," said Pattie, lighting a cigarette. "It's a fashion that's come down from London and it's all the rage now, a cross between 1940s spiv[14] and what posh boys used to wear in the 1930s. I was helping out at a jumble sale in the Drill Hall a few weeks back and the

---

14 Slang for a wartime petty criminal who dabbled in illegal, usually black-market goods, and typically dressed in a striped double-breasted, or long-jacketed "zoot" suit, trilby hat and a loud tie. Generally had a moustache.

young lads were practically fighting over the old tweeds and zoot suits that the grannies had donated."

"How strange that they want to dress so old-fashioned," I said.

"I kind of get it," said Pattie. "Pre-war clothes were good quality and it makes them look well-off and attractive to girls. How many youngsters can afford decent new clothes at the moment?"

"Well, I think they look jolly smart," I said.

"Don't be fooled though, Gwen, some of them are nasty little sods. My uncle says they go around in gangs in his part of London, with bicycle chains, razors and flick knives, beating up old ladies when they're not beating up other Edwardian gangs."

I found it hard to imagine the streets of London being terrorised by brawling Duke of Windsor look-alikes. But it wasn't long before the Edwardians' behaviour, as well as their fashion sense, arrived in Wokingham.

I popped into the station on a break. Higgs was covering the front desk as Sarge and Bob were in the station yard on essential business, apparently.

"Anything of interest happened?" I asked him.

"Nah, nothing much," said Higgs, "apart from that old busybody Miss Major Ironside, or whatever her name is, coming in to complain about some kids being rowdy outside the WI meeting in Emmbrook last night. I said I'd pass her concerns on to the Emmbrook beat officer and off she went."

Major Gertrude Ironside, who was as formidable as her name, was a wartime veteran of the Auxiliary

Territorial Service,[15] chairman[16] of Emmbrook Women's Institute and all-round tireless mover and shaker of local voluntary services. It wasn't like her to complain about anything. I made a mental note to call in and see her about it sometime that week.

Bob and Sarge came through to the front desk, muttering.

"Trust that new mechanic Trevor to do something so bloody stupid," grumped Sarge.

"What's happened?" I asked.

"He only went and dropped a monkey wrench down the gents' lav. Smashed the bowl to smithereens. I've got to get it replaced, pronto."

"In the meantime," said Bob, "police have nothing to go on."

Even Sarge laughed. With all the hilarity around the broken toilet, I'm embarrassed to admit I completely forgot to go and see Gertrude Ironside.

The following month, I was on late turn when a call came into the station.

"Some sort of rumpus at the Women's Institute Hall in Emmbrook, WPC Crockford," said Sarge. "Could you pop round and see what's going on?"

It's probably those rowdy kids again, I thought, as I cycled out of the station yard. As I arrived outside the hall, the doors were wide open, lights blazing. Two

---

15 Created in 1938, The ATS was the women's section of the army, tasked with vital support roles during the war, although not allowed to engage in combat.

16 A WI leader was, and still is, in some groups, called the chairman.

elderly women stood outside, like samurai warriors armed with umbrellas. Another woman was struggling to hold back two barking Alsatians that were straining at their leashes.

"We got some of them, officer! They're inside. Ricky and Rinty here caught one of them, but the others ran off," said Alsatian Woman.

"I'm sorry, I'm a bit confused," I said. "What have Ricky and Rinty got to do with a WI meeting?"

"I'd just come back from walking them – I live next door to the hall, see – and there was this terrific racket, shouting and swearing – oh, the bad language! The WI ladies have had enough of this group of horrible little hooligans that keep on disturbing their meetings and throwing stones at the windows, and they came outside to deal with them once and for all. Miss Ironside dragged one of them off of the flat roof by his trouser leg and got him in an armlock, Mrs Endersby here grabbed one by his ear, and when the others ran off I released the dogs, and they caught a third one. The other two older ones were too fast and ran away."

"Thank you," I said, my mind reeling, trying to take in this surreal scenario. "I think I need to go inside the hall and see what's happening there. Would you mind telephoning the police station and asking for a car?"

"Will do," said Alsatian Woman.

One side of Emmbrook WI Hall was set up for its monthly meeting as usual: a long trestle table covered with red gingham tablecloths, set with rows of green cups and saucers, and two Victoria sponge cakes, pre-cut into slices. So far, so normal.

On the other side was a ring of standing Women's Institute members who turned to look at me and moved apart as I entered. They encircled three silent youths sitting back-to-back on a triangle of three wooden chairs. I thought for one horrible moment they were tied up, but they weren't. Two of the youths glared at the floor, legs apart, arms folded and bottom lips stuck out. The other was tear-stained and sniffing, cradling a hand with a bloodstained bandage competently wrapped round it. All were wearing tweed jackets and shirts with thin ties, thick-soled shoes, and had put Brylcreem in their hair.

"Ah, at last!" boomed the cut-glass voice of Major Gertrude Ironside. "Our toothless police force has sent an officer to take our reports of hooliganism seriously!"

Her eyes blazed and the other members muttered among themselves.

"And at least with a policewoman we might actually get something done about it," she continued.

"It's certainly a first for me to attend an incident at a WI meeting, that's for sure," I replied, taking out my pocketbook.

"I reported last month's disturbance to that dopey young PC of yours on the front desk at the police station," continued Miss Ironside, "but I got the impression he couldn't be bothered to do anything about it."

I felt myself blushing. I knew I ought to 'fess up for forgetting to follow up with her that week, but I was too scared of the doughty Miss Ironside to say anything. I repeated Alsatian Woman's version of the evening's events and asked Miss Ironside for hers as I scribbled notes.

"Well," she began her account. "We started the meeting in our customary fashion, with a lusty rendition of 'Jerusalem', and even then, they were outside, making howling noises like wolves by the windows as we sang. Mrs Endersby went to the door, but couldn't see anyone. Then, right in the middle of Mrs Pocock's demonstration of how to preserve autumn fruits, we heard the clattering of stones being thrown at the windows, followed by clumping about above us. They'd obviously climbed onto the flat roof and were running up and down. Lord knows how they didn't put their feet through the ceiling."

"Go on," I said.

"Well, we figured that if the police wouldn't do anything about these hooligans, we would, so we dashed outside, grabbing umbrellas and brooms as weapons in case we needed to fight. Luckily, Mrs Ravens came round the corner and blocked two of them from escaping the premises, then sent her dogs after the other three. Ricky and Rinty only got one, more's the pity."

"They bit me really hard," came the plaintive voice of the youth with the bandaged hand.

"What do you expect, you little troublemaker?" snarled Miss Ironside.

"And I understand there was a lot of swearing and obscene language?" I asked. There was a silence.

"Ah, well, yes, that was probably me," replied Miss Ironside. "You can take the girl out of the army, but you can't always take the army out of the girl." She shrugged.

"And did anyone see the other two who got away?" I asked.

"Only one," said Mrs Endersby. "He was tall and athletic with a gap between his teeth and unruly hair that even Brylcreem couldn't tame."

Hmm. I could think of a youth who possibly fitted that description: John Carroll.

"Answer me one question, officer," said Miss Ironside. "Why are they all dressed like King Edward VIII after the abdication?"

Shortly after, Bob turned up. After going over the incident yet again, Miss Ironside announced that we all needed a refreshment break and we tucked into the cakes and a welcome cup of tea. Even our tough, hard, scowling Edwardian hoodlums couldn't resist a slice of Victoria sponge.

As Mrs Pocock resumed her demonstration on how to preserve autumn fruits, we escorted the three forlorn youths out of the hall.

"What are you going to do with us?" asked one.

"This," said Bob and he cuffed the two bigger youths round the sides of their heads. He raised his hand to the lad with the bandage, then decided against it.

"Is that all?" one said.

"Yes, now get off home, the three of you, and don't you dare come anywhere near the WI hall again. Just one of those women in there has more guts and gumption than the five of you put together and you will treat the WI with respect from now on."

"Yes, sir," they murmured. "We will, sir."

"Now bugger off before I change my mind and charge you with breach of the peace."

Back at the patrol car, I asked Bob why we didn't arrest the Edwardians.

"I reckon being roughed up and humiliated by members of Emmbrook Women's Institute is enough of a cruel and unusual punishment for young lads, don't you?" He chuckled. "They won't be doing that again."

And they didn't.

Major Gertrude Ironside tugged my sleeve at a WI bring and buy sale a few months later. "No more trouble from those Teddy youths, or whatever they're called, since you dropped by, Miss Crockford. We've been singing 'Jerusalem' in peace ever since."

Unfortunately, even the long arm of the Women's Institute wasn't enough to quell the rising tide of misbehaving Edwardians or "Teddy boys" as the *Daily Express* chose to call them. I was on a late turn with PC Jones when we got a call about a disturbance at one of Wokingham's dance halls. We drove there, went in and crossed the packed, smoky, stuffy dance floor, where oblivious couples were energetically jitterbugging to a live swing band and through to the manager's office at the back. I couldn't see any obvious disturbance.

"What seems to be the trouble, sir?" Jones asked Mr Jackson, the dance's organiser, who had rung us.

"We've got some troublemakers in tonight, officers. At about seven forty-five, eight or nine youths in that Edwardian dress arrived. I think they may have come in on the train from Reading – I don't recognise them as local. At the interval, my Master of Ceremonies, Mr Lovegrove, asked me to come over to the band area where these youths had been arguing with some local

223

lads over some girl or another. One Wokingham lad had blood streaming down his face – he'd obviously been punched. I asked the biggest bloke, who looked like the ringleader, to leave with his mates, but he refused and called me all sorts. That's when I rang you."

"Well, let's go and talk to these characters, then," said Jones. "Lead on."

We dodged around Lindy-hopping couples to a group of glowering Edwardians standing in a dark corner with their backs to the wall.

"You there!" said Mr Jackson to the chubby ringleader. "I've done what I said and called the police. I want you all to leave."

"We don't care you've called the coppers. Anyway, what's she . . ." he jabbed a finger in my direction "... going to be able to do about it? We ain't leaving, and you can fuck right off!"

I don't know what shocked me more: his aggression, his disrespectful attitude to police and authority, or his casual use of that horrible f-word that I had heard used only a handful of times. Things then happened fast, but seemingly in slow motion.

Mr Jackson grabbed the ringleader by his left arm to pull him off the dance floor, but he wheeled round to plant a right hook on Jackson's chin, missed and punched his shoulder. Jackson staggered backwards and PC Jones leaped into action. Someone behind must have kicked his legs out from under him, as Jones went tumbling over the youth's head, landing on the floor and dragging him down with him, where the two of them ended up scrabbling about.

I found myself surrounded by the youth's tweedy friends. Out of the corner of my eye, I saw one of them kneeing Mr Lovegrove in the face and they all cheered. I'd had enough. Using my jujitsu from training school, I grabbed the nearest one and got him into an armlock so he couldn't move without his shoulder dislocating. The other youths backed off, mouths gaping.

The main lights went on, but incredibly, the band carried on playing – 'Ain't Misbehavin', I think it was – making the scuffle feel like a badly acted bar-room brawl scene from a movie. Several of the lads who had been dancing turned out to be squaddies from Arborfield Garrison on a night out and boy, was I glad they were there. They saw what was happening and piled in, grabbing the troublemakers. I passed my armlocked Teddy boy to a burly army mechanic and ran to the front door. Blowing my whistle as hard as I could, I conjured up Bob, who was in the area, cycling down the next road. One phone call to Sarge and the Black Maria van and an ambulance drew up outside the hall within minutes. With the help of the squaddies, we bundled the troublemakers inside.

"Who needs Gertrude Ironside when we've got you on the team?" Bob chuckled all the way to the station. If Gertrude had been available, I'm certain my Teddy boy would have had a broken shoulder.

Mr Jackson was right. The troublemakers weren't local, but a gang of 17-year-old Edwardian youths from Reading who had come in on the train, deliberately looking for trouble. Even before the magistrate, the ringleader, Robert Scott, and his sidekick Stanley Morris oozed disrespect for authority in their electric blue suits with bright orange ties and higher-than-usual Brylcreemed quiffs. They chewed gum with their mouths open throughout their hearings and refused to stand when the increasingly exasperated chairman addressed them. I'd never seen such bad attitude from juveniles before.

So I was not surprised when it came out that Scott had no less than five previous juvenile convictions for larceny, street fighting and demanding money with menaces, had been on probation twice and spent three months at a detention centre. Even his defence solicitor seemed apologetic. Scott momentarily stopped chewing when his consecutive sentences were passed: two months in prison for assault and battery on the local lad and six months for assaulting a police officer.

The chairman was more lenient with Stanley Morris, even though his knee had sent Mr Lovegrove to hospital with concussion. As he had no previous convictions, he was put on probation for three years, with strict orders not to go near any more dance halls or associate with Robert Scott.

And it wouldn't be a Wokingham Magistrates' hearing without a classic pompous summing-up from the chairman. He didn't disappoint:

"I understand that the dress of this party of youths visiting that dance is referred to as 'Edwardian'. This term is evidently used by people too young to have lived at that time, but I did. I would point out that there is no sartorial resemblance whatsoever between the somewhat effeminate costume adopted by these young men and the Edwardian attire worn in those days."

PART 2

CHAPTER 19

The mystery of the skeleton

Autumn 1953

October brought dull weather to Wokingham, with a blanket of mist hanging over the Emm Brook fields most days. There was little to look forward to as the nights drew in and daylight saving time ended near the beginning of the month. Most of our lates would have to be done in darkness until next spring, but the earlies at least briefly had more light in the mornings. Not that there was much sun to get us out of bed enthusiastically.

Now, remember that skeleton we found in the woods?

Pattie and I had been asked to come in together for a rare station briefing with DI Dankworth, Inspector Beeton and even The EF. Miss Robertshaw was there too, so something significant involving us WPCs must have happened. She was half-smiling at us, so it couldn't be anything too bad, we thought.

Dankworth kicked off the briefing. "As some of you know, the group of kids we collectively refer to as the Ferals came in recently to report that they'd found a skeleton in High Copse woods. Well, incredibly, this time it wasn't a fox, or a deer . . .

"Or Mrs Watkins's St Bernard," said Sarge.

THE MYSTERY OF THE SKELETON

"Or a pig's head," chipped in Bob.

Everybody laughed.

". . . But, in fact, human – an adult male," continued Dankworth.

The light-hearted atmosphere became more serious. Officers were aware that human remains had been found in circumstances not considered suspicious. This would be the first time the human backstory would begin to be told and everyone fell into a respectful silence, attentive.

Dankworth continued, "We've no idea whose body it might be yet, but we think it's that of an old roadster. It was well decomposed, indicating that he probably died around June time, and we found an empty pill bottle and two empty bottles of whisky – particularly fine single malts – around him, indicating he probably committed suicide. We found no identifying papers or personal effects on him, so we are currently at a loss to know who he was to inform his family – if he even has any next of kin. These wandering types often don't."

Dankworth shuffled some papers.

"I have here the post-mortem report from our pathologist, Dr Sladen," he continued. "Bear in mind that Dr Sladen can't complete the post-mortem report until identity is confirmed and we have a name. It will have to be left open until then. The report confirms, however, that the body belonged to an elderly male, probably in his seventies, small build, five feet seven inches tall, white-haired, but seemingly in good health before he died, judging by the state of his bones and teeth. Blood extracted from tooth pulp indicates he was blood group O positive. No signs of trauma or struggle or fractures. Bunions on the feet, which we would expect in someone itinerant, walking from place to place over a period of years.

"Clothing unusually high quality – the labels still intact are from top-end tailors, which indicate he was either once well off or had been given charity clothes from someone well-to-do. A bag he had with him was empty, but is the type of large canvas kit bag issued to British soldiers in the war. Toxicology obviously very difficult with so little flesh remaining on the body, but we can assume that he combined prescription medication – probably barbiturates – with spirits, indicating a successful suicide attempt in a time-honoured fashion. This may explain the comfortable sitting position the body was found in.

"We believe he sat down at the base of the tree, took the tablets, drank the alcohol and simply passed away where he sat. He may have been finished off by hypothermia when the temperature dropped during the night. It's perfectly possible to get hypothermia in the summer, especially considering how wet, cold and miserable June and July were. The woodland insects and animals did what they do best and attempted to return him to the earth. Reason for suicide? Who knows? Perhaps life on the road got too much for him, perhaps the ghosts of war haunted him for too long, like so many of his generation. We've checked the missing persons register and nobody has reported a gentleman of this age or description missing. Age-old story, I think – an itinerant roadster with no family or friends to care for him or notice his absence. Forgotten by society."

We were silent. It was always an affecting moment when an investigation began to recreate a real person from the biological components of human remains. Whoever he was, he had died alone, for whatever reason. A lone death didn't seem right, somehow, and it challenged us to give the person an identity, a proper funeral, and bring to justice anyone complicit in their death – unlikely in this case.

Bob broke the thoughtful silence. "Do the newspapers know about this yet?"

"We haven't given a press release, partly because we have just missed the deadline for this week's edition of the *Wokingham and Bracknell Times*," Dankworth said. "Fowler, the farmer, wouldn't want the press all over his land, and even if the Ferals ran into the *Times* office saying they'd found a skeleton, nobody would be in a hurry to follow up that old chestnut."

"The *Wokingham Courier* has a later deadline than the *WBT*," said Higgs.

"In that case, I'll get on to Conrad Jardine on the news desk so they can put out a plea for information in the next edition."

Oh no, not Conrad Jardine and that rag, I thought.

"Sir, could you encourage him to play down the more gruesome aspects of the case?" I asked. "Jardine does tend to sensationalise deaths and suicides just to sell more papers."

"The more people notice the headlines, the more likely they are to come forward with information," answered Dankworth.

"WPC Crockford's right," said Sarge. "I worry that

Jardine's exaggerated reporting appeals to the more, shall we say, voyeuristic members of our community."

"I'll see what I can do, but Jardine is a law unto himself, unfortunately," replied Dankworth. "But before we move on, I do have a special mention. WPC Crockford and WPC Baxter?"

Pattie and I looked up in surprise.

"Thank you for your sterling efforts investigating and retrieving the skeleton from the woods once Dr Wickes had been in and we'd done all our scene work. I realise the body wasn't easy to get to or retrieve, and I also understand that we are sorely lacking in resources such as plastic sheeting, stretchers, etcetera – because we so rarely have use for them. And long may that continue to be the case."

"And ladders," said Pattie. "You all drove off with the stepladder before we went back in the woods to get the old boy out so we had to climb over the barbed wire twice more and ripped ourselves to shreds."

I saw Miss Robertshaw roll her eyes and shake her head in resignation. I wondered if she'd had experience of being disregarded or left behind in an investigation. It was 1953 now – no excuse for hampering the WPCs' contribution to crime scene work. No doubt she would be having words with Dankworth.

"And we got corpse ... er ... bodily fluids all over our uniforms too, sir," I added.

I heard Higgs snigger.

"Did you?" queried Dankworth. "I can only apologise for taking the ladder. Buy yourselves some new stockings and get your uniforms dry-cleaned, and give me the bill," he said in a rare display of generosity. "You both demonstrated remarkable practicality finding that sheet of corrugated iron to move him on and tenacity getting him out of the wood. Yes, we could have left it to the undertaker, but I much prefer bodies to be moved by trained officers who know what they're doing – and I know you found another bottle underneath the body. So I think your efforts deserve a round of applause."

The men in the room all clapped. Miss Robertshaw gave us a thumbs up and mouthed, "Well done, girls."

Pattie and I blushed, a mixture of pride at being singled out for some rare praise, and embarrassment because only we knew how much we had mishandled, sworn at and broken the unfortunate man's body getting it out of the wood. The head fell off and rolled down a path, for goodness' sake! I hoped they hadn't asked Fowler or the undertakers too much about our retrieval process.

"And moving on. The Ferals are back at school, or should be, so keep an eye out for the inevitable truanting. Our WHSmith-embezzler Bernie Carroll is still in the care of her probation officer, the marvellous Hilda Bloom – we are all familiar with Hilda, aren't we?" Everyone nodded. "So Crockford and Baxter, if any issues with the Carrolls crop up you know which probation officer is keeping an eye on the family?"

"Yes, sir,' we answered. *Of course we bloody know Hilda*.

"And now, onto Ascot races . . ."

Monday's edition of The *Wokingham Courier* screamed the headline:

HORROR ON THE FARM!

Shocked children discover decomposed body of a mystery old man in woodland

It was supposed to be a pleasant woodland stroll in the late autumn sunshine for a group of Wokingham youngsters walking their dog, but it soon turned into a something from a Gothic horror story when they stumbled across the horrifying, decomposed remains of an old man propped up against a tree deep in the woods on High Copse Farm.

The terrified children ran to Wokingham Police Station in panic, where policemen were dispatched to investigate what they had found and call in CID to secure the scene. Once foul play was ruled out, policemen investigated then extracted the body from the wood for further investigation and a post-mortem.

Detective Inspector Larry Dankworth, leading the investigation, appealed for information:

"Our investigations reveal that the gentleman in question was probably in his late seventies, medium height and slight in stature, wearing a quality tweed jacket, moleskin trousers and heavy walking boots and carrying an empty WW2 canvas kit bag. He had nothing on him by way of identification and we know of no missing person locally fitting the description. Items found with him, and the post-mortem, suggest that he committed suicide sometime in June. Our best guess is that he was an itinerant, travelling from place to place on foot, but we would appeal to anyone who may have seen someone fitting this description to get in touch with Wokingham police."

We tracked down some of the traumatised children who found the remains. "It was really scary and he smelled horrible," said pretty little Dora, 6. "I thought he was going to get up and chase me," said Dennis, 9. "We had to run for our lives," said Charlie, 10. When we approached Farmer Greg Fowler, owner of the woodland, for a comment he responded, "Please get off my land."

If anybody has any information about the possible identity of the remains found in High Copse woods, please get in touch with Wokingham Police on 4065.

Sergeant Lamb knocked on the door and came into the women's office with that morning's copy of The *Wokingham Courier*.

"Can you believe this?" he asked, handing it to me.

As I read, I picked out the numerous inaccuracies. "No dog ... it's hardly a public right of way for an afternoon stroll, Fowler will hate that ... why is it always a Gothic horror story ... It wasn't police *men*, it was police WOMEN who investigated then extracted the corpse."

"Thought you'd like that bit," chuckled Sarge as I tutted.

I continued reading. "Foul play can't be ruled out until AFTER a post-mortem, for goodness' sake ... Dankworth ... blah blah ... WHAT is Jardine doing tracking down the Ferals and getting them to comment, as if those children would say something helpful? Good old Fowler, I'd have told him to sod off my land too."

Sarge laughed. "Six travesties in four paragraphs – is that a record?"

"Sounds about normal to me," I said. "My dad always

told me never to trust anything you read in the papers. I get that now. The Ferals don't have a dog, do they?"

I was beginning to doubt my own knowledge in light of the *Wokingham Courier's* reporting.

"Not unless they stole one or found a stray – and I wouldn't put it past them," said Sarge. "Jardine is just doing that lazy 'body found by a dog walker' cliché."

"Dankworth is going to have to have a word with him about his reporting," I said.

It also didn't help that the *Wokingham Courier's* early sandwich boards outside the newsagents' starkly stated SKELETON FOUND IN WOODS. This immediately set the entire town achatter and the police station switchboard on fire, with people ringing in asking if it was animal or human.

"It's disgusting! I had to steer my Millie away from the boards," Doris Savin complained to me outside Sketchleys. "I didn't want to explain what a skellington is, or give her the frightening idea that there are dead people in the woods. Millie's worried enough about the state of the world as it is."

The sandwich boards were changed to read ELDERLY MAN'S BODY FOUND IN WOODS. Dankworth must have had a word with Jardine. The street gossip carried on as Wokingham's inhabitants pondered who had died on the outskirts of our town, although fewer people rang the police station.

We weren't strangers to people who were a bit different: tramps like Georgie Lawes and other itinerants passed through from time to time and over the years we had a few of our own treasured local characters.

"Sir John" was a man with wild hair and bushy muttonchop whiskers who wore full hunting pinks and would ride around the town on an old bicycle festooned with silver paper, coloured ribbons, metal buttons on strings and sometimes root vegetables dangling from the handlebars. He blew incessantly on a hunting horn, shouting "Tally ho!" and had been known to crack a bullwhip to get people to move out of his way. He had a habit of cycling through Woolworths, scaring shoppers and small children with blasts of his hunting horn, before taking his bicycle to the old water fountain by the town hall "for a drink" from the horse trough. Hilarious and legendary as "Sir John" was, his eccentric behaviour resulted from brain damage from a hunting accident when he was young.

Another much-loved Wokingham character was Pepsi, the newspaper seller. Nicknamed because of his favourite fizzy drink, he was a cheerful, energetic young lad, who would these days be termed "learning disabled". In the 1950s, he was referred to as "simple but harmless". Pepsi, his hair heavily Brylcreemed, dressed every day in a shirt, tie and belted mackintosh, even in 90 degrees of summer heat. He would leap out and flourish a folded newspaper elaborately at passers-by to get them to buy one and jump on and off the buses with an armful of papers, joking with the drivers.

Mr Bischoff, the bank manager, called in to say he thought he had seen a man fitting the newspaper description change some money at the bank at the beginning of March, but he hadn't struck him as being the dirty old tramp type. Because he had simply exchanged coins for notes there was no record of who he was.

Gradually, the phone calls stopped and the inquiry went cold. We still had no idea of the skeleton's identity.

Pattie and I chatted to Dankworth in the canteen.

"How long are they going to keep this gentleman's body before it can be buried?" I asked.

"There are no hard and fast rules, oddly. We're going to have to give it a few weeks for any relatives to come forward and we've alerted other constabularies to make inquiries too. If nobody does and we've exhausted lines of inquiry, Reverend Tucker says we can inter him in a single marked grave, and he'll do a simple burial ceremony, in case we need to exhume him in future. But I don't think we'll need to."

"Don't we have to keep any sort of samples from the body?" I asked.

"You're thinking like a detective, Crockford! We'll keep his dental records, of course."

I cringed inwardly as I remembered how many of the skeleton's teeth fell out when his head came off.

"Identification through dental records makes me laugh," said Pattie. "If we don't know who you were, how the hell do we know who your dentist was?"

Dankworth gave a rare chuckle.

"If you have an idea where the victim came from – and we don't – you can ask the local dentists. Theoretically, we could X-ray his jaws and send them off to be published in the *British Dental Journal*," he said. "See if any dentists recognise their work or patient. But generally, that's only done in high-profile murder cases."

"But we know his blood group?" Pattie asked.

"Yes – O positive."

238

I did a rough calculation in my head, remembering the blood group percentages from Forensics Week at training school.

"Great. So our skeleton could belong to any one of 18 million people."[17]

"A detective's heart sinks when the blood group is O positive, that's for certain," said Dankworth. "But when a bloodstain is AB negative and your main suspect is also AB negative, that's a result, eh?"

"Have you ever come across that, sir?"

"Er, no, I haven't."

"I think it's dangerous to use blood groups to identify people. Especially when we have the death penalty. We have to be 100 per cent certain that we get the guilty individual," added Pattie.

No relatives came forward. No other constabularies had anyone fitting the description on their missing persons lists. In relentless, soft soaking rain one Thursday afternoon, Pattie, Dankworth, Bob and I stood beneath umbrellas by the graveside as Reverend Tucker said the simple burial ceremony from the *Book of Common Prayer* over the skeleton's coffin. We each threw a handful of soil in at the "earth to earth, ashes to ashes, dust to dust" bit and I noticed Pattie had a teardrop on the end of her nose.

---

17 The population of the UK in 1953 was around 50,750,976.
Thirty-five per cent of the UK population has O positive
blood group.

CHAPTER 20

Indecencies

I don't know what it was about some men in the mid-1950s, but indecency was something us women officers dealt with on a regular basis. We knew from our studies during Sex Crime Week that there was no standard definition of indecency in statute: it was generally left up to magistrates, or jurors on more serious trials, to agree that acts or assaults would be "considered indecent by right-minded people". We had the common law[18] offence of "outraging public decency", which gave us three parameters to work within:

• An act must be indecent, lewd or obscene, and likely to disgust and annoy, outraging the minimum standards of public decency. Magistrates or juries were entitled to infer disgust and annoyance, without evidence that anyone was actually disgusted or annoyed.

• An act must take place in a public place, or a place that is accessible to, or within view of, the public.

• An act must take place where at least two members

18 Common law, or case law, consists of unwritten laws based on legal precedents, as established by courts. It derives from interpretations and opinions from public juries and judicial authorities.

of the public *might* see it; it was irrelevant whether these people actually saw the act or were outraged by it.

One person's upsettingly indecent act was another person's comedy gold. An example of this happened within the seemingly safe confines of our women's office. I was working with Miss Robertshaw one evening when the telephone rang. She picked it up.

"Wokingham Police, women's office, Sergeant Robertshaw speaking ... Yes ... I beg your pardon? ... How dare you ... I insist you get off the line this very moment . . ."

I heard a click as the caller rang off. Miss Robertshaw stood stock-still, looking at the purring receiver, her cheeks flaming red.

"Well, I never . . ." she stammered.

"Are you all right, Miss?" I asked.

"I think I've just had one of those obscene phone calls. A man has just said he wants to do the most disgusting things to me."

Miss Robertshaw sat down and looked close to tears. I had never seen her this upset by anything before. I took out my pocketbook to make notes, treating it like any other offence.

"We need to file this, Miss. What did he actually say?"

"He had a horrible squeaky voice. He said ... 'I'd like to give you a really good ... f ... f ... fuck – I'm sorry, there, I've said it – from behind.'"

I winced as I wrote down the f-word. Poor Miss Robertshaw. Nobody deserved to pick up a phone call and get that.

Pulling herself back together, Miss Robertshaw added, "I'm not sure that what just happened was actually an offence. Are we the public? Is this a public place?"

"I suppose if we caught whoever did it, it would be up to the magistrate to decide," I replied. "I can't believe the chairman *wouldn't* consider it indecent and disgusting."

We had no reliable way of tracing calls back then. Incoming telephone calls were routed through our main switchboard and connected through, literally, a series of mechanical switches. I mentioned it to our duty switchboard officer, who didn't recall a man with a squeaky voice. Whoever it was, he didn't ring again that week and we put it out of our minds.

A few weeks later, I was in the women's office with Pattie, doing a shift handover when the telephone rang. She picked it up.

"Wokingham Police, women's office, WPC Baxter speaking … Yes … You what? … From behind what? … The sofa? … The desk?" She was shrieking with laughter. "Oh, you sad little man, you must have a very tiny John Thomas . . ." She wiggled her little finger at the receiver before putting it down.

"What was that, Pattie? Another of those lewd telephone calls?"

"Best offer I've had all week." Pattie cackled. "Shame he sounded like Mickey Mouse."

If the caller wanted to outrage or disgust someone this time, he got the wrong person. We didn't receive another dirty phone call.

Flashers were something else, though. The "dirty mac brigade", as we called them, could pop up anywhere to outrage public decency. At least their offence was covered by the Vagrancy Act of 1824: anyone "wilfully openly, lewdly, and obscenely exposing his person in any street, road, or public highway, or in the view thereof, or in any place of public resort, with intent to insult any female . . ." would be considered "a rogue and a vagabond" and arrestable under the Act. Wokingham wasn't short of leafy lanes, alleyways, copses and parks thickly planted with bushes where such rogues and vagabonds could loiter.

I was about to leave the station for my patrol one dark, drizzly afternoon when Sarge beckoned me over. He'd just put down the telephone receiver.

"WPC Crockford, since you're just heading out, could you call in and see a Mrs Pearson as a matter of urgency?" He gave me an address off the Barkham Road. "Seems some creature flashed at her daughters as they walked home from school, then ran off in the direction of the allotments."

I was outraged on their behalf. Lots of people made jokes about indecent exposure, but I understood first-hand how upsetting it was for a young girl to have a man expose himself to her. During the war, aged 14, I was walking home late from the railway station in the blackout when I noticed a Hillman Minx parked up outside Westcott Road School, engine running. The passenger window was open, and as I passed the car, I heard a male voice.

"Miss! Miss! Excuse me, miss!"

Keeping a careful distance from the car door, I stopped, noticing that there were no passengers, only the driver on the other side, so I peered in through the window.

"Yes?" I said.

"I wonder if you could help me with something, miss?" said the voice.

"What's that?" I asked.

"This."

The driver flicked on a pocket torch and shone it at something pink that he was holding in his lap. As he stroked it, it seemed to get bigger. I realised what it was. I'd only ever seen a penis on an encyclopaedia photograph of Michelangelo's statue of David and I had no idea one could be this size or this animated. Gasping with revulsion, I recoiled from the car window just as an ARP warden rounded the corner shouting, "Put that bloody light out!" and the driver engaged gear and sped off into the gloom. I'd run all the way home, stumbling on the kerbs and potholes, and locked myself in the bedroom, too scared to tell Mum in case she said I had somehow encouraged it.

So I really felt for 11-year-old Tilly and 12-year-old Jemima Pearson, still in their Holt School uniforms and wide-eyed as I took their statements. Their kindly mother sat on the arm of the sofa next to them, wringing her hands anxiously. They were sensible girls, clearly shaken up by what had happened, but able to give a detailed account. Apologising for having to make them go over it again, I summarised their account back to them:

"So you were walking towards your house together and you heard a man's voice behind you making 'twutting' or kissing sounds, and saying, 'hello,' and 'hello, girls.' You turned round and there was a middle-aged man wearing a wide-brimmed trilby hat and a long brown overcoat standing under the street lamp. It was difficult to see his face properly. He opened his coat with both hands and you could see him exposing his, er, person, which was standing up . . ." Mrs Pearson put her face in her hands.

"Then he danced about, flaunting it, before closing his coat and running towards the allotments. He was naked from his waist down to his knees, and had cut-off trouser legs tied just above his knees with string." *Clearly, he had specially made attire for going out flashing*, I thought.

I rang Sarge from Mrs Pearson's telephone and asked him to alert all the beat points to be on the lookout for this character.

"How are the girls doing?" he asked.

"They've been very brave and they're better witnesses than most grown-ups," I said loudly, more for Tilly's and Jemima's benefit than Sarge's.

The two girls managed a smile.

"You might want to walk the girls home for the next week or so, Mrs Pearson, and I'll make sure a beat officer covers your road around this time," I said as I was leaving. "I'll be in touch when we have any news of an arrest."

Before I left, I felt I ought to check the allotments at the end of the Pearsons' road to see if the flasher might be hiding in there. The entrance gate was open and I stood for a moment to listen for any movement. Nothing. It was pitch-dark inside and I reached for my torch.

Switching it on, I circled the allotment plots, checking behind blackcurrant bushes and Brussels sprout plants and peering through the windows of the little sheds. Some roosting chickens in a henhouse shuffled and pock-pocked to each other as I crept past.

Don't worry, I'm not a fox.

As I rounded a large shed, my torch beam briefly illuminated a figure wearing a hat and an overcoat, standing slap-bang in the middle of a plot. At that precise moment, my torch battery chose to die and I was back in darkness again. I retreated behind the shed, back pressed to it, trying to control my racing heart and fast breathing. With trembling hands, I fumbled in my pockets for my spare battery and somehow managed to replace it without dropping any components on the ground.

I stepped out from behind the shed and flicked on the torch. The figure was still standing there. *He's just toying with me*, I thought, *he's going to make me get close to him, then he's going to grab me*. I gripped the torch tightly. I could use it like a truncheon if necessary. I approached the motionless figure.

"You there! What are you doing loitering about here in the dark?"

There was no response. I moved closer. It was my opportunity to make an arrest and get this rogue off the streets. I brought my hand down hard on his shoulder. He fell over sideways and his hat rolled off, revealing two bamboo sticks tied together in a cross shape, a frame to hang the hat and old coat from.

I don't bloody believe it! A scarecrow!

I exhaled with pure relief. I wished Pattie had been there with me – it's not the same laughing hysterically on your own.

We immediately telephoned all the schools about the allotment flasher. Through assemblies and letters home, the girls were made aware that if they heard a man behind them making "twutting" or kissing noises, and saying "hello, girls", they were to run and find the nearest police officer.

To have one flasher at large in your town may be regarded as a misfortune, to have two looks like carelessness on the part of the police.

Not long after the Pearson girls' incident, Pattie and I were called to the manager's office of Heelas department store early one morning before opening. Mr Norris the manager was standing over a sobbing shop girl, who was sitting on a chair.

Classic stealing scenario, I thought.

"What seems to be the problem, sir? Are you all right?" I asked the girl.

"Something outrageous has just happened to one of my staff." Mr Norris puffed and handed the girl a glass of water and a tissue. "Lucy, are you able to tell the officers what happened?" Lucy nodded and blew her nose.

"I was dressing the womenswear department's front windows. We're changing the display from autumn to winter, you see, so I had undressed the dummies down to their underwear ready to put on their cocktail dresses and Christmas party outfits. I was on my knees rolling some stockings up the legs of the dummy nearest the window and I got this funny feeling someone was watching me. I looked up and there was this bloke just standing there, grinning. There was nobody else about outside, just him. I thought he might be perving at the dummies in their underwear, so I ignored him and carried on putting the stockings on. Then I heard a clunking sound and he'd pressed himself up against the window."

"Pressed himself against the window?" asked Pattie.

"Yes," continued Lucy. She took a sip of her water. "He'd undone his coat, and unbuttoned his trousers, and he was ... you know ... rubbing himself ... right up against the glass, just above my head."

"He was rubbing against the glass?" I asked, feeling disgusted myself.

"No. He was doing it with his hand, but he'd wrapped some red lacy women's knickers round it. He didn't seem to care if anybody saw him."

"And did anyone else see him?"

"I think there were a couple of people walking on the opposite side of the road, but they weren't taking any notice. It probably just seemed as if he was taking a close look at something in the window."

"Can you give me a description of him?" I asked.

"Probably in his thirties, quite thin, medium height, wavy brown hair, blue trousers, grey, single-breasted overcoat, no hat," said Lily. "To be honest, I didn't want to stay in the window any longer so I went and called Mr Norris. When he came down, the man had gone."

"What is the world coming to when my young window dresser can't go about her job without some pervert doing disgusting things through the window?" said Mr Norris.

"I know, sir," I said. "It's completely unacceptable behaviour. I'll put a call out and ask my fellow officers to keep an eye out for anybody matching his description." It didn't help that half the thirty-something men in Wokingham wore grey overcoats and blue trousers.

"We're not doing very well on the pervert front, are we?" said Pattie on the way back to the station. "Allotment flasher and window wanker – two, Police – nil."

A few days later, a Saturday, Pattie and I were starting our late turn.

"The strangest thing has happened today," said Bob. "We've had three separate reports of an unseen person saying, 'Hello, hello, come on then,' to women and young girls at the bus stop along Reading Road. We've had beat officers check the area three separate times, but they've seen nothing untoward. I think you know what I'm going to ask you . . ."

An hour later, Pattie and I were standing at the bus stop, our civilian coats, scarves and woolly hats covering our uniforms. It was a chilly, grey afternoon, few people about. With the churchyard opposite and a wooded copse bordering school playing fields behind us, it was a flasher's paradise.

"He must be desperate if he's willing to get his todger out in these temperatures," complained Pattie, stamping her feet.

Several buses arrived and left. Cold and bored, we were about to call it a day and hop on the next bus.

"Gwen! Did you hear that?" said Pattie.

I listened. I could just about make out a male voice saying, "Hello! Hello! Come on then!"

I grabbed Pattie's arm. "I think it's coming from the copse. Let's just stand here, pretend we haven't heard, and see if that draws him any closer."

A few minutes later we heard the male voice again, but louder, nearer.

"Hello! Hello! Come on then!"

"I think he's behind that cedar tree. He wants us to go over and look."

"Hello! Hello! Come on then!"

The voice was incredibly close now.

"Let's go," I said.

We hurried to the cedar tree and peered round it. Nothing. There was no one in the copse, on the playing field or along the road.

"Hello! Hello! Come on then!"

The voice was so loud this time, it made us jump.

"Oh, bloody hell, don't tell me he's hiding up the tree!" cried Pattie.

We looked up into the tree, but we couldn't see a human crouching among the branches. However, there was a large black bird hopping about in it.

"Hello! Hello! Come on then!" it said.

"Hello! Hello!" called Pattie.

"Come on then!" it replied.

"Is that ... a jackdaw?" I asked. With the light fading, it was quite hard to get a good look at it.

"Could be, but my money's on a mynah bird. My aunt's got one. It says all sorts of swear words and she's

250

got to put a cloth over its cage if polite company comes round. Come on then!"

"Hello! Hello!" it responded.

Pattie carried on this conversation for a while. She held out her wrist to the bird, hoping it would come to her, but it kept its distance.

"C'mon, Dr Doolittle, talking to the animals," I said. "We'd better get back."

"I take it no joy with our indecent exposure merchant?" asked Sarge as we returned to the station.

"No, but do you know anyone who's lost a talking mynah bird?"

CHAPTER 21

Two tyrannical fathers

It was pretty clear that most of the Ferals behaved as they did because of their chaotic home lives. The police, social and welfare services even had a specific name for them: "problem families". The exception was Roger Wickes, living a comfortable, middle-class life as the GP's son. I sensed he was a clever boy who craved risk and excitement, and the only way he could satisfy these was by hanging around with the mischief-making Carrolls and Feltons. Nowadays, he would be channelled into extreme sports or volunteering expeditions, but in 1950s Wokingham, he had to find his own adventures in the gravel pits and woodlands, with the luxury of returning to a comfortable home environment every night.

In contrast, Bernie Carroll appeared at the juvenile court pleading guilty to stealing money from WHSmith, but still maintaining that she had never taken more than 2s.6d. at a time. The chairman ruled that she was to pay all the missing money back to WHSmith in instalments. Hilda's probation reports meant that Bernie avoided being sent to an Approved School and instead, was put on probation for two years, checking in with Hilda once a fortnight. But hindsight being a wonderful thing, we would come to realise that Bernie would have been better off at an Approved School.

While it was important to keep a professional detachment, I couldn't help becoming quite invested in some of the youngsters I dealt with. Bernie was one, not only because she was my first juvenile arrest, but also because I felt she wasn't a bad girl and something bigger was going on in her life. And because her father was a creep.

I voiced my concerns with Hilda when we caught up over a cup of tea one day.

"You know, I feel the same, Gwen," she replied. "I can't put my finger on what it is about Rodney Carroll, either. He always brings her to the probation interview, usually with Dora, and every time he wants to sit in on our meetings, flashing what he thinks is a persuasive grin at me. Every time, I insist he stays outside in the corridor, while I talk to Bernie in my office. I interview her at the desk furthest from the door – I wouldn't put it past Carroll to have his ear pressed to it, listening."

"There is something unsavoury about him, I agree. How's Bernie doing, Hilda?"

"She's never a picture of rosy health, is she? I thought she looked tireder than usual last interview, with puffy bags under her eyes and her loose-fitting dress quite grubby. I asked her about her job at the stables – she finds it all right, mucking out and grooming the horses, and the money all helps, she says."

"When she comes home, can she get some rest?" I asked.

"If nobody's home from school and Carroll and John are out, she might get a quick forty winks. She says the washing doesn't do itself and it's hard to get stuff dry with just the paraffin heater, so she waits for a dry day to hang it out."

"Any help from her father and John with the chores? I'm expecting the answer no here."

"She says her dad goes shopping on his bike, but he and John don't lift a finger with the housework. Women's work, they call it. But they like wearing the clean clothes, apparently, John being an Edwardian and all. Carroll's shirt and trousers look clean, but the girls' clothes need a wash. I wonder if Bernie only does his and John's clothes to stop them complaining and neglects the other children's."

"Hmm. Do you think there's enough money coming into the household to cover the basics?" I asked.

"Carroll gets five shillings a week each for his younger three children from Family Allowances. Bernie has now managed to pay all her WHSmith takings back in compliance with her judgement and her stables money helps keep the family afloat. But it's nowhere near as much as she earned at WHSmith."

"And everything's all right at home, is it?" I asked.

"I always ask that question," replied Hilda, "knowing full well that Bernie is unlikely to say no. I reiterate that she can talk to me about anything and she *says* that she trusts me. I always finish a session by saying she can telephone me at any time."

"She's not going to feel comfortable opening up with her dad hanging around outside the door, is she?" I said.

"I know! When I opened the door last session, he jumped back, with that insincere grin all over his face. I'll bet he was listening at the door. He asked me, 'Everything go all right?'"

"Did you mention that you thought she looked tired?"

"I did, but then noticed her little sister Dora scratching the back of her head like mad. I asked if I could take a look at her and honestly, Gwen, I was quite disgusted – under her long hair was like a hard mass of beige louse eggs, with hundreds of lice of varying sizes scuttling about. Where she had been scratching, her skin was red. This level of infestation clearly hadn't happened overnight and puts her at risk of infection. You know, it reminded me of when I was working around the Paddington slums one hot summer. I dealt with a neglected child who had fly strike, her hair and scalp crawling with blowfly maggots. The sight and smell of it gave me sleepless nights for weeks."

"That's dreadful," I said, appalled that this was even a thing. "But how could Dora's have got past the school's nit nurse?"

"I asked her that and she said, 'I hided in the toilets when Nitty Nora came round.'"

"The Ferals' ability to truant any situation is legendary, after all," I said.

Hilda smiled. "Then Carroll chipped in, glaring at Bernie, asking her why she hadn't been sorting Dora's hair out like he asked her to. She said, 'I couldn't find the nit comb. And we've run out of shampoo.'"

"Do you think they even had a nit comb in the first place?"

"I doubt it. I couldn't help myself and said, 'Mr Carroll, you are the responsible adult here, not Bernie!' He stared at the floor like an overgrown schoolboy."

"What did you do?" I asked.

"I went back in my office, into my desk drawer where I keep some spare nit combs, soap, shampoo, crème rinse and packets of army-issue louse powder. Old Paddington habits die hard. I thought I would give the Carrolls a second chance with the nit comb before going in with chemical warfare, so I pressed a comb, shampoo and crème rinse into Carroll's reluctant hands. He immediately handed them to Bernie. I gave him instructions how to comb Dora's wet hair regularly to catch the lice as they hatch, but I would be surprised if he does it properly. I said I would be checking up in a fortnight's time."

"It'll be interesting to see if he brings Dora to the next probation meeting," I said.

"If he doesn't, it's a red flag, don't you think?" replied Hilda.

As well as Rodney Carroll, there was something about the Ferals' Carl and Dennis, the Felton brothers, that bothered me. They didn't have the resourceful swagger of John and Charlie Carroll, or the privileged daredevilry of Roger Wickes. They seemed scared, deceitful, easily manipulated by the others and eager to please. Their clothes were tatty and ill-fitting, and somehow Dennis always managed to lose his shoes. When Bob and I had encountered them at the gravel pits, they were desperate that we didn't arrest them because their dad "would go berserk". The Felton family lived in Wokingham's historic Rose Street, not in one of the lovely Tudor timber-framed cottages, but in housing that was considered slums, earmarked for demolition.

One afternoon, Miss Robertshaw took a call.

"Yes … yes … So the mother put in a report to the NSPCC? All right, I'll meet you there with one of my WPCs … goodbye now."

She turned to me. "We've got a potential care or protection case, Miss Crockford. We're meeting an NSPCC Inspector and Dr Wickes to attend a property in Rose Street right now."

We met Inspector McGinley and Dr Wickes on the junction of Broad Street and Rose Street, then walked to the house. The inspector knocked on the door. It opened a fraction and a bloodshot eye appeared against the crack.

"Mrs Dorothy Felton?" said McGinley. "It's the NSPCC, with a doctor and the police. May we come in?"

Felton. That name's familiar, I thought.

A frightened-looking young woman in a stained housecoat opened the door and we trooped straight into a dank living room. Before closing the door, Mrs Felton peered up and down the street.

The sooner they demolish these hovels, the better, I thought, looking round the dingy room. Flowery wallpaper was peeling off in sheets, revealing deep cracks in the plaster underneath. A dented saucepan in one corner caught water dripping through a blackened hole in the ceiling. The only furniture was a rickety formica-topped table with four small wooden stools round it and a moth-eaten settee that had springs sticking up out of the seat cushions. Nobody wanted to sit on the settee, so we stood.

Two boys were sitting on the stools at the table. I recognised them immediately as the Ferals' Carl and Dennis. Carl had a bruise along his cheekbone. Dennis stared at us vacantly, mouth hanging open, but recognition sparked in Carl's coal-black eyes when he saw me.

"You're the lady policeman from the library," he said. He glared at me hard, eyebrows raised, as if pleading with me not to say why I'd seen him in the library.

I had no intention of elaborating.

"Yes I am. And you are … Dennis?" I asked the other brother, smiling. He nodded.

"And this is his brother, Carl," chipped in his mother.

"We're here, Mrs Felton, because you've reported that your husband Saul has been hurting your sons," said Inspector McGinley, "and we need Dr Wickes here to examine them and assess what sort of injuries they've received." The inspector took out a notepad and a pen, and nodded to Dr Wickes.

"Can I have a look at you first, please, Carl?" asked Dr Wickes. "I'll need you to get undressed."

"What? In front of all these people?' whimpered Carl.

Mrs Felton sighed. 'Just bleedin' do what the doc tells you."

Carl pulled off his shirt, dropped his trousers and underpants and stood with his eyes closed, hands covering his nudity.

I can't believe children have to be examined like this, I thought.

Dr Wickes knelt in front of Carl and gently turned him round as he checked him over.

"We've got some minor bruising on the back and some more significant bruising on his right thigh, which could have been caused by a whip or a strap," he said. "I'm even more concerned about these bruises on his face, which suggest blows from a clenched fist."

My tummy turned over. *Who would punch a child in the face?*

"You can get dressed now, Carl," said Dr Wickes. "Can I have a look at you, please, Dennis?"

"I don't wanna! I don't wanna!" cried Dennis, cringing into the corner.

"Oh, don't be so ridiculous, Den, these people are here to help us," said Mrs Felton, grabbing him by the wrist and dragging him into the middle of the room, where he sobbed as he removed his clothes.

We gasped as Dennis stepped out of his underpants. His bottom was criss-crossed with angry, purple-black bruises and he had another purple bruise on his shin.

"Extensive bruising to the buttocks, consistent with being hit with a blunt object such as a stick. Bruise on the shins that appears to have been caused by a kick," said Dr Wickes, looking Dennis's back up and down. "Ah – what's this?"

Dennis winced as the doctor lightly touched a bruise under his left shoulder blade.

Dr Wickes took a deep breath. "These look like human bites. If you look closely, you can see the individual teeth marks."

The room started to spin slightly and I heard a

whooshing sound in my ears. I could deal with a post-mortem. I could deal with road accident injuries. I could deal with a dance hall brawl. But injuries to a defenceless child like this made me sick with fury. I leaned against the settee, grateful that nobody else, silent in their own private horrors, noticed my unsteadiness. The only sound was a plip of water dripping into the saucepan.

Mrs Felton broke the silence by rolling up her sleeves to reveal five circular bruises paired with five semi-circular nail cuts on each arm. "It's where he grabs my arms and shakes me when he's had a few. I try to get between him and the boys but he just flings me out of the way."

At that moment, we heard a key in the lock. The door opened and in walked a man who I assumed to be Saul Felton. He was short and wiry, with an angular face and shark-like eyes – coal-black, like his son's. He had a newspaper under his arm and in his hand was a paper bag that looked as if it contained a bottle. He hesitated when he saw he had visitors.

"What the hell's going on here?" he demanded.

Dorothy Felton gathered the boys to her. "Get upstairs, you two – right now," she said.

Dennis and Carl scrambled away up the rickety staircase.

"Mr Saul Felton?" said Inspector McGinley.

"Yeah, that's me," he replied.

"I'm Inspector McGinley from the NSPCC. This is Dr Wickes, WPS Robertshaw and WPC Crockford from Wokingham Police. We need to have a conversation."

"What about?"

"Your wife tells us that you regularly beat your sons. Upon medical examination, the doctor has found injuries on the boys consistent with being hit with a stick and a strap, and even bite marks on one. Can you explain?"

Saul Felton sat down on one of the stools and rubbed his forehead. "It's from me lorry accident, officers. Me nerves have been giving me trouble ever since and I fly into sudden tempers. I can't help it. You know how badly-behaved them boys are and Dot here is too soft with them, letting them get away with murder, so it's left to me to sort them out."

"By hitting and biting them?" asked McGinley.

"Well, yeah. I don't deny it, but I only ever hit them with me hands."

Dorothy, standing behind Saul, stared at us meaningfully, shaking her head.

"Doc, is there anything you can give me for me nerves?" Felton asked.

"Well, you would have to make an appointment and come and see me at the surgery," replied Dr Wickes.

Inspector McGinley turned to Miss Robertshaw and me. "I think this is now a matter for the police, officers, if you would take over now. I'll file my report for you and Dr Wickes, if you'll be kind enough to write up your findings too."

We took our own statements and Saul Felton was charged with two counts of child cruelty under section 1 of the Children and Young Persons Act. He pleaded guilty in front of the magistrate and following psychiatric reports, was placed on probation for three years. A condition of his probation order was that he should not ill-treat his wife or children.

The chairman said: "You must get it out of your head once and for all that treatment can help you. It rests entirely with you to control your sadistic and criminal intentions and your emotions. We have decided after much thought to give you a chance, if you are prepared to take it."

And Saul Felton returned to his family.

Meeting Hilda for coffee in the canteen, we discussed the Felton case. Felton had been placed for three years with Hilda's colleague, Terry Fulford, as his probation officer.

"The strangest thing happened, Gwen, with those two Felton boys," she said. "Terry did a home visit and he knew he recognised them from somewhere. It bothered him all day. Then he exclaimed, 'I remember where I've seen them before. They were the two little sods who set the swan's nest on fire and were about to shoot the female with a catapult!'"

Of course. Terry had seen and reported the attack on the Emm Brook swans. And I had a sudden revelation: the Felton boys had catapults when I made them turn out their pockets at the library. But most boys did back then.

"Does Terry want to do anything about the swan attack?" I asked. "I mean, it was over a year ago."

"Ach, no. He feels, as I do – and I believe you do too – that those boys have been through enough. I have read though that children who grow up with violent fathers can also be cruel to animals. Terry will keep a close watch on the Felton family. I don't believe the boys will be setting fire to another swan's nest."

Less than six months later, Saul Felton was back before the magistrate for breaching his probation order; he admitted twisting Dorothy's arm and punching her in the face. Dorothy asked the bench to withdraw the charges against her husband "for the sake of the children". The exasperated chairman adjourned the case indefinitely, telling Felton, "I don't know for how long you are going to be able to hold your temper."

Shortly after, the Feltons moved out of the town, when their housing was finally condemned, and the Ferals lost two gang members. I would occasionally see Saul Felton going into the probation office for his meetings with Terry Fulford and I heard later that he left Dorothy for another woman. I was relieved for her, Carl and Dennis, but fearful for his new woman.

A leopard like Saul Felton doesn't change his spots.

CHAPTER 22

Burglaries

Burglaries were rare in Wokingham, but we suddenly had a spate of them. I'd spent a good hour of one early turn checking the doorknobs and window latches of central Wokingham's shops and businesses before patrolling the residential roads. In my day, if your house was going to be unoccupied – you were going on holiday, or away for a longer period – you could ask the police to check on it every day. I'd visited and crossed off every unoccupied property on my list just as the sun started to rise above the tree line and warm the quiet streets.

The familiar figure of Mr Finch, the butcher, came striding towards me. I knew him well as I'd had a wartime Saturday job at his shop while I was at school. I'd been in charge of mincing up the offal, fat and unsold mouldy pies to go into his sausages.

"Gwen, love!" he called out, "me shop's been broken into!"

There had been nothing untoward when I checked the back of the butcher's at 6.10 a.m., near the start of my shift. I rang into the station to report the incident and headed off to the shop with Mr Finch. The rear door had been jemmied open and was swinging in the breeze, the broken padlock on the ground. It would have been impossible to miss at 6.10 a.m.

I tiptoed gingerly round the scattered wood splinters and kept my hands away from the door frame. "Mind the splinters, Mr Finch, and don't touch anything yet. What time did you discover this?"

"About a quarter past seven. I was going to get them pigs portioned up before I open at nine."

"Anything stolen?" I asked.

"I haven't checked the cool store yet," he said. "I saw I'd had a break-in and rushed straight to the police station."

"Looks like they jemmied that as well," I said. "There are marks round the frame."

"You're right, there are." Mr Finch looked around his shop. "I'm missing a couple of fresh rabbits I was hanging in the window for a few days ... Look! Buggers – excuse my language – managed to get the till open, not that I keep any money in it overnight ... Oh dammit! My big Sheffield butcher's knife and filleting knife have gone."

An enormous meat cleaver hung alone on the wall above the butcher's block without its usual companions.

I scribbled notes in my pocketbook. "So, damage caused by breaking and entering at the rear of the shop. Stolen: two rabbits, two knives – one large, one filleting. Do you want to check the cool store while I'm here? Careful not to disturb any fingerprints on the handle."

Mr Finch pulled the heavy door open by its edge. A cool blast of meaty-smelling air reached my nostrils. There was a side of beef and two bisected pigs, the halves hanging from meat hooks in the ceiling like some medieval execution scene. I noticed the pigs' heads were still on, so they wouldn't end up being dangled from a bus shelter roof.

"Two legs of lamb missing."

"That's probably all they could carry away," I said.

"Yeah, it would be a bit bleedin' obvious walking through Wokingham with a side of beef over your shoulder." Mr Finch managed a smile.

"I'll have to pop round to the carpenter's to order a new door with bolts and a sturdier lock today. What a bleedin' nuisance. And you bobbies, check my locks, an' all."

"I checked it myself at around 6.10, so it happened between then and 7.15."

"Did you see anyone while you were on your beat?"

I'd passed a couple of building labourers with plaster-encrusted boots and tool bags heading to the bus stop around 6.45 a.m. They had given me a cheery "Morning, officer, miss," as they passed by, smoking their first roll-up of the day; hardly the reaction of men who had just burgled a butcher's shop or were about to.

"Only a couple of labourers, but if I see them tomorrow, I'll ask them if they saw anyone."

Bennett appeared on his bicycle with his wooden box of crime scene materials and tools on the front, camera and flashgun slung diagonally across his body. We showed him the crime scene, then left him alone to take photographs and begin dusting for fingerprints.

Mr Finch's neighbours in the houses facing the rear of the shop were beginning to stir and show interest in the police presence. Several ladies, still in their curlers and housecoats, cigarettes dangling loosely from the corners of their mouths, came out, pretending to sweep their doorsteps. An elderly gentleman on two walking sticks stood on the pavement watching the goings-on. Some little children had ducked under the lace curtains of their bedroom windows, their noses pressed against the glass, fascinated, until their mothers shooed them away.

I conducted a textbook investigation, just as we'd been taught at training school, noting the time, date, place, name; asking onlookers politely to keep back from the scene and going from house to house to ask if anyone had seen or heard anything. Jemmying the doorframe would have been less noisy than breaking a window, and predictably, no one had seen or heard anything.

A harsh, quite unnecessary jangling of a bell cut through the neighbourly chats as a police car roared up and skidded to a stop outside Finch's shop. Dankworth leapt out. He ignored me and, crunching straight through the wood splinters, ran straight in to see Bennett.

"Ooh, who's he when he's at home? Sam Spade?"[19] laughed one woman, pointing.

Dankworth really needs to stop pretending he's some hard-boiled gumshoe from an American film noir, I thought.

Beckoning me over, Dankworth began to organise the crime scene that I had organised perfectly well before he arrived.

---

19 A classic fictional detective character in *The Maltese Falcon* by Dashiell Hammett, played by Humphrey Bogart in the 1941 film.

"Crockford, you need to check the shop interior. Ascertain what items are missing and whether money has been taken from the till."

"Yes, sir, I've—"

"Then afterwards do house-to-house inquiries. Someone must have seen something."

"Sir, I've—'

"I'm going to take a statement from Mr Finch just now—"

"Young lady's already done that, Inspector," said Mr Finch with a twinkle. "She was quicker off the mark than you."

"Oh well ... all right, then," grumbled Dankworth. "I'll take over from here, Crockford. Fill me in on what's happened."

I went over my findings with Dankworth.

He nodded and, unusually, had little to add once I had finished. "That's all fine, Crockford. If you could type all that up as a report, attach Mr Finch's statement and have it on my desk this afternoon." *Yes, I know what to do.* "You can get back to your usual beat now. Dismissed."

Dismissed.

I thanked everyone for their help and cooperation, smoothing the hair of one frightened little girl who was clinging to her mother's skirt crying because she "didn't like bugglars". With that, I returned to pounding my early turn beat.

A few days later, I was in the middle of collating a bundle of summonses that Bob had asked me to hand-deliver when the front desk telephone rang. I half-heard the conversation from the back office.

"Burglary, you say … no break-in … what time was this? They got in how? What was taken? Mmm … uh huh … righto. Can I take your address? Of course, Mrs Cripps, please don't upset yourself … we'll get an officer over to you right away."

Sarge popped his head round the door. "WPC Crockford, we've got another burglary, and not very far from here. Mrs Esme Cripps in Osborne Road."

"Another one? Oh, I know Esme. How upsetting for her."

"I know – she's very upset as she thinks the burglar got in while she was upstairs and the boys were in bed. Go and do your magic. I'll let Dankworth and Bennett know."

Osborne Road was a leafy street, 10 minutes' walk from the police station. Esme lived in a detached house, opposite the telephone box. She was standing on the pavement outside, hopping from foot to foot, her two bored teenage sons lounging on the kerb.

"Oh, officer, I'm glad you've come," said Esme. "I hardly want to go back into the house in case he comes back."

"I don't think you've got a lot to fear with these two strapping lads by your side," I said, winking at the youths.

"Oh dear, this is all my fault."

"What do you mean, your fault, Mrs Cripps?"

"I think I was stupid enough to leave the kitchen window open overnight and he just must have gone round the side and climbed in, took my purse off the table and my engagement ring off the mantelpiece and must have gone out through the front door, which I heard slam, which was when I got scared, came downstairs and saw my purse and ring had gone, grabbed the boys and ran out to the telephone box to ring the police."

"Take a breath, Mrs Cripps," I said. "This is not your fault. Anyone can be burgled. No one has the right to come into your house and steal, whether you've left a window open or not."

"My husband will be so cross – there were four pounds in my purse. I'd just been to the bank. And he keeps telling me to either wear my engagement ring or lock it in the safe." She was close to tears. "What's going on in this wretched town? We've had a little girl murdered, there's been skeletons in the woods, there's these Eddy youths . . ."

"They're called Teddy boys, Mum," said one of the twins, rolling his eyes.

"Whatever they're called, running out of control and fighting, the butcher's shop gets broken into, now my house gets burgled. I hate to say it was better in the war, but it was!"

I could see her point, but I couldn't believe anyone would really want to return to the days of blackouts, bombers thrumming overhead, full rationing, fear of invasion and not knowing whether your loved ones would come home. On the contrary, I felt that the country was on the cusp of something revolutionary and exciting, and it just needed a little more time to shake off the last vestiges of wartime doldrums.

Just then, Dankworth arrived in a patrol car. At least the bell wasn't ringing this time.

He got out and flashed his warrant card flamboyantly at Esme. "Detective Inspector Dankworth, Wokingham CID. And you are . . .?"

"Mrs Cripps. Esme Cripps."

"Right, Mrs Cripps. If we could go inside, you can make us a nice pot of tea and show me where he got in and what has been taken."

"Excuse me, sir, shouldn't we wait for Bennett to examine the scene before we go in?" I asked.

"No need," said Dankworth, taking out a packet of cigarettes and placing one in his mouth. "Bennett can dust the front door latch and the window sill whether we're in there or not. Oh, and can you keep the children occupied while I talk to Mrs Cripps? Lead the way, Esme."

And I watched as the four of them trooped through Esme Cripps's hallway, obliterating a perfect sandy footprint by scuffing it into the brown carpet. I stood on the doorstep, looking at its faint trace, fascinated by how easily a vital clue could just disappear. I opened my mouth to speak, then thought better of it: the damage had been done.

Bennett arrived shortly after.

Interview completed, statement taken and awkward conversation with two unforthcoming teenage boys attempted, Dankworth, Bennett and I finished up at Esme Cripps's. Dankworth's parting words to a crestfallen Esme were a lecture on the importance of keeping downstairs windows closed. I still had to go door to door, asking the neighbours if they had seen anything.

As Dankworth prepared to drive back to the station, he regaled me with his usual bleeding obvious. "What we have here is a classic opportunistic burglary, Crockford. The kitchen window was left open and the burglar thought he would chance his arm. Fingerprints look doubtful so he probably wore gloves. Just indistinct muddy footprints in the sink and on the kitchen floor as he climbed in, and some mud in the hall."

"Sir, forgive me if I'm speaking out of turn here," I said, reddening slightly at my own bravery, "but I think a decent damp footprint in the hall may have been trodden over and smudged when we came into the house. I do think we need to tread very carefully through crime scenes so as not to destroy evidence."

"If you saw a footprint, you should have pointed it out, shouldn't you, Crockford?" snapped Dankworth.

"You'd walked over it before I—"

"Bennett, what did you make of that muddy mark on the hall carpet?"

"Pretty indistinct, sir," replied Bennett. "If it was a footprint, it could be anywhere between a size seven and a size 11. I would have been able to measure it accurately if it hadn't been scuffed."

There was an awkward silence as Bennett looked at Dankworth and Dankworth looked at me.

"Any idea who the burglar could be, sir?" I asked, changing the subject.

"Hmm. Got a few ideas. The fair's in Wokingham and we usually get a – shall we say – advance party, checking the place out."

The funfair came to Wokingham's Carnival Field four times a year, with its thrilling octopus, headache-inducing waltzer, underwhelming haunted house, dodgems spewing showers of sparks and charming, tinkling Victorian carousel.

Rather than letting me, Pattie and Higgs simply patrol the funfair, Dankworth gave us a task: we were to question the funfair workers about whether any of their number had arrived a few days early, hinting that there had been some burglaries.

I felt deeply uncomfortable about these burglary inquiries. I'd come to the funfair myself as a child with my sisters and I knew the travelling fairground families. They were decent people, from generations of fairground owners. True, some terrifying scallywags sometimes hitched a ride to get away from certain areas, no questions asked, but those were unlikely to talk to the police, or tell the truth anyway, so what was there to gain?

Pattie, Higgs and I had split up. As I crossed the fair, breathing in its familiar smells of diesel fumes, trodden grass and frying onions, I saw Higgs in the distance talking animatedly to Gilderoy Lovell, the fairground manager.

Oh no, why did Higgs get to him first? I thought.

From his body language – feet wide apart, arms crossed in front of him, cigar clamped between his teeth – Lovell was on the defensive. Higgs flapped his hands about nervously. As I approached, I caught the conversation, mainly Lovell's side of it.

"So, sonny, you're suggesting that a load of us came up to Wokingham early to burgle our customers' houses?"

Gilderoy Lovell didn't defer to anyone, least of all a callow, wet-behind-the-ears PC who had clearly put his foot right in it. He had his own morals and ethics, forged from decades of travelling with his fairground and he didn't like Higgs's insinuation. He pushed his leather trilby to the back of his head and puffed furiously on the cigar that was on the verge of going out.

"No, that's not what I'm saying, Mr Lovell," flapped Higgs. "I'm just asking if you possibly knew who could have been in the area on the mornings of the burglaries?"

"How the bleedin' hell should I know who was in the area, when we weren't even here?"

"There's … there's no need to take that tone with me, Lovell. In fact, I've got a good mind to—"

"To do what, sunshine?" Lovell was pulling himself up to his full height of five feet six inches. Higgs was pulling out his pocketbook.

"Everything all right here, gentlemen?" I asked.

"Gwendoline! Or should I say WPC Crockford? How lovely to see you! How are you, gorgeous?" gushed Mr Lovell expansively, completely ignoring Higgs now.

"Hello, Gilderoy. I'm very well, thank you. I can't believe the holidays have come round again so fast," I said.

"And I can't believe that little girl with ribbons in her hair what threw up all over her sister on the waltzer is now a lady policeman! How's your dad? Still a special?"

"Yes, still a special. And still picking tomatoes from his special supply."

Mr Lovell roared with laughter. He had also been a receiver of Dad's sewage farm tomatoes.

I turned to Higgs. "PC Higgs, could you possibly go and have a scout around near the dodgems? A lady thinks she dropped her purse in the long grass and she's having problems finding it."

"But I . . ." said Higgs.

A hard stare from me had him obediently scurrying off to the dodgems.

"What's that dinlow[20] on about? What burglaries? Do you gavvers[21] think we're a bunch of robbers now?"

"No, the town's had a couple of break-ins recently. I think they're homegrown burglars, but our DI is always quick to blame the out-of-towners."

"Well, Miss Gwendoline, I can assure you I don't know nothin' about any burglaries, but I will keep my ear to the ground – just for you." Lovell winked.

"Thanks, Gilderoy. I know you don't stand for any nonsense. I reckon that concludes my investigations."

"Kushti," he replied, ambling off.

I stood for a while, surveying the thronging fairground, everyone having a lovely time. Mr Bischoff, the bank manager, uncharacteristically tie-less in an open-necked shirt, shared an enormous pink candy floss with Mrs Bischoff. A huge, bald-headed, tattooed man with rings in his ears lifted Millie Savin onto a prancing carousel horse. Doris one-handedly arranged her splinted legs on its dappled flanks, her other hand clinging onto ancient, blind Foxy's lead. Even Hilda Bloom had taken a break from probation duties and was

---

20 Romany for fool or stupid person.

21 Romany for police.

flinging her father around in a dodgem car. John Carroll and Roger Wickes hung around the base of the helter-skelter, no doubt hoping to see girls' knickers as their skirts blew up on the way down.

In a corner was a bell tent, the entrance hung with gaudy, sparkly material and little crystals threaded onto strings. I caught a heady waft of incense emanating from inside, reminiscent of tedious childhood church services.

The handwritten sign by the entrance read:

Madame Pasqualina Tarot Card Reader
Will Tell YOUR Fortune
1 shilling

Out of the tent emerged Pattie, her face red, doubled over with laughter, staggering towards me. She could barely speak through her mirth, tears streaming down her face.

"That was so rubbish!" she wheezed.

So infectious was Pattie's giggling, I was chuckling even before she started her story:

"So, I was walking past that tent and I heard this wobbly voice going, 'Come in, child, and you will know your fortune.' I thought, why not? 'Close the portal behind you,' the voice said, a ghostly finger pointing to a ribbon holding the tent flap open. I pulled the bow and the flap fell across the entrance, shutting out the daylight.

"Inside was this funny lady wearing a green-and-gold brocade dress, with frilly sleeves and a white lace veil thing over her head and shoulders, sitting at a scarlet-fringed table. A single candle burned in the centre. There was a glowing incense burner on the ground, fuming. I was worried it would topple over and set the whole bloody tent on fire.

"'Cross my palm with silver,' said Madame Pasqualina, holding out her hand.

"I took a shilling and made the sign of a cross on her open palm, then pressed it into her hand, which closed a bit *too* quickly around the coin.

"'Be seated,' she said, and I sat down opposite her.

"'What do you come here seeking?'

"Well, I didn't bloody know! 'When would I meet my true love,' I said, for want of anything better.

"'We call upon the Tarot to help you in your quest!' she wailed. 'Shuffle the cards to release their power.'

"She passed me the Tarot cards to shuffle and cut, then laid out 10 in a cross shape. Pretty bloody creepy pictures. They looked like medieval woodcuts, with a man hanging upside down by one foot and a skeleton riding a horse.

"Madame Pasqualina looked at them for a bit, then pulled a black shawl from the back of her chair and covered herself completely with it. She started rocking from side to side, her dress making rhythmic rustling sounds, then she made these strange cooing sounds that went on for a few minutes. I wondered what on earth she was doing, and honestly, Gwen, if you'd been in there with me, I'd have wet myself. I was about to ask her if she was all right, when she flicked back the shawl and cried, 'Cups! You have a predominance of cups!'

"'Well, I know I've got a decent collection of brassières,

love, but what's that got to do with anything?' I said. She went blathering on about the nine of cups, the six of cups, the seven of swords, the eight of wands, the knight of tentacles, or testicles or something else-icles … Then there was this loud bang from under the table as if someone hiding there popped a balloon. I said, 'What was that?' and she said, 'What was what, dear? Only you can hear the spirits knocking.' Honestly!

"But then, get this, she was waving a finger at me, and just when she was telling me I was going on a journey over water to be reunited with a true love, two things fell off her lap – a torch and a book called *Tarot Reading for Beginners*.'"

As we left the fair, we noticed Sabina Lovell, Gilderoy's wife, and their young son Noah creeping out of the back of the bell tent.

"Well, Madame Pasqualina, my arse," said Pattie.

CHAPTER 23

Gloria Gilmour, Hollywood starlet

One slow day, after the fair had left town, Pattie and I were on shift together. After typing reports, we tidied our office, then the front office; not as a favour to the untidy male officers we shared the station with, but to ourselves so we could actually find things.

I say "we" – but I had pulled all the box files down from the top shelf to brush the thick dust off, whereas Pattie had found a pile of *Picturegoer* magazines in a cupboard that needed archiving in date order, apparently. As I coughed and spluttered in a dust cloud, Pattie sat cooing over the glamorous film actresses on the covers.

"Ooh, that Grace Kelly – look at her in this off-the-shoulder gown! What I wouldn't give to wear something like that for an evening . . ."

A knock on the door and Sarge came into the back office with a piece of paper.

"Another burglary," he said, "but you're going to love this one, ladies . . ."

"Another one?" we exclaimed.

"Afraid so. Near Remenham, this time. The house, or should I say mansion, of – wait for it – Gloria Gilmour!"

"Gloria Gilmour? You're joking!" exclaimed Pattie.

"Blonde Bombshell" Gloria Gilmour, as I shall call her, was one of Berkshire's many local celebrities. Originally a theatre actress, she had appeared in several British film comedies, via some questionable "glamour" movies that she would come to wish she'd never been involved with.

More recently, she had starred in a couple of Hollywood B-movies that had paid for her house on the hill and she was often mistaken for Marilyn Monroe, with her huge blonde beehive, pouting lips, curvaceous figure and cheeky humour.

"Can you two do the initial visit? I'll let Dankworth know and he can follow on with Bennett?"

"Yeah – to tread all over the crime scene again," I murmured to Pattie. "Is there much of a mess?" I asked Sarge.

"Sounds as if an upstairs window was forced open to gain entry, so no broken glass, but there's money, jewellery, a valuable antique clock and a couple of fur coats missing."

"Wow, who has a *couple* of fur coats?" asked Pattie, wide-eyed and star-struck.

"A Hollywood actress, clearly," I said. "It'll be a chance to have a little peek into the life of the rich and famous. Let's go!"

"Eek! Do you think we'll meet her?" Pattie hopped up and down like a little girl, clasping her hands in front of her.

"Don't get your hopes up. Us mere mortals only usually get to meet the housekeeper," said Sarge.

We went out into the yard to collect a patrol car.

"You drive, Pattie, now that you've passed your test at last."

"Ooh, I don't know, Gwen, I'm all a-flutter with the anticipation of possibly meeting Gloria. I might forget what I'm doing."

"It's good practice. You only really start learning to drive once you've passed your test," I said, pressing the keys into her hand.

"Yeah, Simpson couldn't pass me fast enough once I'd had a go at him for shooting his mouth off to his mates about me. Good riddance. That Jones still gives me funny looks, though."

After a few gear crunches, Pattie and I took the A321 out of Wokingham towards Remenham. Gloria Gilmour's white bow-fronted Regency mansion on the hill was clearly visible from the road below, shining through the golden leaves in the pale autumn sunshine.

"I'd always wondered who lived up there," said Pattie.

The ornate wrought-iron gates at the bottom of the drive were open and we followed the gravel up the hill through what looked like acres of parkland, with colossal cedar trees and banks of rhododendrons on either side. We arrived at the house and parked next to a magnificent dove grey R-type Bentley.

"Burglars obviously didn't find the car keys," I said.

We jangled the doorbell and a frenzied yapping started up deep within the hallway. After a minute or so, we heard the shuffling sound of footsteps. A tall, pale, mousy woman wearing a housecoat and fluffy slippers opened the door. Three Pekingese dogs tumbled out, snuffling at our ankles, yapping madly.

"Trixie! Dixie! Pixie! Shut it, for Christ's sake!" yelled the woman. *The housekeeper,* we both thought.

"Good morning, madam," I said. "We've had a call about a burglary at this address? We're here to see Mrs Gloria Gilmour?"

"Is she here today?" butted in Pattie.

"Yeah, that's me. You better come in. Get in here, you lot," she shouted to the Pekingese posse and they eventually trotted back in, the last one stopping to cock his leg against the Bentley's wheel.

We looked at each other in surprise and with a single thought: *This woman looks nothing like the glamorous pictures of Gloria Gilmour we were used to seeing.* If you queued up behind this ordinary-looking lady at the butcher's, you'd be none the wiser who she was. Except she probably doesn't have to stand in a butcher's queue any more.

We stepped onto the black and white tiles of the cool hallway. I took out my pocketbook and prepared to ask the set burglary questions.

"So, Mrs Gilmour, are you quite certain that you have been broken into?"

"Well, I wouldn't have called you if I hadn't, would I?" she snapped.

"I know this is upsetting for you, Mrs Gilmour, but there are certain questions I do have to ask to ascertain the nature of the crime."

"Yeah, I'm sorry to be rude. Bit of a shock." Gloria reached for a packet of Balkan Sobranies on the polished walnut hall table, took out a cigarette and lit it with an enormous crystal lighter. She didn't offer us one.

"What, to your knowledge, has been stolen?"

"About £300 in cash from a jar on the landing table . . ." We struggled not to flinch. That was a huge amount of money to have lying around.

"My square-cut diamond earrings, necklace and bracelet were in my jewellery box on the dressing table – they're gone. They've taken my little ebony-and-gilt Tompion mantel clock from my bedroom, and when I checked the wardrobe, my mink and silver fox jackets have gone. They left the big mink. Perhaps they couldn't carry it."

The big mink. I could read the incredulity on Pattie's face.

"So, it sounds as if it's only property in the upstairs rooms that's been taken?" I continued.

"Yeah – the dogs were shut in the downstairs rooms while I was out – I guess the burglar didn't chance coming face to face with them, terrifying brutes that they are." Gloria managed a smile.

"Burglars don't like coming across dogs and they say it's the little ones they're most scared of," I said. "Where did they get in?"

"Bedroom window has been jemmied open. I forgot to lock it properly."

"Do you mind if we take a look? We'll be very careful not to touch anything."

We tiptoed along the edge of the stair carpet, up the sweeping cherrywood staircase and along the landing. The Oriental money jar with its lid off sat empty on the table. We followed Gloria into a vast bedroom with an unmade bed, clothes and underwear strewn everywhere, overflowing ashtrays and a selection of dirty coffee cups and lipstick-smeared wine glasses. Wardrobe doors hung open, couture gowns tumbling out of them. A Victorian plate camera stood on a tripod in the corner, its lens pointing towards the bed, and two blonde beehive wigs sat on stands on a mahogany chest of drawers. A cold draught blew in through an open sash window.

"Blimey, they've really made a mess of your room," said Pattie.

"Er, I'm afraid it was like this before it was broken into," said Gloria sheepishly. "My housekeeper's on holiday, see. Your sergeant on the telephone told me not to touch anything so I couldn't tidy up before you got here."

I picked my way to the open window and looked down. A thick lead drainpipe fixed to the wall with several substantial brackets ran down to the ground. *As good as a ladder for climbing up*, I thought.

"Certainly looks like they could have climbed up the drainpipe, forced the window and got in and out this way. Clues will dust for fingerprints and it looks like there may be some footprints on your rug. Are you sure there's nothing else missing?"

Gloria blushed furiously. "Funny thing – all my French letters have disappeared out of my bedside table drawer." I noted this down, blushing myself. Pattie was trying hard to keep a straight face. "I checked the other upstairs rooms, nothing else has gone that I can see. All the valuable stuff is – was – in my bedroom and downstairs, which wasn't touched. Thank God for the Pekes, really."

"So, your housekeeper is away?"

"Mrs Anderson. Yes."

"Would you know if there were any pedlars or fortune-tellers[22] doing the rounds? They're sometimes casing a joint?"

"I don't know. Fair's gone, hasn't it?"

"Any tradesmen?"

"Apart from the gardener? He's been here donkey's years and he's 65, so I don't see him shinnying up no drainpipes. He wouldn't, anyhows. And he doesn't come much in October, apart from to sweep the leaves." Gloria rubbed her chin. "Oh wait. I did mention to Mrs Anderson that some gutters needed attention. She said she would get some local handyman to do it while I was in Los Angeles. Not sure if she organised it or not."

Pattie and I exchanged glances.

"Can you get hold of Mrs Anderson to ask?"

"Not really, she's on her holidays in Skeggie. She did leave me a note of where she would be staying but Lord knows where I put the piece of paper." Gloria surveyed the wreckage of her bedroom.

"How would we know if the work has been done?"

"Well, if it rains and the guttering on the east wing doesn't leak, it's been mended. Been dreadful the whole summer."

"I guess we'll need to wait for some rain, unless you can get hold of Mrs Anderson," I said.

At that moment, the doorbell jangled. Trixie, Dixie and Pixie kicked off again, and the three of us tiptoed gingerly down the stairs. Gloria opened the door to DI Dankworth and Bennett.

---

22 We had to ask this question as part of burglary investigations.

Dankworth came in, stepping over the yapping Pekingeses, and made the same mistake Pattie and I had.

"Oh, you look very different in real life from how you do in the movies," he said, barely keeping the disappointment out of his voice. Pattie and I rolled our eyes at each other.

"Make-up, darling," purred Gloria, putting on her trademark husky voice. Magically, she became the starlet we all recognised. "Not forgetting great corsetry and a good dresser," she added and we laughed. Clearly an appreciative man in the house cheered Gloria up a bit.

I ran through everything I'd noted down with Dankworth and he listened as attentively as he could with a Hollywood starlet nearby. When he and Bennett went upstairs to look at the entry point, I was quietly delighted that Dankworth tiptoed along the edge of the carpet rather than dashing upstairs like a Home Counties Sam Spade.

Leaving CID to it, we said goodbye to Gloria and Pattie drove us back to the station to get started on the burglary report.

"That gorgeous house! But I'm gobsmacked at how ordinary she seemed . . ." said Pattie, looking at me and failing to observe a Halt sign.

"Pattie, you've just—"

"Thing is, though, it must be exhausting getting dolled up like she is in the posters all the time," she continued. "Swanning round the house in a dressing gown must be so liberating."

Pattie swung into the station yard, narrowly missing the parked pursuit car.

"Are you thinking what I'm thinking about who-dunnit?" I asked when I'd finished wincing.

"Rodney Carroll?"

"Yes, but at this stage we have no evidence it's him."

"Wonder if he's been doing the other burglaries too?"

"Wouldn't surprise me."

"How did you get on with our very own Marilyn Monroe?" asked Sarge eagerly as we came back into the station.

"How the other half live!" gushed Pattie. "Massive house, but you should have seen the state of her bedroom – worse than mine! Beautiful Bentley in the drive, antiques, cocktail dresses and furs all over the place. Gloria herself looked completely different without the make-up and beautiful gowns, quite plain, actually, and she was a bit grumpy. And do you want to know a secret?"

"Go on."

"Her blonde beehive hairdo isn't real – it's a wig! We saw two blonde wigs in the bedroom. Her real hair is even mousier than Gwen's here."

"Thanks for that," I said.

"Well, who'd have guessed?" Sarge chuckled. "Any clues about the burglars?"

"We're not sure yet," I said, "as Gloria hasn't been able to get in touch with her housekeeper who's on holiday, but I have an inkling who we should be looking closely at. A certain local handyman?"

"Good luck pinning anything on that slippery bugger," said Sarge. "But he'll get his comeuppance for something, one day, mark my words."

When Dankworth and Bennett returned, we had a case conference about Gloria's burglary in the back office.

"Marvellous lady, that Gloria Gilmour," enthused Dankworth, "although until she put on that trademark sexy voice, she could have been anyone in the bus queue."

"It's certainly interesting to see the real person behind the Hollywood glamour," I said. "How you don't notice someone until they put a big blonde wig on."

"Yeah – funny that. Anyway, we've dusted and photographed fingerprints, which we'll get checked against Mrs Gilmour's, her husband's and her housekeeper's elimination prints. If he's any sort of decent burglar, he will have worn gloves. Footprints too indistinct once again to get a decent measurement. All we've really got to go on is the testimony of the housekeeper, letting us know if she got a local handyman to come round or not, and who that was."

"Are we thinking along the lines of Rodney Carroll, sir?" I asked.

"Well, he's the obvious local handyman, isn't he? His Bernie has got form for sticking her fingers in the till at WHSmith. But until we've got some hard evidence it's even him, we can't go crashing in there, searching their home."

The next morning, Dankworth received a telephone call from Gloria Gilmour.

"Inspector," she'd purred. "I managed to contact Mrs Anderson in her Skegness B&B and she confirmed that it was indeed Mr Carroll she had used to fix the guttering above the East Wing where my bedroom is and she paid him five pounds for the job."

"I think we need to go round and have a chat with Carroll," said Dankworth, "if only on the pretext of asking him if he saw someone dodgy hanging around the house when he was working there. And to gauge his reaction to our question, of course. Crockford, if you can come with me as I expect there to be children on the premises."

Dankworth and I drove in an unmarked police car into the woods and down the overgrown track towards the Carrolls's caravan. The leaves had completely turned shades of orange, red and yellow, and for a brief time, it almost looked to be quite an attractive place to live. The caravan itself still looked tatty and mouldy.

"Is this it?" asked Dankworth, turning up his nose. "Where all the Carrolls live?"

There was no sign of anyone in – no washing on the line, no distinctive smell of the paraffin heater being on, no windows open to let out fumes. Dankworth rapped on the door. Usually there would be scuffling before the door opened if someone was in, but there was silence. There really was nobody home.

Dankworth rattled the door handle while I inched through the nettles and brambles to get behind the caravan to the rear window. I spotted a small gap where the thick yellowed lace curtain didn't quite cover all the windowpane and stood on tiptoe to peer in. I could see the small table with its banquette, and some pillows and blankets. Above the banquette was a shelf with some tatty dolls made from clothes pegs, a piggy bank, some children's comics and a particularly ornate, shiny black and gold clock on it that seemed utterly out of place among the other grimy objects.

"Sir! Sir! Can you come round here?" I called to Dankworth.

Dankworth picked through the nettles and brambles, cursing as the thorns tore at his trouser legs.

"What is it?"

"Look through here."

Dankworth stood on tiptoe to squint through the window, looking around. Being taller than me, he could see more. "You mean the clock? That looks like Mrs Gilmour's Tompion."

"That's what I thought, sir. It doesn't really fit into these surroundings, does it?"

"That's several hundred pounds worth of antique mantel clock right there, if I'm not mistaken. Bingo! I think we've got enough evidence to search this caravan when Carroll's back. If he's uncooperative, we can approach the magistrate for a search warrant to see what else he's got inside here."

On our way back to the car, Dankworth shook the caravan door handle viciously, hoping it would just come open. It didn't.

"I'll hide myself here on observation and wait for Carroll himself to come home," said Dankworth. "I don't want to give him a chance to fence the stolen property. Damn radio isn't working in my car. You go back to the station and get a team together in the van and meet me back here."

My blood was up. I was so excited about getting a team together for a search and possible arrest that I spun the police car wheels on the gravel in my haste to get back to the station.

CHAPTER 24

Catching a thief

I flung the unmarked CID car into the station yard – narrowly missing the pursuit car myself – squeezed in next to the Black Maria van, cut the engine and ran into the station.

"Whoah, where's the fire, WPC Crockford?" said Sarge.

"Sarge! We think we've found stolen property at the Carrolls's caravan. Dankworth's waiting there for Carroll to come home. We'll need backup to make an arrest. Who's around?"

Sarge didn't even need to ask. Bob and Higgs had heard me rush in and appeared from the back office.

"Let's go!" said Bob. "Dankworth will search the caravan. I'll make an arrest if necessary. WPC Crockford, you deal with the children, and Higgsy, you can provide some extra brawn."

He certainly won't be providing extra brain, I thought.

"Are there enough of us to do this, sir?" I asked.

"Under normal circumstances we'd have Henry Falconer as well, but we don't," said Bob, "and Sergeant Robertshaw's tied up at another station today with a woman prisoner."

Sarge smiled. "I'm sure our A-team will be able to cope."

"I'll take the pursuit car," said Bob. "WPC Crockford, you know the way – can you follow behind in the van with Higgs?"

Sarge tossed the van keys to me. Higgs went to grab them at the same time and we had a microscuffle over ownership of the keys, which I won.

"I should be driving the van," moaned Higgs as we hurried into the station yard. "I bet you haven't even driven it before."

"Of course I have, loads of times," I fibbed.

Bob had already turned the pursuit car round and was waiting for us by the yard entrance as we climbed into the van. I turned on the ignition, pressed down the clutch, engaged first gear ... and shot backwards. I stamped on the brake before we hit the wall behind.

"What the hell?" cried Higgs.

I looked at the gearstick. *Bugger, it's three gears, not four.* R for reverse was forwards, where I expected first gear to be, although the other gears made some sense. As long as we didn't have to stop and start too much, and I remembered to pull the gearstick back into first to move off, we would be all right.

"And you say you've driven this before?" Higgs sneered. "Women drivers, I don't know . . ."

I ignored him.

Our convoy crept along the track towards the caravan. We could see Dankworth ahead of us, hiding behind a beech tree, gesturing at us to pull into some thicket down from the caravan and wait. After some minutes, in the distance, I saw the caravan door open and Charlie Carroll come out. Perhaps the children had returned home before their father, oblivious to Dankworth hiding in the copse opposite.

Then everything happened quickly. Rodney Carroll, cycling back home along the track, came across our two black vehicles, threw down his bicycle and immediately legged it into the woods before we could even get out of the van. Charlie Carroll saw his father running and without hesitation ran in the opposite direction. Bob ran after Carroll. Higgs dithered about, not knowing whether to join Bob or head off after Charlie. He chose Charlie, his deliberation giving the lad a head start.

I caught up with Dankworth by the caravan door.

"Now you're here, we can speak to the kids," he said. "Clearly their father's got a guilty conscience."

He flung open the caravan door and we came face to face with Dora on the double bed, wrapped in a silver fox fur jacket. She screamed, dropped the jacket and, like a circus acrobat, threw herself out of the open side window and ran after her father.

Good God, these Ferals are lithe, I thought.

Chasing after Dora, the youngest of the children, was my priority. The wood was hard to run through, deep with fallen autumn leaves and a summer's worth of bramble overgrowth; I kept tripping and stumbling. *I seem to spend my life in these bloody woods*, I said to myself. The Carrolls had the advantage over us, living here and knowing every inch of the tracks, the copses, the ways out. After a while, I could hear Bob's distant voice shouting at Carroll to stop and the screams of a small girl.

I followed the sounds to the edge of the wood and stopped to catch my breath. The run had left me lightheaded and out of puff. Although I was light for my height, I did no physical exercise apart from walking my beats – it was unheard of for women to go out running – and I felt my lack of fitness. As I caught my breath, I saw to my dismay that I had come out alongside a wide river, near its weir pool. Weirs and their rushing, tumbling water were the stuff of my nightmares. I'd heard tales of people being sucked under them and drowned.

Rodney Carroll stood in the middle of the concrete weir, the rushing water flowing either side of his feet, with Dora in his arms. Higgs was on the opposite bank: he had clearly lost Charlie and had run across the footbridge to the other side, cutting off Carroll's escape route. Carroll was caught like the proverbial deer in the headlights, hesitating from left to right, clearly weighing up which officer – Higgs to the right of him, me to the left – he had more chance of escaping from. Dora struggled in his arms, screaming over the rushing water.

I have no idea to this day how I found the courage to do it, but I stepped onto the weir and, holding out my arms, shouted, "Police! Rodney Carroll, give me the little girl NOW!"

Carroll, sensing a weakness and seizing his chance, rushed at me. Swinging Dora's legs as a weapon, he knocked me off the concrete into the churning waters of the weir pool as he escaped back to the wooded side.

I fell, knocking my back on the sharp edge as I went in. Winded, and shocked by the cold water, my bubbling vision became beige and blurry, and I could hear nothing but a muffled distant roaring as rushing brown water poured on top of me and closed above my head. I was back in Martin's Pool, aged eight, drowning as holidaymakers played around me.

I felt myself being tumbled over and over and over, gulping in water. Eventually, I couldn't even summon up the strength to gasp as my face briefly surfaced, before being tumbled back round again. I felt remarkably calm and my thoughts were coherent: *I can't swim. I'm going to drown. I should never have avoided swimming lessons. This is what dying feels like. It's not so bad. Dad, Barbara, Ron and Jean, I love you and I'm sorry to leave you. Henry, it was never to be, what a shame . . .*

Beatific Jesus from my bedroom picture beckoned me to enter His world of tropical birds and I felt a sensation like a train rushing towards me. Then everything went black.

The next thing I remember was taking a monumental, shuddering gasp that pulled me upright and set off a series of body-racking coughs. I found myself on a muddy riverbank and everything around was hyperbright. *Are there muddy riverbanks in heaven?* I thought. A wingless angel who looked remarkably like Bob Hartwell crouched over me, a worried frown on his face.

"Oh, thank God for that," he said. "You've come round. I was worried I was going to have to give you mouth to mouth."

"What's happened?" I whispered.

"We got the bastard, but you fell in, that's what," said Bob. "Resisting arrest, assaulting a police officer and a minor. And that's just this morning. He's over there."

I looked round, painfully. Rodney Carroll was lying face down on the grass, his hands cuffed behind him. Higgs, his trousers sopping wet, sat astride his legs. Beside him, Dora rocked backwards and forwards in a foetal position. *Poor little mite to witness all this*, I thought. Carroll seemed to have a swollen eye and a split lip.

"He happened to bang his face on my boot," said Bob. "Oh dear, too bad, never mind."

"How did I get out of the river?" I murmured.

"Higgsy here saw you go in," said Bob. "I'd grabbed Carroll and got the cuffs on him first, so he could jump down into the weir and pull you out."

"It's only three feet deep, called Higgs. "But once you fall and get caught in the weir's tumbling motion it's impossible to stand up, which is why you couldn't. I grabbed your collar and dragged you to the bank, then pulled you out."

Three feet deep. Well, this is embarrassing, I thought.

"Thank you so much, PC Higgs. I thought I was drowning."

Feeling suddenly queasy, I got onto my knees and threw up brown river water, fragments of rotten leaves and a water snail. Bob looked away. He wasn't good with vomit.

"Are you OK? Ready to walk this villain back to the van?"

"I think so, yes," I said, getting unsteadily to my feet and wiping strings of mucus from my nose. I realised

I had lost a shoe in the river and would have to limp through the brambly woods, tearing my foot to pieces. I noticed Dora wasn't wearing any shoes at all.

"We've only got one shoe between us, haven't we? Silly us!" I said to Dora, holding out my hand to her. "Can you show me where the soft bits of the woods are to walk on?"

She took my hand without hesitation and uncurled out of her foetal position.

"Leave my fuckin' daughter alone," growled Carroll, thickly.

"Language in front of a lady and a minor, Carroll," said Bob, digging him in the ribs with the toe of his boot, before dragging him to his feet.

Our cold, wet, bruised crew somehow managed to limp back through the woods to the police van, escorting Carroll: Higgs on one side holding him firmly by his right arm, and Bob holding his left, supporting me on his free arm. In turn, I held Dora's hand. We must have looked like the ragged survivors of an endurance ring-a-ring o' roses game.

Bernie Carroll had arrived back from the stables and sat passively on the caravan step with a scared-looking Charlie, who clearly hadn't fancied the life of a runaway and had returned to face the music. Carroll gazed pathetically at them as we frogmarched him past. Charlie shouted "Dad!" and started crying. Bernie looked at her father, her face unreadable, emotionless, and said nothing. Dora ran over to her sister and flung herself into her arms.

"You got him! Jolly well done!" called Dankworth to our bedraggled group as Bob shoved Carroll roughly into the back of the van and Higgs clambered in after him. Dankworth followed us, carrying several evidence bags full of Gloria's lovely things that Carroll had brought home.

"What happened to you, Higgs and Crockford? Fall in a ditch?"

I was shivering now. Bob took his police cape out of the pursuit car and put it round my shoulders as he explained to Dankworth what had happened.

"Well done, Higgs, for your quick thinking and rescuing Crockford. Well done, Hartwell, for taking the bastard down, and well done, Crockford, for having a go. You probably could have got yourself out of the water anyway – you *can* swim, can't you?"

I didn't say anything. I knew that without Higgs I would have been a goner, even in three feet of water. He had probably saved my life. Perhaps that made him slightly less of an idiot.

"Now, we've somehow got to sort this mess out," Dankworth continued. "Get the detainee and the recovered property back to the station, get our fellow officer checked over and organise some care for these kids. How are we going to do it? We can't leave Crockford here with the kids in her state, and I don't feel we can drag them out just now and put them in the van with their father – too distressing."

Bob Hartwell raised his eyebrows. "Sounds like that puzzle – getting the fox, the chicken and the bag of corn across the river in one boat," he said.

I got halfway through trying to say, "We need to get a warrant from the magistrate before we can enter and remove the children," before throwing up again, and I became the priority instead.

"It's OK, mister," piped up Bernie Carroll. "You don't need to drag us nowhere. I'm used to looking after everyone when Dad's not here. I do it all the time. We ain't going nowhere. We're all going to live here now. Together.' Bernie looked happier than I had ever seen her.

"I want my dolly and my bed," grizzled Dora, snuggling into Bernie's shoulder.

"And I want my museum," added Charlie. "I hope the prat in a hat hasn't taken it." Bernie shushed him.

It was often the case with deprived, neglected and abused children that no matter how bad and squalid their home was, the thought of going to another one was even worse and they would do anything they could to stay in it. I'd had a conversation with Hilda Bloom about the phenomenon.

"Home Sweet Home. Its concept is a powerful thing for children," Hilda had said, "and the worse home is, often the more they'll resist leaving it."

I would come across this time and time again in child care or protection cases.

"There's a fourth Carroll, isn't there?" I said, wiping my mouth on my sleeve. "John?"

"He could be anywhere," said Bernie, "but he usually comes back when he's hungry. I'll make sure he don't do nothing stupid like a runner."

"So let's get going. First stop Wokingham Hospital, I think," said Dankworth. He jabbed a finger at the Carroll children. "You lot, stay here."

Bernie, Charlie and Dora nodded.

I took Dankworth aside and spoke to him quietly. "I think the children are all right to stay here for a while today, but not too long, and they certainly can't carry on living here like Bernie thinks they can. I'll speak to Hilda Bloom when I get back."

Bernie was coming to the end of her two years' probation with Hilda, who was still responsible for her.

"You're going straight into the Accident Unit for a check-up, Crockford."

Because of my history with the Carroll children, I was determined to get back and support them through whatever decision was deemed best for them. I was touched today that Dora had taken my outstretched hand and even Bernie seemed to have forgiven me for the WHSmith episode. I didn't want to be in Wokingham Hospital for too long.

As it turned out, I wasn't. Once I'd warmed up with a bath and cup of hot sweet tea, I began to feel a lot better, especially when Suzette appeared on her afternoon shift with my spare dry uniform and shoes.

"That lovely desk sergeant of yours telephoned Mrs Cunningham's, saying you'd fallen in the river," she said, beaming. "I hear you are quite the heroine, trying to rescue that little girl from being dangled over the weir. You go, girl! Proud of you."

"I wasn't a very good one, Suz, falling in and needing rescuing myself," I said.

"Everybody's fine, and that's what matters," she said, squeezing my arm.

301

Suzette stayed with me while the doctor examined the purple bruise across my back where I'd hit the concrete weir on the way down.

"There's nothing broken, but you're going to ache a bit in the morning," he said. He jabbed a couple of injections into my arm. "With any luck these should stop you being sick from ingesting the water. Filthy river, that one."

Suzette laughed. "If you were, it wouldn't be the first time I've cleared up your vomit."

"And I wouldn't be able to blame you for it this time, Suz," I replied.

I limped back into the station to an unexpected round of applause.

"We didn't expect you back quite so soon," said Bob.

"All I've really injured is my dignity and I can live with that," I replied to laughter.

"I'm afraid your day's not over yet," said Bob. "Hilda Bloom has approached the magistrate for a warrant for the removal of the Carroll children. Because Pattie is on annual leave and Miss Robertshaw is busy in Crowthorne, she's put your name on it as you're the only available woman officer."

In the CID office, Dankworth had laid out the items retrieved from the caravan: Finch's butcher's knives, Esme Cripps's empty purse and her engagement ring, Gloria Gilmour's Tompion clock, her mink and silver fox jackets that Bernie and Dora had obviously been sleeping under and her diamond jewellery. There were also several French letters and three tattered editions of *Frolic* magazine. There was no sign of the legs of lamb or £300 – Carroll could have hidden that anywhere.

"Caught the bugger red-handed! Well done," said The EF, emerging from his office to admire the retrieved haul. "He's going to go down for a five-stretch at least. I'd put him on an attempted murder charge too if I had my way, trying to drown my WPC like that."

CHAPTER 25

Care or protection

In the 1950s, a WPC's dealings with children and young people were more about advice and prevention than resorting to law enforcement. Particularly in cities, women police would watch out for and befriend runaways, neglected children and "girls in moral danger",[23] referring them to organisations that could help, rather than criminalising them.

If we had stuck to the letter of the law, we could have arrested members of the Ferals many times for criminal damage and various public nuisances, but we didn't. Sleepy Wokingham had few runaways, but we did have, I realise now, substantial child neglect and abuse. And with Arborfield garrison on our doorstep, we had our fair share of underage girls, plastered with their mums' make-up to make themselves look older, chatting up the squaddies and putting themselves in "moral danger". We would regularly shoo tutting, tottering-on-high-heels girls away from the garrison gates and back home.

Before that makes us sound as if we encroached into welfare or social work, we were careful to keep

---

23 This usually meant underage sex.

our distinct police identity – only we had powers of arrest and authority to remove child victims to a place of safety. Our sacred text, as I have mentioned before, was the Children and Young Persons Act, which laid out legislation covering child cruelty, child sexual exploitation, begging, alcohol and tobacco, and safety issues. It had raised the minimum age for the death penalty to 18 and criminal responsibility to eight. We relied on the Act to decide if children were being treated badly enough to need "care or protection" by authorities other than their parents or guardians.

When I'd finished in the CID room, my next stop was Hilda Bloom in the probation office to fill her in on the day's developments.

"Before we start, how are you, Gwen?" she said. "You were incredibly brave tackling Carroll – he's a lumpen monster at the best of times."

"I'm all right, thanks, Hilda. Nice to be in a dry uniform. A wet one's dreadfully itchy."

"I'll bet! I have a warrant to remove the Carroll children from home," she said, handing me an envelope. "That's the easy bit. The hard bit is finding a place that can take them together."

Hilda busied herself on the telephone, making enquiries. I sat on a chair in the corner of her office and closed my eyes. I may have drifted off, as before I knew it, she was making her last call.

"I really hoped it wouldn't come to this," said Hilda, cupping her hand over the receiver while she was waiting to be connected to the Children's Department. "I've had my doubts all along that a girl of Bernie's age could look after her siblings, keep house and go out to work, although with Carroll being around in a nominal father role we couldn't remove them."

"We can't leave them overnight," I said.

"No, we can't. It's unlikely Carroll will get bail, and even if he did, he's not demonstrated he's a fit parent. I've been monitoring Bernie for a while and I'm not sure she's particularly well. She's been looking pale and exhausted lately, and I feel that she's keeping something back when she talks to me. Problem is, I don't have a foster or care home that can take four of them in together right now. I've got one place in a probation hostel for Bernie; Dora and Charlie can go to one foster placement and there's a council home in Maidenhead with one place that will take John. I will have to split them up and I know they will hate that."

"We've got no choice but to remove them though, have we?" I asked.

"No. Shall we get it over with? Are you up to another trip to the woods? I promise you won't have to go anywhere near that river again. I'll need you, and probably three other officers, ideally ones who aren't too heavy-handed, to help remove them."

An hour later, Hilda arrived in her car at the caravan, at the same time as two police cars with me and three PCs I didn't know that well – Jones, Webb and Sansom. With the warrant in my hand, and Hilda beside me, I knocked on the caravan door. Bernie opened it, with Dora peering round her legs.

"What's them lot doing here?" Bernie asked, nodding towards our police presence.

"Well, we can't leave you all alone in the middle of the woods when your dad's at the police station, can we?" I said.

I hadn't been in a fit state to notice the condition of the children when we arrested Carroll. Hilda gave me a grimace that told me she was concerned. Bernie looked hollow-cheeked and shabby in a loose, sack-like, manure-stained smock over a pair of boy's ripped moleskin trousers. Dora's unbrushed hair stuck out in clumps, still full of nits, with large, obviously picked scabs on her scalp, and she had an oddly septic smell about her.

"Can I have a look at your hair, my love?" asked Hilda, as she checked Dora's head warily. She winced. "Not quite Paddington levels," she murmured to me, "but she'll need some medical attention."

Charlie and John, somewhat lean and grubby, looked in reasonably good health, although Charlie was scratching his head. He wore his trademark shirt and short trousers, his leather satchel slung firmly across his body. John, more subdued than usual, and chewing gum, wore typical jumble sale Teddy boy attire: a long, oversized jacket with velvet lapels, stripy tie and white shirt, holey knitted waistcoat and pleated black wool trousers. Brylcreem barely tamed his wild, wiry hair, which stuck up in spikes.

"When's Dad coming back?" asked Charlie.

"You're going to have to come with us, my darlings," said Hilda. "Your dad isn't going to be back for a while and we've got some lovely people who are going to look after you. Can you get your things together?"

"You ain't taking us away, are you?" asked Bernie.

"Yes, I'm afraid we are. We have a piece of paper giving us permission. We can gather up your other things and bring them along later."

"I ain't leaving my museum!" Charlie leapt towards the eclectic collection of natural and man-made artifacts lining the windowsill and scraped them into a shoe box, which he slammed shut and clung to as if his life depended on it.

"My dolly!" Dora pulled her doll off the bed.

"Have you two got anything you particularly want to take?" Hilda asked.

John and Bernie shrugged.

"We are going together, though, ain't we?" asked Bernie.

"That's the plan to get you all together eventually," replied Hilda. 'Although you'll have to bear with us for a week or so while we find somewhere with spaces. Bernie, there's a safe hostel for you where you can get some rest; John, one of our homes in Maidenhead will look after you, and Dora and Charlie, we've got a lovely foster family in Wokingham who'll look after you together."

"You can't split us up, you can't!" shrieked Bernie, rooted to the spot in fury.

"I don't wanna be away from my sister!" cried Dora.

"And I ain't going in no home!" shouted John.

Then our worst nightmare happened. John leaped up and sprinted towards the woods, followed by PC Jones, who rugby-tackled him to the ground. Bernie seized Dora and tried to scramble back into the caravan to lock them both in. PC Webb roughly grabbed Bernie, and

Sansom seized Dora: there was an almighty screaming tussle as they separated the two girls. Bernie's face was uncharacteristically red with fury as Webb restrained her, and Dora scratched, bit and shed lice like a wild animal as Sansom carried her, struggling yet clinging to her doll, to the police car.

"Bleedin' wildcat, this one," he muttered, stuffing her into the back seat, leaving me to get in beside her and try to calm her down. She pushed herself as far away from me as possible against the door, sobbing. *There must be a better way of doing this.*

Charlie stood wordlessly in shock, clinging to his shoe box, looking from side to side, wide-eyed like a terrified rabbit, trying to take in what was going on around him. Hilda gently shepherded him into the car beside me and Dora, who had curled into a ball around her doll, her head on her knees.

Bernie, slightly more composed now, having been shoved into the back of the second police car, sat glowering and breathing hard, gnawing at her thumbnail. As PC Jones manhandled John past Hilda to join Bernie in the back seat, the boy's dark eyes glowed with hatred and he spat at her, saliva hitting Hilda full in the face. She took a step back, pulled out a lace-edged handkerchief from her coat pocket and wiped the spittle from her face.

"You absolute little shit," muttered PC Jones at John, crushing into the back seat of the police car with him and Bernie. "Just for that, I'm sitting in with you. Are you all right, miss?" he called.

"I'm fine, thanks. Par for the course in my job, I'm afraid," Hilda said. "I'm coming with you so we have a

WPC and a female probation officer with the children in each car. Can we pick up my car later? We have to come back to collect the rest of the youngsters' things anyway."

Hilda closed the caravan door, checked she'd locked her car and slipped into the front seat next to PC Sansom, to accompany John and Bernie back to Wokingham station and then to their temporary homes. The second police car with me, PC Webb, Charlie and Dora followed behind.

The next morning, the telephone rang.

"Gwen, it's Hilda. The Carroll children are in their homes. Would you be kind enough to take me to collect my car and retrieve their belongings from the caravan?"

Hilda and I arrived at the caravan, opened the door and looked around its tatty interior.

"What on earth can we take from here that's going to be any comfort for those poor children?" I asked.

"They took what was important to them earlier," replied Hilda. "Dora has her dolly and Charlie has his box of weird stuff. I hope he hasn't got a dead rat in it. Bernie and John didn't want anything, but we ought to find them something."

I sighed. "I don't think these youngsters have had the best start in life, have they, Hilda? I really hope getting them away from Carroll will give them new beginnings."

Hilda pulled a couple of damp, tattered *Dandy* comics off the shelf and picked up the piggy bank. She shook it. It didn't rattle. The clothes peg toys, made without glue, fell apart in her hands and reduced to their component parts – just wooden pegs with sad faces pencilled on them and a pile of wool and fabric scraps.

We looked at the small, sorry pile of playthings from a home of four children.

"I doubt the foster homes will entertain these grimy items for long, before they put them in the dustbin," she said, her eyes filling with tears. She sat down wearily at the caravan table and took her glasses off.

"You've been working all night on the Carroll case, haven't you, Hilda? Are you all right?" I asked.

"Ach, Gwen, I have. For me, this is so, so personal. It reminds me of the morning when Mutti, Vati and I left our beautiful home in Berlin for an uncertain journey to England. I had to choose two toys only to take with me in my little suitcase and leave the rest behind. I had a treasured collection of model farm animals, bought with pocket money, and received as presents. I sobbed my heart out as I chose the kind-eyed bull with his nose ring and lawyer's wig hair, and the shire horse with her huge, fringed feet, abandoning the geese, the sheepdog, the farm cat, the cows and the goats."

Hilda, you're about to make me sob my heart out too, I thought.

She continued, "But I like to believe that somewhere on the Russian steppes, a little girl like me played with my toy farm animals that her papa had found in Berlin and brought home after the war."

I was too choked up to say anything. Then, in true Hilda style, and with her German accent getting stronger, she eloquently turned her creeping melancholy into a more present, righteous anger:

"*Mein Gott*. I really struggle with these sorts of cases, Gwen! What have two world wars and Attlee's social revolution really achieved? They haven't stopped a conniving, self-centred layabout like Carroll, with no appreciation of how precious family is, driving a horse and carriage over the childhoods of his children. No matter how much social science and psychology we deploy, how much goodwill we have, all we can ever do in cases like these is pick up the pieces."

If we'd have been in the canteen on a happier day, I would have challenged Hilda. I saw lots of good things happening as a result of the social revolution, but now was not the time for debate.

She sniffed deeply to pull herself back together. "Let's get these things packed up and out of this cursed place," she said, opening a brown paper carrier bag and putting the meagre items in it.

"You all right driving back, Hilda?" I asked. "You haven't had any sleep."

"Of course I am. I can't leave my car here again, I need it later. But I *am* going to have a stiff gin and tonic or two and a nap when I get home."

"If I see your car out and about, I'll turn a blind eye," I replied.

Hilda laughed, for the first time in days.

It had been an emotional week. After a couple of days off, most of which I spent sleeping, I went through the back office and my heart did a little skip as I saw a familiar face at a previously long-empty desk.

"Hello, Henry, you're back!"

"Hello, Gwen, thought I'd sneak in with as little ceremony as possible."

Henry had been invalided off work for a full year after his accident, then seconded to recuperative desk duties at the new Berkshire County Police headquarters in Sulhamstead.

"Bet you feel you're back to slumming it here after being in the swish new HQ?" I joked, "and you're using just a walking stick?"

"Yes – look at this," he said.

Henry pulled up his uniform trouser leg to reveal a shoe with a spring on the front attached to a brace round his lower calf.

"It picks my foot up for me. I still have to do strengthening exercises every day, but at least I can come into work without dragging it around like Quasimodo."

"You won't be chasing criminals for a while."

"It's not certain whether I'll ever be able to chase criminals again, but I'll have a bloody good try."

"It's nice to have you back, Henry," I said.

And it was.

A couple of weeks later, the women's office phone rang. I picked it up.

"Hello, Gwen, Hilda Bloom here. We've got a situation with one of the Carroll children. Perhaps two, if my instincts are right. I'll need a female officer as I think it's a police matter now."

"Can you tell me what it's about on the telephone?"

I heard Hilda take a deep breath.

"Bernie Carroll's pregnant. The hostel matron spotted the signs immediately and alerted us."

I was silent for a moment. *Oh, Bernie. What more could go wrong for that poor girl?*

"OK. Do you have any idea who the father is, Hilda?"

"I wondered if it might have been one of the young grooms from the stables having a tumble in the hay, but she's absolutely tight-lipped about who the father is. Won't say a word."

"Of course, it's a police matter as she's below the age of consent," I said. "Although I'm not sure she'll open up to me any more than she will to you. She doesn't really trust the police."

"It's not actually Bernie I need you to talk to. It's the little girl, Dora. Mrs Chalmers, her foster mother, noticed that she's displaying what we call 'sexualised behaviour' to her teenage son and her husband, although he didn't see – taking off her knickers and lifting her skirt to them, and gyrating in a suggestive way."

"Oh, my goodness," I said. "She did that to me and Sergeant Hartwell when we first went to the Carrolls' caravan the day Straffen got out. I had no idea what she was doing – I thought she was just being mischievous and showing off. Carroll was furious and dragged her back inside."

"That's very interesting," said Hilda. "You see, we observe this typical sexualised behaviour in incest cases and systematic indecency with children. The children want attention from adults and they've learned that the quickest way to get it from these wicked people is to expose themselves. They carry on doing it even when they're in a place of safety. Learned behaviour."

"Oh, dear God. I had no idea Dora's behaviour stemmed from that kind of experience. So, are we thinking that Rodney Carroll may be committing incest with his children?"

"It's a distinct possibility and my instincts are saying he is," replied Hilda. "And in these cases, I don't wish to shock you, but we need to know whether he's interfering with the boys as well as the girls."

I took a moment to absorb this information. "We need strong evidence it's him, Hilda. It's a serious accusation to make, so we need to make sure we've got a watertight case. So what are we going to do?"

"I need you to use all your gentle touch skills and interview Dora and Charlie Carroll," said Hilda. "See if you can get them to tell you about what's been going on behind that caravan door."

"Goodness, this goes beyond most of my training. I don't think we've got official procedures in place on how to do this properly, without traumatising the kids. Us policewomen are thrown in at the deep end and expected to deal with women and children, but we really haven't been around and doing the job for long enough to have official guidelines for something like this. I really would be taking a stab in the dark."

"That is why I am asking *you*. Not Pattie, and not Sergeant Robertshaw, although I would have to clear the interviews with her, obviously. I wouldn't ask Pattie because not only does she tend to have, how do you say, the bull-in-the-ceramics-shop approach sometimes, but also because I hear she has a reputation for playing fast and loose with different male officers. Her credibility, though it pains me to say it, might not stand up in court as well as yours would."

That bastard Simpson, I thought. *Boasting about Pattie to his cronies has got her station reputation round even as far as the probation office.*

"And Sergeant Robertshaw doesn't really like working with young children – she is better with teenagers and women. But you have a way with these children. They trust you. See yourself as pioneering the process. You have the opportunity here to make the protocols and procedures depending on how you get on with this case for future childcare or protection investigations. This isn't really Probation Service territory – it's crime investigation and falls squarely under the police's remit. It's just that we need a special kind of officer to do this job, and some new thinking, and I feel you are that officer."

I felt flattered and more than a little nervous. I hadn't interviewed children in the context of sexual crimes before and I had no idea where to begin. I remembered a bizarre woman police inspector at training school teaching interview techniques. She had held up a large photograph of an elephant and we all laughed.

"To get the best from an interview, you have to be like an elephant," she said.

"What, and eat all the buns?" cracked one wag.

"No," said the inspector. "An elephant has enormous ears and must use them for listening. An elephant has a long trunk for being nosey. And an elephant has a tiny mouth to say as little as possible. Be more like Jumbo when you interview."

We had exchanged glances and nudged each other in amusement at this strange simile, but now I could see what she was getting at. I thought it wasn't a bad simile to start with, and I didn't have anything better.

CHAPTER 26

Show me with the dolls

I used my 20-minute walk to the foster-carers' house on Reading Road to come up with some sort of strategy for interviewing Dora. Us WPCs usually did little more than take witness statements and occasionally make the notes in CID interviews. Was I straying, untrained, into CID territory? Was it even my place to do this? Miss Robertshaw had seemed happy for me to do it: she was busy with a case of a brothel allegedly being run in Sunningdale.

Would Dora find my uniform intimidating? The Carroll children hadn't had the best encounters with uniformed police, after all. Should I have come in civvies? Too late to change now. Perhaps I should take off my tunic and tie and interview just in my shirtsleeves. How would I record the conversation in my pocketbook? Should I have brought someone to take notes? But then two of us would be doubly intimidating … So many things to think about.

I arrived at a generously-sized, bay-windowed Victorian house and rapped the knocker. A slight lady with salt-and-pepper hair and a toothy smile opened the door.

"Mrs Chalmers? Hello, I'm WPC Gwen Crockford from Wokingham station. Hilda Bloom from the probation office sent me. About Charlie and Dora Carroll?"

"Ah yes, do come in, WPC … Cracknell, you say?"

"Crockford."

I stepped into the cosy hallway, all shiny wooden floorboards and burgundy oriental rugs. It smelled of beeswax polish, cinnamon and apple: perhaps Mrs Chalmers had just baked a cake. *How different this is from that dank caravan*, I thought.

"Charlie and Dora are playing in the garden. They're eating the last of the plums off our tree." Mrs Chalmers giggled. "I don't think they've had much fruit before."

I followed her into a warm, bright reception room overlooking the garden. In it was a tall bookcase full of books for children – *Robinson Crusoe, Swiss Family Robinson, Alice in Wonderland*, and picture books for younger children. A toy box was filled to the brim with dolls, teddy bears, tops, musical instruments and Dinky toy cars. A Meccano set and Charlie's cardboard museum box sat on a sideboard and a large doll's house sat on the floor. On the table was a half-finished jigsaw puzzle.

I saw Dora through the window, her hair wrapped in an orange headscarf, sitting on the swing, Charlie twisting the ropes so she spun round fast when he let go. Both children were laughing, oblivious to their visitor.

"It's probably best if we chat first before I call the children in," said Mrs Chalmers, "then I'll make us some tea. Have a seat."

We sank into two comfy armchairs in the bay window.

"Miss Bloom has given me some background on what Dora has been doing and the possible reasons for it," I said.

"So she's told you? Good. Showing ... you know ... themselves, is a classic sign of children who've been interfered with, particularly girls. Sometimes they've only witnessed the acts rather than been made to take part, but it affects them all the same. I've fostered some little mites whose stories would make your hair curl."

"I can imagine. And how is Charlie? Has he shown any signs of 'sexualised behaviour' as Hilda calls it?"

"Ah, Charlie's a funny one. He's outwardly quite a sunny, chatty boy. He's got this leather bag slung across his body that he refuses to take off. He even sleeps with it. Brian – that's my husband – and I have decided to leave him be and not force the issue. I mean, what could be in it that's so bad? It doesn't smell. A few shells, some fossils, some coins? Just like what's in his box. It's the equivalent of a comfort blanket and, dear God, he needs that right now."

My police radar was piqued: I wondered why Charlie kept his bag so close to him.

"But no, no sexualised behaviour as yet," continued Mrs Chalmers. "Now that doesn't necessarily mean he's *not* been interfered with . . ."

"Why's Dora wearing a headscarf?" I asked.

"Poor wee soul. That chubby little coloured nurse at the hospital shaved her head and she's got antibiotic salve on the sores where she'd been scratching. It doesn't look too pretty, so it's to preserve everybody's dignity while it heals."

"That would have been Nurse McDaniel," I said. *And my dear, caring friend you're talking about here,* I thought. "She's brilliant with children. Can I talk to Dora in here?"

"Yes, of course."

"What are her favourite toys?"

"She loves the little bitty things in the toy box – the drum and the teddies and the dolls," said Mrs Chalmers, pulling the toy box into the middle of the rug. She then went into the kitchen to put the kettle on and bring Dora in from the garden.

I watched. Charlie looked delighted that he now had the swing to himself. I took off my tunic and tie and hung them on the back of a chair.

Despite her headscarf, Dora looked cleaner and healthier just in the short time she had been with the Chalmers. Mrs Chalmers brought a cup of tea for me and a glass of milk for Dora, then sat on the stairs within earshot.

"Hello, Dora," I said.

"Hello," said Dora, contemplating me with her head on one side. The last time I saw her I had been soaking wet and covered in river weed, my hair plastered against my head. "You the police lady what falled in the river."

That's incredible she recognised me in just my shirt sleeves and not soaking wet, I thought.

"That's right, Dora. I'm a bit drier now."

"Why you here? Where's Bernie?"

"Bernie's being looked after in another place but you'll see her again soon, promise. I've come to play with you today. Why don't you choose us some toys?"

Dora was just as trusting as the day she took my hand to walk through the woods and seemed to accept what I said. We did some more of the jigsaw, banged a drum with some wooden drumsticks, spun the top a few times, then took the teddies and dollies out of the toy box. I noticed a tube of crayons on the bookcase and had an idea.

"I'm going to do some drawing while you're playing. Is that all right?" I asked, taking the crayons. Dora nodded. "What colour should I choose?"

Dora pulled out a green one. As she turned to play, I took my pocketbook out of my tunic on the back of the chair.

"We playing families now," said Dora. "While you draw."

"Good idea! Are these your family?" I asked, pointing to the toys. I hardly dared believe that the golden opportunity I'd hoped to engineer might just have presented itself.

Dora picked up a small teddy. "This is me." Then, picking up a larger one, she said, "This is Charlie."

She then chose a medium-sized doll with articulated arms. "This is Bernie," and picking up a wooden soldier, "And this is John."

"And where's Daddy?" I asked.

Dora shook her head and said nothing.

She played for a good hour, chatting away to me and the toys – mainly with the two teddies together and the doll stationed by the doll's house. Her play seemed innocuous and typical of a child her age: the toys playing "it" in imaginary woods, paddling in a stream, making

322

cups of tea and cooking. The soldier stood alone from the group, unplayed with.

I kept quiet, pretending to draw, but I observed and made green crayon notes in my pocketbook.

"I like playing with you," said Dora.

At midday, a key turned in the lock as Brian Chalmers came home for lunch. A loud, affable man with thick grey hair and a bushy moustache, he popped his head round the door.

"Hello, officer. Hello, Dora," he boomed. "Bit of a blustery day out there! I think we've seen the last of the warm weather and it's downhill all the way to winter now ... I must say how lovely it is having Dora and Charlie here to stay, and I hope we get some snow soon so they can build snowmen and we can have snowball fights . . ." Mr Chalmers barely drew breath. All I could do was nod – no chance of getting a word in.

As he blathered away, I noticed out of the corner of my eye that Dora was staring intently at me. She had picked up a wooden drumstick and was rhythmically poking it between the legs of the medium-sized doll. I turned to look. While Mr Chalmers had been in full flow, she had arranged the teddy bears so they were looking in the opposite direction and had moved the soldier so he was standing near, watching the doll.

It took some moments for Mr Chalmers to notice what Dora was doing, but when he did, his face turned red with embarrassment.

"Don't do that, Dora, it's not very nice!" he boomed. "Poor Dolly. Put that stick down!"

Dora jumped at the tone of his voice, threw down the doll and drumstick and knocked over all the toys before running out of the room. Mr Chalmers followed her. My spirits sank. I would have been so close to asking Dora what she was doing and why she'd arranged the toys in the way she had if only he'd kept quiet and not admonished her. Now that opportunity had gone and although I could put my own interpretation on what I had witnessed, there was no way these scattered toys could be considered as evidence against Rodney Carroll.

"How did you get on, dear?" asked Mrs Chalmers, coming in.

"I'm really not sure," I replied.

"I think Dora might be a bit tired just now. She's sitting in the kitchen. How about I make us all a nice cheese sandwich? We can have a slice of the apple cake I baked this morning as well. Then you could talk to Charlie."

The five of us sat round the little wooden table in the kitchen eating sandwiches and cake, glassy-eyed as Mr Chalmers breathlessly regaled us with stories that he found hilarious about his job at the paper mill. The two children ate in silence, Dora periodically yawning and rubbing her eyes.

"I think Dora needs a nap," said Mrs Chalmers, taking her by the hand and leading her upstairs.

"And I must be getting back to the coalface," replied Mr Chalmers, getting up from the table to fetch his coat. "Nice meeting you, officer. Cheerio."

That left just me and Charlie in the kitchen.

"Would *you* like to come and have a chat with me, Charlie?" I asked.

Charlie momentarily pulled his rabbit-in-the-head-lights expression and gripped his leather pouch closer to his body, but then seemed to relax and nodded. We went into the playroom.

"What toys do you like to play with?"

Charlie shrugged.

"Do you like Meccano?"

He shrugged again.

"Cars? There are some Dinky toys here."

Charlie shook his head and looked at the floor. *How on earth can I engage him?* I thought.

"I could show you my museum if you like," he said, smiling.

"I would really like that, Charlie. Could you get it for me?"

Charlie lifted his box off the sideboard and set it down on the table carefully, away from the unfinished jigsaw. He took the lid off. Inside was a whole load of curios.

"This is from a badger," he said, lifting a clean white skull out of the box. "And this is a snakeskin," he added, uncoiling a waxy, scaly length of something unspeakable.

I shuddered.

"You haven't killed a snake, have you, Charlie?"

"Oh no." Charlie laughed. "I wouldn't do that. Snakes moult their skins off every year. It's called sloughing. I found this skin by the riverbank. That means it's a grass snake's. They live near water."

Charlie proceeded to pull out a tiny green bottle, with bubbles in the thick glass, three Victorian pennies, some multicoloured snail shells and a desiccated stag beetle, describing each item and its provenance in detail – a process that took about half an hour.

All fascinating stuff, I thought, looking surreptitiously at my watch, *but we're no nearer to finding out if Carroll has been interfering with the children.*

"Does your dad like your museum?" I broached.

"Nah. He's not really interested."

"What is he interested in, Charlie?"

"He likes smoking, having a drink, going out on his bike . . ."

"Does he do anything at home?"

"He likes going behind the curtain with Bernie."

I wasn't expecting that so soon. I reached for my pocketbook and green crayon.

"What curtain is that, Charlie?" I felt some beads of perspiration prickle on my forehead.

"In the caravan. Bernie and Dora pull it across their bed so they can be private. But Dad sometimes goes in there with them."

"Why does he go in there?"

"He likes giving the girls cuddles. But I don't think they like him cuddling them because he makes Bernie cry. He's laughing, but Bernie's crying."

"And what about Dora?"

"He cuddles her a bit but Dad says he's not going to give her a really special cuddle yet."

"What's a really special cuddle?" I asked, feeling slightly sick.

Charlie was silent. Then, "Do you want to see what's in my bag?" he asked brightly.

I couldn't have been more surprised, or frustrated, by Charlie's offer. I felt privileged to be offered the chance to know what was in his precious brown bag, but my professional head said I was also on the brink of hearing the evidence needed to charge Rodney Carroll. I decided to go with it as I was gaining Charlie's trust.

"Yes please, I'd love to."

Charlie opened the flap of the bag. He pulled out and explained more artifacts – broken clay pipes, a fossil, another coin. *More of the same*, I thought. *So why is he so reluctant to take it off?*

Then I glimpsed something dark red, right at the bottom.

"What's that red thing, Charlie?"

"It's like a little book."

"May I see it, please?"

Charlie pulled out a tatty red driving licence. The annual renewal slips inside were stuck together, black and mouldy, the lettering obscured.

"Where did you get it?"

"I found it."

"Where did you find it, Charlie?"

"Er, I think it was near the gravel pits."

"Do you mind if I take it? Someone might need it to be able to drive their car."

"Yeah, s'pose."

"Thank you."

I put the licence into a brown envelope I had in my handbag.

Charlie looked directly at me. "I don't like it when I hear Daddy cuddling Bernie. And I don't like the way John sometimes peeks through a gap in the curtain at them. I don't understand why he finds it so interesting."

"Have you ever peeked through the curtain?"

"No! I haven't! I wouldn't! I don't want to see!"

"See what, Charlie?"

"Dad's wee-wee. Dora says she sees Dad's wee-wee when he's behind the curtain."

This was just the information I had been hoping for and I scribbled it down. I would have to hear it from Dora as well for her to give in evidence as a witness.

"Nobody wants to see anybody's wee-wee, do they? Thank you so much, Charlie. You've been really brave and helpful."

Charlie blinked at me, not entirely comprehending the significance of what he had just said.

"And I love your museum. All those interesting things!"

"Can I go and play outside now?" asked Charlie.

"Of course you can," I replied and he scampered off. I took a long, deep breath.

Mrs Chalmers came in again. "How did it go?" she whispered. "I heard some of your conversation."

"I think you're right that Carroll has been interfering with at least one of the girls. Not with the boys, I think. I'll need to have another chat with Dora when she's less tired."

"Come back whenever you need to. The little 'uns like you."

I took my time walking back to the station, glad of the fresh change-of-seasons breeze and the skittering autumn leaves, my head buzzing with that afternoon's events. The only person I really wanted to see was Hilda, to hold my focus and help me make sense of what I had just seen and done.

The only other person I didn't mind seeing was Bennett. Always diligent, always punctual, analytical, calm and knowledgeable, it was high time he got moved from clues officer into proper forensics, an area he probably did more than his pay grade in anyway. I was relieved he was the only person in the CID office when I dropped the driving licence off.

"Ah yes," he said, squinting at the blackened document. "I've got some solvents that'll be able to loosen the renewal slips and clean them up so that we can at least read a name and address. Leave it with me."

Hilda and I sat in the probation office, chain-smoking her mouth-desiccating Camel cigarettes and drinking cups of tea. I'd spent the last hour going through my interview notes with her, once she'd stopped laughing at my green crayon scrawl.

"So, now we have, in effect, a double investigation going on with Mr Carroll – burglaries *and* incest," said Hilda. "What a charming man! I spoke to Mrs Chalmers earlier and understand that Dora got upset when you interviewed her? What was that all about?"

"*I* didn't upset her. She was fine with me up until then, playing. Mr Chalmers butted in and wouldn't shut up, taking my attention away, and she displayed what I believe was sexualised behaviour – poking her doll between its legs with a drumstick until she got my attention back. Unfortunately, Mr Chalmers thought she was doing something dirty and told her off, then she ran away."

"How can we stop that happening again?"

"I'm not sure he was fully briefed about why I was there. I'm not convinced Mrs Chalmers told him."

"You may be right," said Hilda. "Mrs Chalmers did say she'd seen Dora pulling her skirt up in the presence of her son and husband, but didn't think they'd noticed. British people can be so uptight about sex things, they probably didn't talk about it."

"As I'm making it up as I go along," I replied, "I would recommend all foster carers understand the nature of a police visit so they don't influence the child's behaviour. And I should really be able to interview a child undisturbed in a private room."

"Now, you may not have seen Dora's behaviour if Mr Chalmers hadn't come in and triggered it," said Hilda.

"Well, that's true, but he also spoiled the moment. I wondered if in other cases like these, could we organise another adult to come in to see if it triggers behaviour, only they would be briefed not to react to it? I'm not sure whether that's ethical or not, though."

"No," said Hilda. "Trying to trigger behaviour is not ethical, as you say. And as evidence it would be inadmissible – it would have to be verbal disclosure of a criminal offence. But let's instead focus on what *did* work and perhaps you could build on that."

"Well, the Chalmers' comfortable playroom was the model for an ideal environment, with plenty of toys, books, crayons and paper, space to crawl around on the floor playing. And I don't think we should be in uniform – civvies would be more comfortable and make us seem less intimidating. I took my tie and tunic off. I was also struck by Dora's explicit use of the doll. Do you think there's any mileage in having boy and girl dolls? Children won't necessarily *tell* us how they've been interfered with, but they might demonstrate it playing with a doll."

"Very interesting, Gwen. Whether the police have enough resources to set up a dedicated room, I doubt. Would there be much call for one? I think you'll be lucky if you get a toy box and a quiet office."

"Do you really think incest and interference cases are that rare, Hilda?" I asked. "Or children are just so frightened they don't come forward? If they're too scared to tell parents, or parents are the perpetrators, do you really think they're going to tell the police?"

"I have thought for a long time that adults are too authoritarian and unapproachable," said Hilda. "Children are scared of their teachers, the police, even the Church, although Reverend Tucker is a nice man. Children still must be seen and not heard. You have in England this 'rigid upper lip' idea that whatever happens to you, you cannot complain. I believe there are many children out there who are being abused by family members, family friends and within organisations, but they are simply too scared to say anything."

"Look at the Feltons and the Carrolls, just in our own small patch. How many more?"

"Exactly. I am unofficially conducting my own research," said Hilda. "I have done since my training in Paddington, documenting the number of abused

331

and neglected children in the families I come across and their circumstances. One day I will try to analyse the information and see what conclusions I can draw. Perhaps you are right that there's a bigger problem out there."

"That is one circumstance where I'd love to be wrong, Hilda. So are you happy with me going back to chat to Dora yet again? I need to hear from Dora herself about what Carroll's doing to Bernie."

"Of course. Hearing your approach, I'm actually quite excited that you are trying something different in the way police deal with children. I can't see that you're doing them any harm. I'll telephone Mrs Chalmers and make another appointment for you – after lunch, when Mr Chalmers is back at work."

Back at the Chalmers' house and getting the soft toys, doll, soldier, drum and drumsticks out of the toy box again, Dora and I set up the previous scenario. For an hour, the teddies played in the woods, went in the doll's house and paddled in the stream.

My knees started to ache from kneeling on the hard floor and I stood up for a stretch. I looked outside. Charlie was in the sunny garden with a plank of wood. He had placed some garden snails on it and was encouraging them to race by waggling lettuce leaves in front of them. *Charlie's fascination with the natural world is boundless,* I thought. He looked up, noticed me in the window and waved. I waved back, smiling, and gave him a thumbs-up.

I felt Dora's eyes boring into me.

"Come and play with me, Mrs Policeman," she said.

"I'm just seeing what your brother's doing," I said. "I think he's found some snails."

"Come and play with me pleeeeeeease," she pleaded.

She's going to try to get my attention, I thought. *I'm going to try something.*

I carried on waving and smiling at Charlie. It was a risky strategy, as he could have construed my friendliness as a cue to come in, but he didn't and turned back to his snail race.

Out of the corner of my eye, I noticed Dora reaching for the drumstick and the doll. As I'd hoped, she began poking the doll between its legs. I didn't look directly at her, but moved away from the window and slowly sat back down on the rug. She was still poking the doll. I sensed Mrs Chalmers moving about outside in the hall and prayed she would stay there.

"Your dolly is Bernie, isn't she?"

"Yes. Is Bernie. My sister."

"What's the drumstick?"

"It's Daddy."

"Daddy?"

"Yes, Daddy and Bernie having a special cuddle."

"Why is Daddy a drumstick, Dora? Why isn't he a teddy?"

"Cos it's Daddy's wee-wee, silly."

Bingo. The evidence I needed. Through my peripheral vision I saw Mrs Chalmers loitering in the hall, her mouth an O of shock. *Good, another witness to this horrible information*, I thought.

"And what does Daddy do with his wee-wee?"

"Daddy puts his wee-wee in Bernie like dis." Dora poked the doll faster between its legs.

"How do you feel when Daddy does that to Bernie?"

"I don't like it."

"Does Daddy do this to you?"

"He says not yet."

"Do you think you could be the bravest girl in the world and tell some important people what Daddy does to Bernie? They will be able to stop him doing it for ever."

"What people?"

"Somebody called a judge and maybe 12 people called a jury. I would be there and so will Hilda, who is Bernie's friend. Do you think you could do that?"

Dora nodded.

I felt a tremendous weight lift off my shoulders that Dora could now give evidence in court against her father, although my heart sank at the thought of that dear little tot appearing in the witness box, probably having to stand on a chair. The Children and Young Persons Act stated that anyone not directly concerned with a case should be excluded from the courtroom when a child was called as a witness. Yet that still left members and officers of the court, counsel or solicitors, and the judge, who were probably, to a child, the most intimidating figures, in their ceremonial robes and strange hairy wigs. And I'd seen first-hand how savage defence counsels could be.

I pretended to draw, scribbling down everything Dora had said while she played with the teddies a little longer.

"Thank you for all your help, Dora, you're a very brave girl."

"S'all right, Mrs Policeman," she replied. "Will you come and play another day?"

"I'll see you again very soon, Dora," I replied, feeling a little stab in my heart that I probably wouldn't play with Dora again but would see her in court. It wouldn't be professional to strike up a non-work friendship with her.

"You heard all that, didn't you?" I asked Mrs Chalmers when I came out of the playroom.

"I did, poor little mite, clear as day. She was very open."

"You could also corroborate the evidence, couldn't you?"

"I could, and I would. What a horrid, horrid man."

"Thank you so much, Mrs Chalmers. Hilda or I'll be in touch and let you know what the next step is."

CHAPTER 27

Cracking the Carrolls

I'd just come into the station for my shift when I heard footsteps trotting down the stairs and Bennett's voice.

"WPC Crockford? I've managed to extract a name and address from that driving licence you handed in."

"Oh, well done, PC Bennett," I replied. "Someone local?"

"Well, no, actually. It belongs to a Mr Herbert Golding who lives in Brunswick Road, Gloucester. It hasn't been renewed for a couple of years."

"Someone from Gloucester? Why on earth would he drop his driving licence by gravel pits in Berkshire?"

"I'll make some inquiries with a contact of mine in Gloucestershire Constabulary, rather than simply posting the licence back to the address," said Bennett.

"And I'll ask the lad who found it again. He seemed oddly vague about exactly where he found it."

I had more pressing issues than enquiring about a lost driving licence that day. Dankworth was preparing to interview Rodney Carroll in prison, where he was being held on remand. We now had enough grounds to question him about the alleged incest with Bernie and possibly indecency involving Dora and Charlie.

Following my brief excursion into interviewing, I was back in my normal WPC role of notetaking while Dankworth questioned Carroll.

A burly prison officer delivered Carroll to the interview room, where he sat slumped in a chair, legs spread, arms folded across his chest. He smelt of sweat and prison-issue carbolic soap, with deep dark circles under his eyes. The wide grin was absent. He made me shudder as much as ever.

"You do know your daughter Bernie is pregnant?" Dankworth opened the interview.

"Why, that little slag," retorted Carroll instantly, oblivious to my presence in the room. Dankworth blinked. "Must have been one of them stable boys what got her up the duff. If I could get my hands on him … except I'm inside and I can't do nothing. Thanks for that."

"I'm suggesting that, in fact, it's you who are the father of Bernie's unborn child," said Dankworth.

Carroll pushed himself back in the chair and stuck his legs out straight. "What, me? Don't be so bleedin' ridiculous. I'm her father."

"It's not unknown for fathers to get their daughters pregnant. We've dealt with cases like this before. It's called incest, Mr Carroll. And it's a serious crime, punishable by a custodial sentence."

"How on earth can you know it's me? Has Bernie told you a pack of lies?"

"Bernie hasn't said anything. She has refused to tell her probation officer or the hostel matron anything about the father of her child."

"Well, there you go, then. It ain't true." Carroll visibly relaxed and sat back, grinning smugly, no humour in his eyes.

"Bernie hasn't said anything," continued Dankworth, "but Dora has."

Carroll sat bolt upright again. "She's just a little kid. What does she know about anything?"

"She says you go behind the curtain in the caravan with her and Bernie. Allegedly, you give Bernie a 'special cuddle'. I'm going to quote from WPC Crockford's notes of an interview with Dora:

"'WPCGC: And what does Daddy do with his wee-wee?'

"'CC: 'Daddy puts his wee-wee in Bernie like dis.'

"'[DC poked the doll faster between its legs.]'"

"That's a load of rubbish!" cried Carroll, beads of sweat breaking out on his grimy forehead. "She's just showing off! Trying to get some attention because she's the youngest. Always wanting attention. It drives me mad. You don't know how hard it is trying to look after four kiddies on your own, officers."

Both Dankworth and I sensed that Rodney Carroll was beginning to crack.

"And not only Dora, but Charlie too." Dankworth turned over his page of notes. "When Charlie was interviewed, he said, and I quote, 'Dora says she sees Dad's wee-wee when he's behind the curtain.'"

"Well, I can't help it if the kid sees it. Don't prove a thing. We all live crammed into one tiny, poxy caravan. They're bound to see me in the buff at some point."

"Why would you be exposing yourself behind the

curtain? Surely the curtain in the caravan is there to give privacy to the two girls? It's round their bed?"

Rodney Carroll shifted uncomfortably.

"Instead of using the curtain for privacy, are you perhaps using it to conceal what you're doing with Bernie and Dora from the boys? About the curtain, let me quote from WPC Crockford's interview with Charlie:

"'CC: In the caravan. Bernie and Dora pull it across their bed so they can be private. But Dad sometimes goes in there with them.'

"'WPCGC: Why does he go in there?'

"'CC: He likes giving the girls cuddles. But I don't think they like him cuddling them because he makes Bernie cry. He's laughing, but Bernie's crying.'

"'WPCGC: And what about Dora?'

"'CC: He cuddles her a bit but Dad says he's not going to give her a really special cuddle yet.'

"'WPCGC: What's a really special cuddle?'

"'No response from CC.'"

"I never bloody touched Dora!"

Dankworth and I exchanged glances.

"But you did touch Bernie?"

Rodney Carroll was silent.

"Mr Carroll, when we searched your caravan, as well as finding property belonging to Miss Gloria Gilmour, we also found a quantity of French letters. May I ask what a widower like yourself would be doing with a supply of prophylactics?"

"Prophy-what?" asked Carroll, visibly irritated.

I had no idea where this intrusive line of questioning was going.

"Rubber johnnies? Condoms? French letters?" continued Dankworth.

Carroll reddened. "Can't a man prepare himself for getting lucky? It's not like I'm married any more."

My stomach lurched at the thought of Rodney Carroll getting lucky with anyone.

"I'm suggesting you didn't care to use them when you had sexual relations with Bernie."

"I did! I mean I didn't! I mean some of the time. I mean I didn't have sex with Bernie . . ." Carroll's lying bluster was digging him into a bigger hole.

"She wouldn't be pregnant if you had, would she?"

"No ... she bloody wouldn't."

There was a heavy silence in the room as Carroll realised what he had said. My pen hovered above my notepad. Dankworth was still as a statue, his pale face like alabaster. Carroll was breathing heavily.

"So ... you admit that you did have carnal knowledge of your daughter Bernie?" asked Dankworth.

Carroll's face screwed up in an ugly grimace, his eyes clamped shut. He started to sob and put his large meaty hands over his face.

"It's because I love her!" His voice was muffled. "I can't think of another way to show how much I love her! I loved my wife so, so much and that's how I showed my affection. I love my daughter and I can't think of another way to show it. What's so wrong about it? It's just an expression of love. I haven't done anything wrong!"

Carroll took his hands from his face, still sobbing. His mouth was flecked with spittle and a string of snot hung out of one nostril.

I felt nauseous and lightheaded, and had to look away from him.

Dankworth had heard enough. "Rodney Carroll, I am further arresting you for incest under Section 1 of the Punishment of Incest Act 1908. You are not obliged to say anything unless you wish to do so but what you say may be put into writing and given in evidence," he cautioned. He walked to the door and called in the prison officer, who lifted the crumpled figure of Rodney Carroll out of the chair.

"Take him upstairs, please," said Dankworth. "I'll be up shortly to get the charge authorised."

Closing the door, Dankworth turned to me and puffed his cheeks out. I was shaking a little.

"Nailed the bastard!" he said, shaking his fists excitedly. "Or rather, he was hoisted by his own petard. Never thought a rubber johnny could be key to getting a confession out of a felon." He chuckled and I blushed slightly. "You all right, Crockford?"

"I think so, sir. That was intense. He's repellent, isn't he? I'm more shocked that he's pleading ignorance – as if he doesn't know that what he's done is wrong."

"He knows damn well what he's done. He's pretending. Well, we all know that ignorance of the law is no defence, so that won't wash in front of a judge."

"Can we also charge him with some sort of felony against Dora or Charlie? Indecent exposure, perhaps? Those kids have been quite damaged by what they've seen him doing."

"I'm not sure that will stand up in court. Charlie only heard what was going on. As far as I can tell he didn't

341

see anything and wasn't touched. Dora could be deemed 'too young' to be 'insulted' by indecent exposure."

I wasn't really surprised. Thinking back, I'd had a conversation with Hilda Bloom about this, who, as ever, gave her sociological insight.

"Our inadequate indecency with children legislation was constructed as a reaction to Victorian moral anxieties, rather than the need to protect and safeguard children from harm," she had said.

"We're still struggling with Victorian moral anxieties, aren't we, Hilda?" *My mother certainly is*, I thought.

Hilda continued, "Do you remember a case as recently as 1951? Magistrates up in Clitheroe, in Lancashire, dismissed a charge of indecent assault on a nine-year-old girl, because they said she had, 'willingly accepted an invitation to touch an adult man who approached her when she was walking along a river bank'. What nine-year-old would willingly touch a stranger's private parts? What creature was he to make such an invitation in the first place? His word against hers, without a doubt. Completely Victorian attitudes, putting the blame on the child rather than the man initiating the contact."

Still musing on Hilda's case, I said to Dankworth, "Well, that's ridiculous! Dora has clearly exhibited sexualised behaviour as a result of her experiences – at her young age. Yet she's not too young to potentially stand in the witness box and give evidence against her father in an adult court. How does that work?"

"Unfortunately, we can only work with what the law gives us."

"Well, if the law supposes that, the law is an ass," I replied. The Victorians had riled me enough to get me quoting Charles Dickens to Dankworth.

He looked at me blankly.

Get over yourself, Gwen, I thought. I changed the subject. "If Carroll's found guilty, sir, how long do you think he'll get for incest?"

"Up to seven years."

"And how much for the burglaries?"

"Anything up to 14 years, I reckon."

"So, he's messed up four young lives, yet gets less time for that than stealing things that were recovered and can be returned to their owners?"

"Yep, that's about the sum of it. I just hope the bastard pleads guilty, otherwise if he puts in a not guilty, we'll have to get those little kids up in the witness box to give evidence against their dad. That's never a pretty sight. It's upsetting for everyone involved, but there's no other way of doing it."

With Carroll charged, I had one thing left to do that day. Dankworth dropped me off in Reading Road. As ever, Mrs Chalmers was warm and welcoming and showed me into the playroom.

"I just need to ask Charlie a couple more questions, if that's all right, Mrs Chalmers?" I didn't divulge that we'd charged Carroll that day. "Hello, Charlie," I said, as he came into the room. "What have you been doing today? Got those snails in training for Ascot?"

343

He laughed.

We chatted for a while about what he had been doing; he was excited that he'd seen a kestrel hovering over the back field that morning and told me all about it.

I guided the conversation round to business. "Charlie, thank you for giving me that red driving licence you found. Can I ask you some more questions about it?"

Charlie looked a little uncomfortable. "S'pose."

"When did you find it?"

"I can't remember. It was the first interesting thing I found and it made me want to collect other interesting things."

"Are we talking weeks? Months? Years?"

"I was in Miss Wallis's class. So that was last school year."

"And did you find it on the shore of the gravel pit, or in the wooded bit, or by the road?"

Charlie was squirming and his face had gone red. He wouldn't look me in the eye.

"Did you really find it near the gravel pit?"

"No."

"Where did you find it, Charlie?"

"In High Copse woods."

Now we're getting somewhere, I thought.

"Can you tell me whereabouts in High Copse woods you found it?"

"It was quite far in, where the big beech trees are."

"Were you on your own?"

"I was when I found it."

"Had you gone into the woods on your own, then, or with the Fer ... I mean your group of friends?"

344

"A whole gang of us gone in. We was playing hide and seek."

A realisation dawned on me. "You didn't just find this driving licence on the ground, did you, Charlie?"

Charlie continued blushing and stared at the table. "No."

"Don't be scared to tell me where you found it, Charlie. You're not in any trouble. And you'll be able to help me a lot."

"I found it on the man."

"Which man, Charlie?"

"The man what died."

"Do you mean the man who was a skeleton?"

Charlie nodded, his body tense with fear.

"And then you were all brave enough to come to the police station and tell us you found him?"

Charlie nodded again, his lip trembling.

"Were you the first one to find him?"

"Yes."

"Were you scared?"

"A little bit. But he looked as if he was asleep, not like he was going to get up and chase me or nothing."

"What did you do?"

Charlie looked directly at me now, his blue eyes filling with tears. "I done a bad thing, miss."

"What was that?"

"The skeleton man's jacket was open and I could see a wallet in his pocket. So I reached in and took it before the others came and found me."

"Why was that a bad thing, Charlie?"

"'Cos the wallet had some money in it and I stealed it. I stealed from a dead man."

"What else was in the wallet?"

"That driving licence I gave you. I'll show you the wallet."

Charlie opened his shoe box and took out a crinkled brown leather wallet that had seen better days even before it had sat for weeks in the jacket pocket of a decomposing corpse. It opened with a sticky cracking sound. It was empty.

"What money was in it?"

"A 10-bob note."

"What did you do with it?"

"I used it to buy some food. After Bernie lost her job, Dad kept going away for days at a time and we didn't have no food. But with the dead man's money I could buy fish and chips for everyone."

I sighed. No decent person could call this stealing. Here was an intelligent, curious boy with a genuine need. The skeleton hadn't needed the money any more.

"You're a good boy, Charlie."

Charlie wiped his tears and a track of mucus from his nose with his sleeve.

"You helped your family, that's the important thing."

"Am I going to go to prison?"

"No, you're not." I lowered my voice. "All I was interested in, apart from you and Dora being safe here with Mr and Mrs Chalmers, was identifying the owner of the driving licence. I've completely forgotten about the 10-bob note in the wallet."

"There was one in there – honest."

"Charlie, I've *completely forgotten* about the ten-bob note," I stage-whispered, winking significantly.

"Oh, yes," said Charlie, the penny finally dropping. "I've forgotten too. What's a ten-bob note anyway?"

I felt a warm, maternal feeling for Charlie wash over me. He wasn't a natural liar or thief.

"Well, thank you, Charlie. You've been really helpful."

"Can I go back in the garden?" he asked.

"Of course you can."

Charlie scampered eagerly out into the fresh air.

"Did you get what you wanted, dear?" asked Mrs Chalmers, popping her head round the door, handing me a cup of tea.

"Charlie was very helpful again, thank you," I said, trying to keep a lid on my excitement that we could at last put a name to the dead man in the woods and perhaps learn a little more about him.

CHAPTER 28

Resolutions

Reader, we identified him.

Dankworth called me, Pattie and Bob up to the CID office. The red driving licence sat in the middle of the evidence table, with the wallet, a piece of stained, folded paper and what looked like a face-down photograph.

"Seeing as you've all had considerable involvement with the gentleman found decomposing in High Copse woods, it seems only fitting that we share with you what Bennett has managed to find out about him," he said.

Bennett cleared his throat and indicated the driving licence.

"Well, WPC Crockford gave me this rather unprepossessing, mouldy document from the High Copse body that one of the Feral boys had retrieved. Using the latest solvents, I cleaned it up and separated the renewal slips so that I could read the name Herbert Golding and an address in Brunswick Road, Gloucester."

"So not a local lad, then?" commented Bob.

"No. I then telephoned the Gloucestershire Constabulary. They sent an officer to Brunswick Road to make inquiries. It's a lodging house run by a landlady named Netty Deacon and Mr Golding had rented the attic rooms off her for a few years. He wasn't a particularly forthcoming man, by all accounts, and deeply religious. All Mrs Deacon knew about him is that he came out of the Army in 1918, a survivor of the Battle of Arras, apparently, and he worked at the Gloster Aircraft Company during the war."

"Luftwaffe tried to take that out a couple of times," said Dankworth.

"Not surprised, they were churning out Hurricanes for the RAF," said Bob. "Unlucky bloke – bombed in the Great War and then again in the next one."

Bennett continued, "Mrs Deacon said he never mentioned a wife or family, but he had a house in Cheltenham which he sold, before taking her rooms in Brunswick Road."

"So why didn't she report him as a missing person?" asked Pattie.

"This is the interesting part," continued Bennett. "Mr Golding was a pilgrim. He rented Mrs Deacon's cheap rooms as a base to go on walking pilgrimages to holy sites around the British Isles. He'd done the Pilgrims' Way to Canterbury, Iona and St Cuthbert's Way, and the North Wales Pilgrims' Way. He could be away for weeks at a time, and then just turn up again, but he would always leave advance rent money in his room."

"That would certainly explain the state of his feet," I said, "but not why he ended up dead in a woodland in Berkshire, his absence unnoticed."

Bennett reached for the folded piece of paper. "This might shed some light," he said, holding it up. "This is a note he left for his landlady."

1 March 1953

My dear Mrs Deacon,

I write to inform you of my intention to fulfil my lifetime's ambition of travelling to Spain to walk the Camino de Santiago de Compostela. En route, I intend to make a sentimental journey to Arborfield Garrison and Wokingham, then visit the Holy Well of St Anne & Reading Abbey before taking the train to Winchester to start the Pilgrims' Trail to Portsmouth, where I hope to board a ship for northern Spain.

Please find enclosed six months' rent in advance, after which I hope to return, unless the delights of Iberia compel me to stay.

Yours, Herbert Golding

"Hmm. That doesn't seem like a suicide note," said Pattie. "He sounds really excited about his foreign adventure."

"And being religious enough to be a pilgrim doesn't sit well with him taking his own life," I said.

"Doesn't seem as if he even got as far as Reading," said Bob. "Something compelled him to take two bottles of whisky and pills into the woods. He sounds quite a loner and he'd been through two wars. Maybe turning up in Arborfield was a tipping point . . ."

"We were never able to ascertain what the pills were, or how many were in the bottle," added Bennett. "Perhaps he took them in good faith as medication and they interacted with the whisky. If he fell unconscious

350

in the woods in March, he would have rapidly died of hypothermia."

"There was no evidence of foul play," said Dankworth. "We'll probably never know and we don't have resources to inquire further just for curiosity's sake."

Bennett continued, "When his rent money had been used up and he didn't return, Mrs Deacon assumed he had started a new life in Spain. She packed up his few belongings in a tea chest and stored them in an outbuilding, in case he come back for them, then re-rented his rooms. She didn't really give him a lot more thought, let alone that he might be dead."

Some things remain mysteries. We would never know why Herbert Golding died in the woods, but at least Dr Sladen could close his post-mortem report and we had a name to put on a gravestone. It was more than I ever believed we would discover.

"And finally," said Bennett, "would you like to see a picture of him?"

We nodded and I'm sure it wasn't just me who expected an oddball.

He turned over the photograph. A thirty-something Great War infantryman, wearing a peaked cap and battle dress, with a strong jaw, dark, intelligent eyes and a rakish half-smile looked back at us.

"He's gorgeous," blurted Pattie.

"Hello, Herbert," I said, a catch in my voice, "lovely to meet you at last."

We stood in silence for a few moments, not one of us, even Dankworth, unmoved. Pattie and I managed to keep it together as we left the CID office and went down to the locker rooms, where we closed the door and had a good cry.

And talking of crying: another person whose vivid, humane storytelling moved me to tears on numerous occasions was Hilda. I was alone in the women's office late one afternoon when she knocked on the door.

"Hello, Gwen. Have you got a moment?"

"Of course, Hilda, everything all right?"

"It's about Bernie Carroll."

We were no strangers to the horrific stories about abuse in some institutions for unmarried mothers and were determined that this wasn't going to happen to Bernie. Hilda had used her contacts to make sure she was initially placed in an approved and inspected home for girls' moral welfare, run by kindly Church of England nuns.

Six weeks before her baby was due to be born, Bernie transferred to Rosebury Heights, another C of E mother-and-baby home with a good reputation and its own maternity unit, personally visited by Hilda and deemed to be the most suitable.

There, Bernie could stay for a further six weeks following the birth and decide for herself whether she wanted to keep her baby, or give him or her up for adoption. "Decide" was perhaps a strong word, as these young unmarried mothers were heavily encouraged to go down the adoption route, but Hilda felt strongly that Bernie should be the only person to make that decision.

She hoped Bernie would choose adoption and then try to get on with her life.

Rosebury Heights was the most humane institution she knew to be able to help her. There would be no shortage of childless couples knocking on the door to adopt a baby; whether the home decided to divulge the parentage of the child was another matter.

Hilda sat in my office chair and offered me one of her Camel cigarettes.

"I have just had a long telephone call with Sister Deborah at Rosebury Heights, about Bernie Carroll," she said.

"Oh right, what did she say?"

"She said, 'Bernadette's going to be all right, I'm glad to say. I can't say the same about the baby, I'm afraid.'"

"Oh?"

Hilda took a long drag on her cigarette and blew the smoke towards the ceiling. She then recounted what had happened in such vivid detail I could almost have been there.

"Bernie had lain awake all her first night at Rosebury Heights in a dormitory with seven other young, pregnant, unmarried women, no doubt processing her arrival with a donated suitcase that smelled of mothballs, and meeting the other girls, all with their own as yet untold stories of illicit or unwise love, unwelcome advances or simply persuasion. She must have looked around at the sleeping forms of her dorm sisters, watching their serene faces and listening to their deep breathing and gentle snores, feeling older and more experience-battered by the ways of the world than she imagined they were, even though she was the youngest.

"Bernie had worked different jobs, looked after a young family, suffered at the hands of her father, been through the juvenile courts and probation system, and she still wasn't 16. She must have missed Dora and Charlie that night, John perhaps less so; he was always in the pocket of his father and had never tried to stop him.

"Bernie shifted uncomfortably onto her side on the hard mattress, her baby settling like a stone inside her. Feeling vaguely sick, she wondered if anyone had experienced the same as her. She felt she could never divulge what had happened and she really didn't want to hear that somebody else had suffered like that. A tumble in the haystack with a strapping young groom seemed a more acceptable version of why she ended up here and she decided to stick to that story if asked, wishing it could have been what happened.

"The nuns woke the girls and got them up at seven by bustling in, pulling the curtains and throwing open the windows to let the fresh, freezing air of a winter morning in. Shivering, the girls strip-washed at huge sinks in the communal bathroom, some choosing to pull the curtain round them for modesty, some not caring who saw them undressed, then filed downstairs to the refectory for a breakfast of bread and jam and tea in enamel mugs.

"After clearing breakfast away, the girls were allotted their chores for the morning. Bernie's task was to clean the large public stairs that curved from the hallway to the rooms and dormitories on the first floor. She was given a stiff brush to clean the stair carpet, a mop to wash the woodwork and a duster and polish for the banister's newels and rail.

"Bernie reached the bottom of the stairs with the brush and stood up to collect her mop and bucket. She felt a twinge of pain and winced. She breathed deeply, recognising the sensation as familiar monthly pain, but deeper and stronger. It subsided, a wave of relief in its wake. Bernie looked around the chilly, empty hallway, felt able to continue and reached for the mop.

"Then she felt it, a trickle running down the inside of her leg. As she leaned on the mop handle, she looked down to see a puddle of blood and water pooling around her feet. Instinctively, she began to mop up the puddle, but the fluids came faster than she could mop, accompanied by pain that was getting stronger and stronger. Silent and barely breathing, Bernie tottered, upright and stiffly, along the corridor to Sister Deborah's office, a trail of blood on the floor in her wake.

"She banged on the door with the flat of her hand. After several agonising seconds, Sister Deborah called 'Come' from within and Bernie fell through the doorway into her office, trying to keep herself on the polished wooden floor so that she would not soil the carpet.

"The next few hours were a haze for Bernie as she was rushed to the delivery room. Urgent voices whispered,

'Not due for at least another month . . .' and '. . . not happy about this amount of blood . . .'

"The pains grew more and more powerful. Bernie felt as if she were trying to pass a football out of her body, yet at the same time as if she were standing at the opposite end of the room, observing as well as participating.

"After one last monumental push, the football was out. There was silence. Bernie gradually came back to herself. One midwife was holding the motionless form in a towel and the other was looking at it in obvious horror.

"'Isn't it supposed to be crying?' murmured Bernie.

"The other midwife hurried to her side and wiped her brow. Her eyes were wide and haunted. 'I'm so sorry, darling, that little bean was never going to be crying anyway. It's been … gone … for a while.'

"'Is it … was it … a boy or a girl?' asked Bernie.

"The midwife looked helplessly towards her colleague, who was now in the far corner of the room, out of sight of Bernie, wrapping the little body in newspaper. She shook her head.

"'We don't know, my love. There were lots of things wrong with this little one. It's a blessing it's passed, if the truth be told. It couldn't live in the state it was in.'

"The door closed quietly as the midwife with the newspaper bundle left the room.

"'Could I see him or her?' asked Bernie.

"'Oh no, that's completely out of the question, sweetheart. You wouldn't want to, either. Just you lay back while I sort a few things out, then you can have a lovely long sleep.'

"The midwife wordlessly delivered the placenta and bundled that in newspaper too. She examined Bernie and cleaned up.

"'You didn't need any stitches, darling. You'll be a little sore for a couple of days, then you'll be right as rain. Here, take these.'

"She handed Bernie two tablets and a cup of water as she plumped her pillow.

"'Get some sleep now. You'll be able to go home in the next couple of days.'

"Bernie had drifted off to sleep, blocking out what had just happened, uncertain as to what the next few days would hold or where she would call home."

Hilda stubbed her cigarette out in my ashtray.

"So that is what happened. Ironically, Sister Deborah said they don't often see birth deformities this bad. They'd only experienced it once before when a girl had been sleeping with her brother. I didn't think it was appropriate to elaborate on Bernie's case. After all, it's academic now."

"Forgive me if I sound callous, Hilda," I said. "But I'm kind of relieved for her that the decision about what to do with her baby has been taken out of her hands. Bernie is free now."

"I absolutely agree with you! Away from her father and no longer pregnant, she can look forward to the rest of her life."

"Where is she going to live, though?"

"That was the second thing I was coming in to tell you. The Chalmers have agreed to foster Bernie as well as Dora and Charlie. The girls can't wait to share a room together again."

"That is really good news. And what about John?" I asked.

"Ach, he is all right in the council home in Maidenhead, where there are boys his age. Getting three Carrolls into one foster home is as good as it gets for now."

With the Winter Assizes approaching, Rodney Carroll finally decided to do something half-decent and plead guilty to all his charges of larceny and incest. Charlie, Dora and Bernie wouldn't have to go in the witness box to testify against their father, at the mercy of savage defence counsels, many of whom couldn't care less who they tore apart, as long as they won their case.

Carroll was sentenced to a total of 10 years in prison.

CHAPTER 29

A dreadful day at the races
Thursday, 14 July 1955

I didn't have another case as complex as the Carrolls, or a mystery as intriguing as Herbert Golding, in my remaining time as a WPC. But I will be forever grateful to them for giving me the opportunity to move onto the next stage of my police career.

"The superintendent wants to see you in his office, Miss Crockford," said Miss Robertshaw one hot summer morning.

My stomach lurched. We only really saw The EF in major incidents or serious disciplinaries. *Why would he want to see me?*

Miss Robertshaw accompanied me up to his office. *Another ominous sign.*

I knocked and went in to find Bob and Dankworth already there. *Has somebody complained? Did they find out I served that summons on a Sunday[24] in 1952?* But they were smiling.

"Ah, Miss Crockford. Do sit down," said The EF. "Don't look so nervous. We've brought you up here to

---

24 Police used to serve summonses in person, but were not allowed to do so on a Sunday. If they did, it could invalidate a case on a technicality.

tell you that we've been watching your work for a while. And, well, we're impressed."

"Thank you, sir," I said, feeling perspiration seeping into my tunic.

"DI Dankworth here tells me you have developed diverse skills: preserving and managing crime scenes, gathering evidence by your extraordinary way with children and solving a cold case by recognising Herbert Golding's driving licence as a significant lead. We also know that you're not afraid to get your hands dirty . . ."

"Or your uniform soaked," quipped Bob.

"And you're not squeamish," said Miss Robertshaw, smiling. "Not many officers come out of their first post-mortem buzzing like you did."

The EF continued, "So, if you are willing, we would like to put your name forward for detective training. Because you've in effect worked as an aide to CID for the last year or so, I have *every confidence* that you'll breeze through Selection Board," – he gave me a particularly noticeable wink – "and onto the 10-week training course at Hendon CID Training School early next year. Up for it?"

I couldn't believe what I was hearing. Me? A detective? I thought that I'd just been finding simpler ways of doing my job, worrying that I often went beyond my remit and hoping nobody noticed. But clearly people *had* noticed, and it hadn't done me any harm.

"Goodness, thank you, sir," I said. "I'm tremendously flattered and it's an incredible opportunity."

"You don't need to give me your answer right away, WPC Crockford," said The EF. "Take a day or so to think about it."

I didn't really need time to think. How could I pass up the opportunity? I took it anyway to make sure I mulled over its implications fully: coming out of uniform, possibly leaving Wokingham, no longer working day to day with Pattie, Bob, Henry, Sarge, even Higgs, relentlessly long hours . . .

Walking back down the stairs with Miss Robertshaw, I asked, "Do you know of another woman detective in Berkshire I could talk to before I formally accept the super's offer?"

"I'm afraid there isn't one," she replied. "Get through Hendon and you would be the first one. You go for it. I think you would be excellent."

The first woman detective in the Berkshire Constabulary. That's what I'd be.

"Really?" I said. "I'm astonished at that. Aren't you tempted to go for CID yourself, miss? You've got more years of experience than I have?"

"Ooh, no – far too many decomposing bodies for me. And anyway . . ." she dropped her voice to a whisper, "I'm staying in uniform as I've got my eyes on the prize of first Woman Police *Inspector* in the Berkshire Constabulary."

I had no doubt she would get it.

It was the Thursday of Royal Ascot, the week when the Queen and various members of the Royal Family usually attended Ascot races, and the weather was scorching. Half the station were off en masse to police Ascot race-course and keep order among the tens of thousands of racegoers swarming over the vast course. I was packed into the back of the police van with Pattie, Bob, Henry and Higgs, sweltering.

Pattie, red-faced and perspiring, tugged irritably at her tie. "Feels like it's going to be in the high eighties today," she huffed.

"I don't think the Queen's even going to be at Ascot today," I said. "She's got a Buckingham Palace tea party instead."

"We should've been doing this back in June, rather than in this July heat," moaned Bob, referring to June's national rail strike that led to Royal Ascot being postponed until now. "Seems that every bugger can go on strike and bring the country to a grinding halt, except us."[25]

The van pulled up in the racecourse's designated police area and Bob handed out our roles for that afternoon:

"WPC Baxter and PC Higgs – general patrol around the course, especially the parade ring, where, as we know, the pickpockets tend to work as people check out the horses before the races. PC Falconer – I've put you on a first aid station with the St John's Ambulance: expect to spend most of your day dealing with heat-stroke and sunburn. And last, but certainly not least, WPC Crockford, I'm putting you on traffic duty outside the London Road car park, so you'll need your white

---

25 Police had been banned from striking since the 1919 Police Act. It was passed following strikes in Liverpool and London in 1918 and 1919 when nearly every sergeant and constable refused to turn up for duty. The police do not have a trades union; the Police Federation represents its members.

gloves. And you can all be in shirtsleeves – it's far too hot for tunics."

I was quite happy to be outside the course today, directing traffic into the car park. The racecourse and enclosures were jam-packed with overheating racegoers. While out here, I was able to move and breathe, stationed by my wooden "Keep Left" police plinth. I didn't even have to shout myself hoarse as the plinths were equipped with modern loudspeakers and hand microphones for broadcasting instructions to pedestrians and drivers, and I had a wooden chair to sit on when it quietened down.

If I became a detective, I wouldn't have to direct traffic again, I thought.

I'd patrolled Ascot races many times. I was always struck by its "all human life is here" panorama: from dukes and fragrant duchesses parading in top hats and couture to grubby, flat-capped tipsters slurping pots of jellied eels and spitting the chewed bones onto the ground. Pattie and Higgs would be ambling through the bustling crowds, past the gesticulating banter of the tic-tac men at their betting boards, signalling horses' odds, and the inevitable evangelical mission decrying the punters and encouraging them to repent of their gambling sins and turn to The Lord instead.

By about three thirty, the heat had become oppressive. In the distance, I could see some dark clouds rolling in and I'd developed a headache. A kindly car park attendant brought me a cup of water and an aspirin. We both looked at the sky.

"Greasy-looking clouds," he said. "This weather's going to break."

And break it did. Just after four o'clock, the sky blackened and huge raindrops began to fall. To call it rain was an understatement – it was a deluge of monsoon proportions. Grabbing my tunic, I ran for cover into the car park and under the attendant's gazebo. We could only stand and watch as the rain beat down on the car roofs and rivers of muddy water swirled between the parked cars and out onto the road.

"There are going to be some soggy top hats and see-through dresses this afternoon," the attendant chuckled, "no way is there enough shelter for everyone on the racecourse, poor sods."

Suddenly, I felt my face prickle, then a lightning fork zigzagged down in the direction of the racecourse with a fizzing, whiplash sound.

"Bloody hell, that's close!" cried the attendant, ducking, his voice drowned out by a monumental crack of thunder a second later. Two more blinding flashes followed straight after and two more immense thundercracks.

"That must have given everyone a hell of a fright!" he cried, straightening his cap.

As the rain eased, a strange atmosphere hung over the racecourse. I swore I could hear distant shouting and intermittent screams, but the car park attendant said he couldn't. I wondered if the thundercracks had messed with my hearing. But soon there was no mistaking the approaching dring of an ambulance bell along London Road, followed by a second one.

I ran back to my police plinth outside the car park. The ambulances slowed as they approached me.

"Everything all right?" I called through the open window to the ambulance man.

"Haven't you heard, love? Massive lightning strike on the racecourse. Multiple casualties."

"Good God."

"What's your first aid like?"

"Pretty good."

"Get in then, we'll need you."

I opened the door and clambered in, not knowing what I was going to deal with. We sped to the Golden Gates entrance onto the course and towards the public enclosure opposite the Royal Box, where a constable semaphored directions to us and the stream of emergency vehicles trundling in behind. We couldn't believe what we were seeing. Ascot races, usually gaily ablaze with colourful flower arrangements and a sea of lovely floral hats and summer dresses, was a muddy battlefield dotted with casualties.

Incongruous, drenched groups of people – book-makers, first-aiders, police and top-hatted off-duty doctors who had been enjoying a day at the races – tended to the injured on the filthy ground before they were stretchered off towards a marquee. I counted at least 20 of these groups.

There were stretchers everywhere. Loudspeakers that should have been announcing the next race's runners and riders instead appealed for off-duty doctors, nurses or skilled first aiders. Many more people wandered or ran around the scene, some crying, some screaming names of relatives, some in a daze.

The worst casualties are the quiet ones, I remembered from training school.

I felt someone grab my arm. It was Pattie.

"What the hell just happened?" I asked her.

Her eyes were wide with the horror she'd just witnessed. "Gwen, it was absolutely bloody horrible!" she babbled. "When the rain started to stair-rod down, everybody who could run for cover ran – into booths, tents, under awnings. A load of people crammed into a tea tent by the metal fence opposite the Royal Box, but loads more, caught in the open and soaking wet, were crushed against it. A bolt of lightning hit the fence and this bright blue light travelled the length of it, knocking anyone in contact with it down like ninepins. I saw it! It threw people out of the tea tent and onto the ground!"

Pattie looked close to tears. And as if to mock the scene of carnage unfolding in front of our eyes, the glowering clouds moved off and the hot sun came out again, warming our backs and causing steam to rise from the sodden ground.

"You two WPCs there!" We heard an authoritative voice behind us and a sergeant from what looked like the Buckinghamshire Constabulary beckoned to us. "We're setting up a casualty clearing station in that marquee over there and we need a ring of police around it to deal with distraught relatives and stop them going in while we process the injured. The more women the better. Off you go."

Pattie and I sprang into action. Pulling our sodden pocketbooks from our tunics, we stood in front of the blue line of policemen forming a protective ring around the marquee.

"You're looking for your young son? Can I take his name and your details … No, sorry, madam, you can't go in there, it's emergency staff only … They're all doing their best, please be patient … I know it's hard … Can you all step back, please! … I believe they're being taken to the Edward VII Hospital in Windsor … You can't go in there, sir! Ah, you're a doctor, that's fine then … Stretchered casualty coming through! Make way! … Mind your backs, please … Yes, madam, we're all soaking wet … Lavatories? Over there by the Grandstand…"

And so on, until all the wounded and walking wounded had been gathered into the marquee for triage, first aid and transport to hospital if necessary. I'd tried to avert my eyes as casualties were stretchered through, but it was hard not to notice scorched clothing, burned hands and bloodied faces.

A steady stream of ambulances passed by the triage marquee, stretcher after stretcher loaded into them, their bells a cacophony of dringing as they sped away to the Edward VII.

"Blimey, I never knew East Berkshire had this many ambulances," marvelled Pattie as yet another one rounded the marquee.

But even the substantial East Berks emergency resources began to run dry after the most serious casualties had been taken to hospital. Now, any available van at the racecourse was commissioned into the transport queue to take the remaining walking wounded.

Our Black Maria arrived, a stony-faced Bob at the wheel, followed by a catering van, and most incongruous of all, an ice cream van.

Most of the upset relatives had dispersed by now and Pattie and I could take a few moments to survey the aftermath of the disaster. The last ambulance pulled off, its bell ringing, followed by Bob revving the Maria. The catering van honked its horn, then behind that came the tinkly, plinking tune of 'Greensleeves' chiming from the departing ice cream van.

"Mr Creamy – the fourth emergency service." Pattie snorted.

You know when something has been so stressful that you're on the edge of hysteria and you don't know whether to laugh or cry? The ice cream van tipped both me and Pattie over that edge into hysterical laughter.

I could barely breathe. "Damn you, Pats," I wheezed. "We are so going to hell."

We struggled to pull ourselves together when we noticed the stern Buckinghamshire sergeant staring at us.

Oh no, we've let our constabulary down, I thought.

"Good job, ladies," he said. "It's been one hell of an operation this afternoon. Completely surreal. Can you believe they've only just decided to call off the last two races? Sometimes this country takes 'Keep Calm and Carry On' a bit too far." And he strutted off.

We helped with the clean-up operation once all the casualties had been evacuated and the racecourse cleared, then regrouped to wait for Bob's return after his final hospital run. Henry stood by the First Aid station, leaning on his walking stick and looking ashen-faced.

"So much for just treating a few punters with sunburn and heatstroke, Henry," I said. "What did you have to do?"

"If it wasn't for this bloody leg, I'd have been kneeling on the ground doing artificial respiration," he replied. "So many people with poor technique doing mouth-to-mouth. But you can't just stand there criticising, can you? I dressed quite a few burns injuries and dislocated wrists instead."

Higgs bounded up, his usual grin plastered all over his face. "Well, that was shocking, wasn't it? Shocking? Geddit?" He giggled.

I was sorely tempted to tell him to shut up, but this manic idiocy was probably his way of coping with the desperate situation, just like Pattie and me losing it over the ice cream van.

Pot kettle black, be a little kinder, I told myself.

Bob drew up at last and we wearily climbed into the van, the back of it resembling a barnyard, as there was so much mud inside. As we left the racecourse, all that remained of the carnage was a charred, twisted umbrella, stuck point-down into the muddy ground.

We didn't chat much on the way back to Wokingham. We were all exhausted, had seen too much and couldn't really verbalise how we were feeling. I noticed Henry's hands were trembling.

The news reports over the next few days revealed the full extent of the tragedy we'd been party to: a 28-year-old pregnant woman standing with her husband by the tea stall took the full force of the third lightning strike and was killed instantly, and a 51-year-old evangelist with a London mission who was standing near her died later in hospital. An AA patrol man on the main road by the racecourse was hit by one of the three flashes, but survived. One hundred people had either been knocked flat or hurled into the air, with around 49 of those sustaining injuries.

"You saw all this at Ascot?" said Suzette, reading out the newspaper report the next evening before supper.

"I saw the three lightning flashes but only the aftermath of the strikes," I replied. "I was more involved in crowd control and the clean-up. Anybody get sent your way?"

"All the hospitals were on standby to receive casualties, but in the end, Windsor had capacity. I think they only admitted around 37 in the end. Tragic about that poor expectant mother and the preacher man, though." Suzette shook her head. "You get to do all sorts of exciting things as a policewoman, don't you? I bet you love the job."

I did, but I felt ready to move on. It was on the tip of my tongue to tell Suzette about my recommendation for detective training, but as it was a few months in the future I wanted to enjoy the time I had left at Mrs Cunningham's, if indeed I had to move on. No point speculating on what might not happen.

CHAPTER 30

The Police Benevolent Fund Show

I said yes to The EF's offer of detective training.

"A wise decision, and good for you, WPC Crockford," he said. "CID could do with a woman's touch. I can get you onto the selection board in the New Year."

Accepting the move to CID was easy. The hard bit was going to be telling my friends and colleagues. I went down into the back office, where Henry was pecking at his typewriter. Sarge trotted in with some tickets and a concert poster that he drawing-pinned to the notice board.

"Hope you two have got your tickets for the Police Benevolent Fund Show?" Sarge asked, waggling the tickets at us.

"Do we get to hear The EF mangling some perfectly decent piece of music on the trombone again?" asked Henry.

"Of course. But it's going to be much, much worse this year." Sarge chuckled at the memory of last year's excruciating evening.

"I can hardly wait," I said.

"Anyway, I thought you, WPC Baxter and Miss

Robertshaw were going to dress up as the Andrews Sisters and do 'Boogie Woogie Bugle Boy'," said Sarge.

"We literally didn't get our act together in time," I replied. "Anyway, I think it would be funnier if Higgs, Dankworth and Beeton did the Andrews Sisters."

We chuckled at such an unlikely drag act.

"We've got the Metropolitan Police Male Voice Choir, who have been on Pathé News, apparently," said Sarge. "They'll be performing, for your delectation, choral pieces old and new."

"Oh joy," said Henry, with a wry smile.

"No, 'Ode to Joy'," said Sarge.

"How much are the tickets?"

"Ten bob each. Two guineas to you, squire."

"Give me two then, Sarge," said Henry, handing over two 10-shilling notes.

I felt momentarily crestfallen. At least Cynthia the attractive physiotherapist would be guaranteed a very tedious evening and a lot of police shop talk.

Henry handed one of the tickets to me as Sergeant Lamb trotted out again.

"Is this for me?" I asked in surprise. "I'll get my handbag and give you the 10 bob."

"No, this one's on me, Gwen. I need a partner in crime to laugh at the worst acts."

"Oh, don't!" I said. "My giggling will get me into some real trouble one day. It doesn't need encouraging. But thank you, Henry, I'm looking forward to it." The prospect of spending an evening listening to the EF parping away on a trombone suddenly seemed more appealing.

The annual Police Benevolent Fund Talent Show was one of those events that everybody, unless they were on shift, was expected to attend. We took over Wokingham's opulent art deco-esque Ritz cinema as a private function for the evening, setting up a donations bar in the foyer. The playbill was of variable quality year on year as officers got on stage and did their party pieces, some of which were brilliant and some of which were dire.

The EF always played his trombone and Bob always performed with Constable P. Nuss – his tatty ventriloquist's dummy wearing a police helmet whose head accidentally kept coming off. At some point in the evening, usually far too early for everyone to be warmed up, the chief superintendent would sing 'The Laughing Policeman', trying to work himself up into infectious guffaws. It was so forced everyone just tittered in embarrassment, desperate for it to be over.

Henry met me in the foyer. "Ready for your annual torture?" He chuckled.

"At least it's for charity," I said.

Pattie, dressed as an usherette in a short skirt and a pinnie, greeted us and showed us to our seats. She looked from me to Henry to me again and gave me a quizzical, raised eyebrow look.

"I've put you on the end of Row F so you can stretch your leg out if you need to, Henry," she said.

"Or make a dash for the bar if the acts get too dreadful," he whispered, "not that I can really dash."

Henry let me into my seat first and I looked around the cinema as I took my coat off. The show was our annual opportunity to take a sneak peek into the personal lives of our colleagues. Dankworth had absented himself as usual, pleading work commitments. A couple of rows in front, Hilda Bloom and Bennett were ensconced, deep in conversation, looking into each other's eyes for longer than was strictly necessary. *Well now, that's a friendship I hadn't thought about, but makes sense.* Miss Robertshaw arrived with Miss Montgomery, who looked disconcertingly like her, except blonde. *Aha, so that's Miss Montgomery.*

Sarge hosted the evening to rapturous applause, a role he relished every year. He'd waxed his moustache, parted his hair down the middle, put on his old scarlet military mess jacket and morphed into a verbose music hall Master of Ceremonies, ramping up anticipatory "oohs" and "aahs" from the audience for even the most modest act.

The first act was The Toolshed Trio – three PCs from Crowthorne who were to play 'The Swan' from *Carnival of The Animals* on a woodworking saw, spoons and the comb and paper.

"But why, though?" whispered Henry as the PCs ambled onto the stage.

I took a deep breath to suppress giggles.

Actually, they were rather good. The otherworldly vibrato of the saw, gentle rasp of the comb and paper and surprisingly sensitive percussion from the spoons made for a lovely piece of music, provoking momentary awed silence when the piece ended, before enthusiastic applause.

"Well, I didn't expect that," I said.

Henry nodded, impressed.

Things got more knockabout with Bob and Constable P. Nuss doing a skit on traffic duty hand signals, with the dummy's hand as well as its head falling off, and Bob himself falling over on the stage. They really should have followed Bob with 'The Laughing Policeman' as the hysterical crowd would laugh at anything now. Instead, a retired officer read out one of Kipling's 'Barrack Room Ballads' in dialect, which wasn't at all funny, and the boredom was palpable.

Special guests the Metropolitan Police Male Voice Choir bookended the interval. The Londoners marched onto the stage and took their positions in four neat rows, some standing on gym benches. Sarge introduced their first song.

"Ladies and gentlemen, the Metropolitan Police Male Voice Choir will sing their homage to Britain's Queen, the specially-commissioned Coronation piece, 'Beautiful Majesty of England'."

"She's bloody Majesty of Scotland as well," I heard my neighbour, gruff Inspector Gregor McTavish, snarl to his wife.

The choir launched into a tuneless, turgid, sycophantic homage to Her Majesty, all "fair as buds in spring", and "noble, kind and true". Henry and I grimaced at each other.

"How much more o' this crap do we have to sit through?" growled Gregor above the polite applause.

Henry and I were shaking with repressed mirth.

"There's an interval now and about another hour of crap after that," I said to Gregor. "Think of the widows and orphans."

"At least time to anaesthetise myself with some Scotch before I carry on suffering for those widows and orphans," mumbled Gregor as he and his wife squeezed past on their way to the bar. He patted Henry on the shoulder. "Good to see you back, matey."

Pattie appeared, carrying a tray with two gin and tonics. "You don't want to be caught up in the crush at the bar, so here's seat service instead. You won't get it when your leg's better next year, though, Henry," she joshed.

"I'll be performing a tap-dancing number, just you watch," he said.

The audience milled around the smoky foyer until the interval bell rang and filed back in to take their seats again.

"And seeing how you all loved their previous number, we welcome back on stage the Metropolitan Police Male Voice Choir to perform that perennial classical favourite, 'Nymphs and Shepherds'," announced Sarge.

The burly policemen launched into:

Nymphs and shepherds, come away,
In this grove let's sport and play;
For this is Flora's holiday,
Sacred to ease and happy love . . .

I sensed Henry shifting in his seat. He sighed and I noticed his hand was gripping the arm of his seat tightly. His eyes were shut and he was trying to control his breathing. Perspiration had broken out on his brow.

While you express your jollity!
Nymphs and shepherds, come away.

Henry hauled himself up out of his seat, took his walking stick and whispered, "Excuse me," before limping out of the door to the foyer. I wondered if he felt unwell or needed the gents urgently. Did I need to follow, or leave him be? I decided to wait a while to see if he came back.

And pass the day in jollity!
Nymphs and shepherds, come away!

The police choir concluded their twee song with a triumphant, harmonic crescendo and their wives cheered.

"Let's hear it once again for the Metropolitan Police Male Voice Choir!" declared Sarge, whipping up applause before launching into a lengthy anecdote about policing during the blackout.

Applause at the end was the ideal time to exit the auditorium and see if Henry was all right. I nipped into the foyer, looking around, but I couldn't see anyone apart from an officer gathering glasses.

Henry's probably in the gents, I thought – *he wouldn't go home without telling me, surely? Would he?*

I walked to the end of the makeshift bar and lit a cigarette, then spotted Henry alone at a far table, with a glass of whisky in front of him and a cigarette in his hand. He did a double take when he saw me, looking embarrassed at being sought out.

"Ah, there you are, Henry. Thought I'd get a breather." I noticed his hand was trembling. "Are you all right? I thought you looked a bit peaky in there for a moment."

"Yeah, can't stand that nymphs and shepherds thing."

He took a deep drag on his cigarette.

What on earth could be so upsetting in a song about Restoration nymphs and shepherds frolicking about in the countryside? I thought.

377

"Your hand's shaking."

"It's the old war wound," he said with an unconvincing laugh. "We've all got 'em."

"I don't understand. I thought you got through the war uninjured? Apart from a bit of buzzing in your ears from when that mortar blew your tin hat off?"

"Figure of speech, Gwen."

I paused for a moment. I'd heard about soldiers from the First World War coming back from the trenches with what they called shell shock, but wasn't that because the trenches, conditions and bombardment were so dreadful they drove many souls mad? Henry wasn't suffering from some sort of modern shell shock – was he?

"Would you like another drink?" Henry asked, his shaking hand beckoning the bartender over.

"I'll have a gin and tonic, please," I said.

"Another single malt, sir?" asked the bartender.

"Please," replied Henry. "Actually, make it a double."

"Are you all right these days, Henry? You seemed a bit shaken up after the Ascot lightning incident back in the summer and I hope you don't mind me asking, but what was all that about in there just now?"

Henry drummed his fingers on the table. "All right, I'll tell you. You've seen my medal ribbons: Defence Medal, 1939–45 Star, 1939–45 Medal, Africa Star, Territorials Medal. I've also got an Italy Star."

I knew some of the war's fiercest battles were fought in Italy. "You weren't at Anzio or Monte Cassino, were you?" I asked.

"Neither of those, thank God. But where I was is now recognised as some of the worst conditions British troops experienced since the Great War. It rained torrentially, continually, and we were stuck in muddy conditions in the freezing mountains in autumn and winter of '44."

No wonder Ascot brought back some bad memories, I thought.

"Where was this?"

"We were with the US Fifth Army on the Gothic Line below Rimini." Ah yes. Sarge mentioned this on the night of Henry's accident. "It's called 'the forgotten front'. Trust me! Was it something I said?" Henry laughed, without humour.

"It was pretty bloody awful," he continued. "We made camp below a ridge, but before we put the tents up, we had to clear away the fragments of some dead German soldiers left after the Canadians had gone through ahead of us. That was the night my greatcoat froze to me, sleeping on top of the traces of those Germans.

"We were mopping up the resistance as the rest of the Allies pushed north towards Bologna. So many pretty, historic little towns reduced to rubble by tanks – Shermans on our side, Panzers and Tigers on theirs, just blasting buildings and people to smithereens. Ruined villages are strange things, you know – you'd get families in blasted buildings just carrying on with their lives even though the back walls of their houses were gone, and the shattered towers and churches are hideouts for enemy snipers. You never know who you'll meet round any corner – friend or foe.

"One particular day, we were fighting house to house in a mountain town. A sniper had been targeting our unit from the hill and we were edging up the rubbled streets to flush him out, on full alert, everybody very tense. Suddenly we hear this jolly, trilling music – a woman singing – coming out of a house with a half-open green door. Bloody 'Nymphs and Shepherds' song. Me and my mate Adam McCairns wonder if this could be a Jerry trap, so we kick open the door, rifles at the ready. We relax. It's just a family: mother, father, two little girls, a grandmother sitting round a table listening to their gramophone playing 'Nymphs and Shepherds', just like they probably always did on a Sunday. Poor buggers, frozen in terror, hands in the air, afraid that we might shoot them. Instead, we shush them, pull the door to and carry on up the street. One of the little girls gives me a thumbs-up as we leave."

Well, this doesn't sound too traumatic, I thought, *it's quite a sweet story.*

"While we're flushing out the sniper at the top of the hill, we hear a commotion down at the bottom, grenades going off – clearly there's close combat between our lads and some Jerries holed up, who we'd probably walked right past. Grace of God and all that. This goes on for an hour or so, then silence. It's gone quiet up at the top of the hill too, so Adam and me, we make our way back down to see if our lads are all right – thankfully, they are, all accounted for.

"Then we see it. The green door blasted across the street … chairs and table just matchwood … the dented gramophone half-buried in the rubble opposite. Then we see them … what's left of them … some bastard Jerry had thrown stick grenades in … they hadn't stood a chance. I sense I'm standing on something and look down at something black and red. It's a gramophone record. Sodding 'Nymphs and Shepherds'. Little dog on the label still looking into the gramophone horn as if nothing had happened. Then other people start emerging from what was left of their homes and the screaming starts ... so much screaming ... and pleading for us to do something . . ."

Henry took a deep draft of his whisky and reached for another cigarette.

"So now you know why I can't abide that song."

I felt my eyes filling with tears at the demise of this poor Italian family who probably thought they were safe when Henry and Adam left. I sniffed them away, embarrassed by my failure to control my emotions. From the auditorium, the sound of the 'The Laughing Policeman' and the audience politely tittering along seemed to be mocking Henry's story.

"I bloody hate 'The Laughing Policeman' as well," said Henry, managing a smile.

"I think I do too, now," I said.

"I'm sorry if I upset you," continued Henry. "I've never told anyone that story before. It always seemed too soon to talk about it, yet here we are nearly 11 years later and it still bothers me. I guess Ascot brought it all back first; the screaming people in torrential rain and mud. Then that damn song tonight."

"I'm glad you felt you could tell me, Henry. How could you have known they were going to sing that song? So, you survived Italy, obviously, where did you go next?"

"We just slogged on through the mud and torrential rain of the winter of 1944. Still bloody awful until they took us out of Italy to Palestine for a rest. Then 1945 dawned and the rest is history."

I sensed that Henry didn't want to say more and I didn't think I could deal with any more myself.

Final applause was coming from the auditorium. The show was, thankfully for many people, coming to an end. Soon the great and the good from the constabulary would be escaping into the foyer. Bob had offered to run us all home.

"Could I ask you something, Gwen?" said Henry.

"Of course," I answered.

"Would you—"

Just then Pattie merrily burst into the foyer with Bob – still holding his ventriloquist's dummy – and headed straight for us.

"Oh my goodness!" she trilled. "Some of the acts were dreadful tonight! People were crying with laughter then having to pretend they were moved to tears by the music!"

"And I thought the chief super was going to give himself a hernia doing 'The Laughing Policeman'," said Bob.

"Wha' you two doin' out here all on your own anyway?" asked the dummy through Bob's clenched teeth. "Our performances no' good enough for you? Gottle o' geer, gottle o' geer."

"Oh, I just needed to move around, got a few pins and needles in the leg," replied Henry.

"You won't have that excuse next year – your leg will be all mended," added Pattie.

"Hope so," said Henry. "It's touch and go whether I end up with a limp."

"With a limp what?" asked the dummy.

Pattie cackled and I grimaced, Henry raised an eyebrow and Bob realised he'd probably pushed the bawdy humour too far.

"Well, on that note," Bob added, "let's get out of here. Gwen and Pattie, I'll drop you off first."

CHAPTER 31

Goodbye, uniform – for now

Christmas 1955 was approaching. It was close to my birthday, so, with Mrs Cunningham's permission, I decided to throw a dinner party for my closest friends, where I would also announce my move to CID. The senior ranks knew, but I'd asked to be the one to tell my close colleagues. By a stroke of luck, Pattie, Suzette, Hilda, Bennett and Henry were all off duty on the evening I chose.

I wasn't the greatest cook, but I managed to knock up a respectable cottage pie with Brussels sprouts and roast parsnips, and Campbell's cream of mushroom soup to start. Suzette, bless her, made sticky black cake: a Barbadian speciality, using dried fruit she'd been soaking in rum for months.

"No problems finding ingredients for my black cake, as you British love your prunes, currants and Guinness," she said.

"We like to stay regular, we do," I added.

"Do you want me to make my rum punch?"

"Do you think that's wise, Suz, seeing how it ended up last time?"

"The difference this time is there's a bottle of rum between six, not two." She laughed.

It was a lovely evening. I was showered with birthday flowers, chocolates and perfume, then everybody sang 'Happy Birthday' and got a bit giggly on rum punch, wine and cake. With everyone relaxed and happy, it was time to drop the bombshell. I felt slightly sick. I stood up and tinged a glass.

"I'd like to propose a toast – to the best group of friends a girl could have."

"The best group of friends a girl could have!" they chorused.

"I've also got some news to share with you. In the New Year, I'll be going in front of the Selection Board for detective training. If I get through that – and The EF thinks I will – I'll be a probationary detective, off to Hendon CID Training School for their 10-week course. And if I pass, I'll be the Berkshire Constabulary's first woman detective."

"Bravo!" cried Hilda, leaping to her feet, applauding. "You will be fantastic!"

"That's amazing," said Pattie. "I wondered when you would get promotion. Are you going to be coming back to Wokingham, though? I'm not sure I'll be able to put up with Miss Robertshaw without you around."

"Think of the forensics!" enthused Bennett. "You'll be working with famous pathologists like Keith Simpson, Francis Camps and Donald Teare! You'll be allowed into Scotland Yard's Black Museum!"

"You kept that quiet," said Suzette, frowning. "Does this mean you'll be moving out?"

"Everything's uncertain at the moment," I said. "I might not even pass selection *or* training. But the plan is to stay with the Berkshire Constabulary and I'll keep my room here while I'm at Hendon, Suz. They might even base me at Wokingham then send me round the county. Who knows? They haven't had a woman detective before."

"And 10 weeks goes in a flash," said Henry. "You'll be back before you know it."

"One thing is very certain," said Hilda, beaming, "you have got to take an opportunity like this. It's huge!"

Everybody agreed. In an instant, my Wokingham friendship dynamic had changed and I knew that would happen. But if I knew my friends, they would all have seized similar opportunities. The rest of the evening passed with anecdotes about detectives that people had known and advice on what I should do to change the status quo. End-of-evening hugs were warm and sincere.

Suzette helped me with the washing up.

"I'm sorry if I didn't sound enthusiastic back then," she said. "I've known since Jersey that this day would come. You're more than a beat officer. You'll be brilliant and I'm really happy for you. I'll just miss you, that's all."

I gave her a huge hug. Hugs with Suzette always soothed the soul.

With the cat out of the bag, I could speak freely about changing the direction of my police career into detective work.

"That's my girl!" said Dad, hugging me when I popped into Seaford Road to tell my parents. "You've always taken the different, more challenging path and it doesn't look like that's going to change anytime soon. Proud of you!"

"Well, you've always been the nosy one, sticking your beak into everyone's business," said Mum. "Being a detective is the perfect job for you, *if* you pass."

"Can't you give it a rest for just one day, Aggie, and appreciate what your daughter has achieved?" snapped Dad.

I left before the row started.

Back at the station, Pattie and I found an imitation Christmas tree in a cupboard and a string of fairy lights that didn't work. Sarge spent most of his shift testing each bulb to find the dud that stopped all the others working before we could decorate the tree.

"Bloomin' good news about CID, WPC Crockford," said Sarge. "I remember your first day in the police – that neat, polite recruit who turned up 10 minutes early for her first duty. I thought you'd go far even then."

"Do you remember my first day, Sarge?" asked Pattie.

"How could I forget? You were very nearly late, all of a fluster, and you saluted me like you'd just joined the Army!" Sarge laughed. "But you've both been great girls to work with. A credit to the constabulary."

Sarge's eyes were moistening a little. We couldn't have adored him more.

I was tidying my desk for the last time in the women's office. Through the open door, I could hear Higgs faffing about with files in the back office and Henry on the telephone going through details for issuing a firearms certificate to a local landowner.

Higgs wandered into my office and over to where I was sitting. He stood a little too close, his trouser fly buttons uncomfortably near my right temple. I pushed my chair back, trying to create some personal space between us.

"I haven't said congratulations on your CID recommendation," he said. "Well done."

"Thank you, PC Higgs. It might be a whole new world for me, come January."

"We've been through a lot together, you and me, haven't we?" he said. "From investigating burglaries, to pulling you out of the river, to the Ascot lightning strikes, we've made a great team over the years."

"I think our whole Wokingham team is great," I replied.

Higgs's fly buttons moved a little nearer and he leaned down. "How about you come out to dinner with me this week and we can celebrate properly?"

I was repelled yet oddly conflicted. Yes, this man had saved my life and I'd read an article in a psychology journal that suggested experiencing a dangerous episode or trauma together was supposed to make you attracted to another person. I looked at Higgs's pale eyes, moist freckled forehead and wiry hair. I couldn't be attracted to him even if he'd climbed up and rescued me from the top of the Empire State Building.

"Thank you, but I'm really busy up to Christmas," I said.

"I'm sure you can find one evening to come out? We could go to the pictures if you'd prefer?"

"No, I really am very busy. I've got a carol concert with Suzette, then Christmas shopping with my sisters, as well as night duty coming up."

Henry had finished talking to the gamekeeper and put the telephone down. Out of the corner of my eye, I noticed he had quietly pushed his chair towards the open door and was peering round the corner into my office.

"Look, I'm going to ask you one last time," said an exasperated Higgs. "Will you go out with me?"

"No, I won't!" I said.

"Will you go out with *me* then?" Henry's voice cut through the awkward silence.

Higgs jumped and turned bright red up to his hairline.

"Yes, I will!" I said, with no hesitation whatsoever.

"She's really busy, you know, carols and Christmas shopping and nights and all," Higgs flapped.

Henry looked at him, half-smiling.

"All right . . . well . . . I – I'd better go and see what's going on with Sarge at the front desk," Higgs stammered and turned to leave my office, tripping over the waste-paper basket, then trying to pretend he hadn't.

I was trying hard not to laugh as he stumbled out of the office, feeling a bit sorry for him for the first time in my life.

"Did you really mean that, Henry, or were you just rescuing me?" I asked after Higgs had left.

"Oh, I was rescuing you all right."

My face must have fallen slightly.

"But I was serious as well," he continued. "I would be delighted if you would be foolhardy enough to go out with me. We can either go to the pictures – *The Night of the Hunter* is playing, or we could have dinner at the Ship Hotel?"

"Ah, that festive favourite, *The Night of the Hunter*," I said. "Nothing says Christmas like a psychopathic serial killer pursuing innocent children."

Henry laughed. "The Ship it is, then. What duties are you working next?" he asked.

"I'm on earlies for the next few days."

"I'll book a table for 7 p.m. on Saturday as you're on the early shift next day. Shall I pick you up from Mrs Cunningham's at a quarter to seven?"

At the end of my shift, I slipped out of the station. I felt compelled to stand beneath the pagoda for a few moments, smoking a cigarette and looking at Wokingham's twinkling Christmas lights and people hurrying home to their families. I was a different person from the nervous recruit who stood on this very spot nearly four years ago. How my professional and personal life had moved on.

I wondered what 1956 would bring.

Acknowledgements

Many lovely people have supported, advised and encouraged me as I wrote the various iterations of *Calling WPC Crockford*.

Special thanks must go to: Pippa Wilson for suggesting I should write my mother's story in the first place; Caroline Hopkins and Wendy O'Mahony, who patiently listened to me read and commented on the whole manuscript as I wrote it; Julie Currie, formerly of the Metropolitan Police, for her procedural advice; the Right Reverend Andrew Rumsey, Bishop of Ramsbury for his ecclesiastical advice; and my critical readers Paul D'Alessandro, Matthew Chatfield, Fiona Murray, Julie Morley, Rose Metalli and Jenny Coates for their honesty. Thank you to Janet Conneely for lending me her 1950s family scrapbooks about the Royal Family.

Special mention to the legend that is my Auntie Barbara for being a good sport about me including the wartime farting anecdote.

My inspirational agent, Kate Hordern of KHLA, for her vision, sage advice, guidance and encouragement throughout the planning and writing of *Calling WPC Crockford* and my ever-supportive, oldest friend

Catherine Cotter, who suggested I approach Kate in the first place.

Welbeck's delightful editorial director Ajda Vucicevic and her team for recognising that the story of police-women in the 1950s is one worth telling; my eagle-eyed editor Victoria Goldman and my proofreader, Jane Donovan, for picking up things I'd missed; Victoria Simon-Shore for her legal read and Millie Acers, Laura Newton and Alexandra Allden for making this book a reality.

Professor Louise Jackson, whose book *Women Police: Gender, Welfare and Surveillance in the Twentieth Century* was the bedrock of my research, for kindly sharing proofs of her book, *Policing Youth, Britain 1945–70* with me; I also reference her 2015 paper, *Child sexual abuse in England and Wales: prosecution and prevalence 1918–1970* on p.228.

The description of the coronation in 1953 was drawn from the ebook *Wokingham in the News: A Chronological History of Wokingham from Local Newspapers, 1858–1999* by Jim Bell, 2016.

The ATV television series, *Probation Officer*, broadcast in 1959/60, inspired and informed the probation service storyline, interview techniques and procedures.

Quotes from the chairman of Wokingham magistrates came from newspaper clippings found in my mother's papers that had neither source nor dates with them. To the best of my knowledge, these would probably have come from *The Wokingham and Bracknell Times* of the period.

The Berkshire Record Office for being as helpful as they could be with the scarce archives and The British Library for being a monumental research resource.